Ṣūfī Thought of
Shaikh Sayyid 'Abdu'l Qādir Jīlānī

Islamic Heritage in Cross-Cultural Perspectives

1. Gandhi's Responses to Islam; by Sheila McDonough (ISBN 81-246-0035-X)
2. Fawā'id al-Fu'ād — Spiritual and Literary Discourses of Shaikh Niẕāmuddīn Awliyā; Originally Compiled by Amīr Ḥasan 'Alā' Sijzī Dehlawī; English Translation with Introduction and Historical Annotation by Ziya-ul-Hasan-Faruqi (ISBN 81-246-0042-2)
3. Change and Continuity in Indian Sūfism — A Naqshbandi-Mujaddidī Branch in the Hindu Environment; Thomas Dahnhardt (HB: ISBN 81-246-0170-4) (PB: ISBN 81-246-0405-3)
4. Islamic Thought and Movement in the Subcontinent — A Study of Sayyid Abu A'lā Mawdudi and Sayyid Abul Hasan Ali Nadwi; Sheikh Jameil Ali (ISBN 81-246-0491-6)

Islamic Heritage in Cross-cultural Perspectives, no. 5

Ṣūfī Thought of Shaikh Sayyid 'Abdu'l Qādir Jīlānī

And its Impact on the Indian Subcontinent

Manzoor Ahmad Bhat

D.K. Printworld (P) Ltd.
New Delhi

Cataloging in Publication Data — DK
[Courtesy: D.K. Agencies (P) Ltd. <docinfo@dkagencies.com>]

Bhat, Manzoor Ahmad, 1960-
Ṣūfī thought of Shaikh Sayyid 'Abdu'l Qādir Jīlānī and its impact on the Indian subcontinent / by Manzoor Ahmad Bhat.
p. cm. -- (Islamic heritage in cross-cultural perspectives ; no. 5)
Originally presented as the author's thesis (Ph. D.) — University of Kashmir.
Includes bibliographical references (p.).
Includes index.
ISBN 13: 9788124605455
ISBN 10: 8124605459

1. 'Abd al-Qādir al-Jīlānī, 1077-1166. — Influence. 2. Qādiriyah members — Biography. 3. Sufis — Biography. 4. Qādiriyah. 5. Qādiriyah — South Asia. 6. Sufism. 7. Sufism — South Asia. I. Title. II. Series: Islamic heritage in cross-cultural perspectives ; no. 5.

DDC 297.4092 22

ISBN 13: 978-81-246-0545-5
ISBN 10: 81-246-0545-9

First published in India, 2010

Published and printed by:
D.K. Printworld (P) Ltd.
Regd. office : *'Srikunj'*, F-52, Bali Nagar
Ramesh Nagar Metro Station
New Delhi - 110 015
Phones : (011) 2545 3975, 2546 6019; *Fax* : (011) 2546 5926
E-mail : indology@dkprintworld.com
Web : www.dkprintworld.com

Preface

Taṣawwuf (Sūfism) as an Islamic science is being studied both by Muslim and non-Muslim scholars and the Orientalists with great interest and curiosity, yet with diverse objectives in their minds. Some regard it as mysticism, a few others categorize it as a form of *ruḥbaniyat* (monasticism), while some treat it as spirituality or *'Irfān*.

In fact, *taṣawwuf* (Sūfism) is a mediator between *sharī'at* and *ḥaqīqat*. Practising *sharī'at* in the most desired form that could guide a believer properly to understand the *haqīqat* (Ultimate Reality) in its totality is *taṣawwuf*. It can also be termed as the esoteric aspect of the teachings of Islam.

In this book, which is a humble attempt to study the Ṣūfī thought of Shaikh Sayyid 'Abdu'l Qādir Jīlānī (Rah.A), highly revered and the most influential Sūfī and Preacher of his times, our endeavour has been to provide a historical perspective while exploring the most recurring themes of his thought, in the light of Jīlānī's original works. An attempt has also been made to provide an insight into the impact of the Shaikh's thought on the Indian subcontinent and the subsequent emergence of various Qādiriyya centres in that area.

The objective analysis leads to this conclusion that the Shaikh has not deviated even in the least from the fundamental teachings of the *Qur'ān* and the *Sunnah* of the Prophet (S.A.W).

This work, originally a doctoral thesis submitted to the University of Kashmir would not have been in the form as it is now, in the absence of the erudite guidance of Prof. M. Ishaq Khan, ex-Dean Academics, University of Kashmir, and Prof. Naseem Ahmad Shah, Director, S.H. Institute of Islamic Studies, University of Kashmir.

I express my deep sense of gratitude to my senior colleagues and scholars with whom I had useful discussion during my research work. The librarians of all those libraries which I visited during my research work deserve my thanks.

Last, but not least, thanks to all my family members who proved a source of inspiration for me and had to suffer a lot during the course of my studies.

May Allāh approve this little and humble effort and prove it a means of salvation for me here and in the *ākhirah.* May He forgive me for my shortcomings and lacuna, if any, committed in this work.

Contents

Introduction

SOME of the biographies of Shaikh 'Abdu'l Qādir Jīlānī (Raḥ.'A) were composed by his disciples including, among others, Qāḍī Abū Qasim Ibn Dirbās and his sons, Abū Muhammad 'Abdu'l Qādir Ibn'Uthmān Ibn Abil Barakat al-Tamīmī al-Bardānī, Abū Manṣūr 'Abdullah Ibn Muhammad al-Baghdādī, Abu'l Farāj Ibn Muhammad al-Baṣrī, and Abū Bakr 'Abdullah Ibn Naṣr Ibn Hamzah al-Tamīmī al-Bakrī al-Siddīqī al-Baghdādī. But none of these biographies is extant.

Bahjat al-Asrār wa Ma'din al-Anwār (commonly known as *Bahjah*) by Nuru'd-Din Abul Hasan 'Ali bin Yūsuf al-Shattanūfi[1] (b. 644/1246, d. 713/1313-14) is the earliest extant and most popular biography of Shaikh 'Abdu'l Qādir Jīlānī (Raḥ.'A). The book exclusively deals with the events and anecdotes connected with the life of the Shaikh (Raḥ.'A). The author has handed down the events with full chain of narrators. The book, however, contains only stray references about the different dimensions of the religious thought of Jīlānī. The chronology of the events, as contained in the book, is separately discussed, here, in Appendix A.

Ghibṭah al-Nāzir fi Tarjamat al-Shaikh 'Abdu'l Qādir (precisely referred as *Ghibṭah* in the text) by Ibn Hajr al-Asqalāni (d. 852/1448) is another work that deals with various aspects of the Sīrah (biography) of the Shaikh (Raḥ.'A).

1. Shattanufi (AH 644-713) was a teacher at al-Azhar.

Tadhkiratu'l Huffāz compiled by Shams ud-Din Dhahabī (d. 748/1348) contains a significant notice of Jīlānī (Raḥ.'A). It was later published by Dāi'ratu'l Ma'ārif in 1355 (AH) from Hyderabad.

The life compiled by Dhahabi contains some of the matter printed in *Bhajah* and was evidently employed by the author of *Ghibṭah*.

Khulāṣat al-Mufākir by Affifu'd-Din 'Abdullah bin Asad al-Yāfi'ī (b. in Yemen, settled at Makkah in 718/1318 and died there in 768/1367) is a collection of two hundred anecdotes (in Arabic) about the Shaikh (Raḥ.'A).

Wafāyāt al-A'yān (vol. VIII) by Ibn Khallikān (d. 681/1282) contains a brief account of the Shaikh (Raḥ.'A).

'Imād ud-Dīn Abū'l Fida Isma'īl Ibn 'Amar Ibn Kathīr (d. 774/1372) gives a brief notice on the Sīrah of the Shaikh in his monumental work *al-Bidāyah wa an-Nihāya* (vol. XII).

'Abdu'l Wahhab al-Sh'arāni (898/1493-973/1565), an Egyptian Ṣūfī writer, gives a brief account of the Shaikh (Raḥ.'A) in his voluminous hagiographic work entitled *Tabaqāt al-Kubrā* (vol. I).

Nafahāt al-Uns by Nur ud-Din 'Abdu'l Rahmān Jāmī (817/1414- 898/1492) contains a precise biographical account of the Shaikh (Raḥ.'A).

Qalā'id al-Jawāhir, composed about AH 980; by Muhammad Ibn Yahyā al-Tādifī, is an exclusive biographical work on Jīlānī (Raḥ.'A). It was later published from Cairo, in AH 1303.

Natījatu'l Taḥqīq by Abū 'Abdullah. Muhamad al-Dilā'I (d. AH 1089) is another valuable biographical account of the Shaikh (Raḥ.'A).

Tafrīj al-Khātīr fī Manāqib Sayyid, 'Abdu'l Qādir al-Jīlānī, translated from Persian by Shaikh 'Abdu'l al-Qādir al-Qādirī Ibn Muhy al-Dīn makes a valuable contribution to the biographical literature on the life of the Shaikh (Raḥ.'A). It was printed at Cairo, in AH 1300.

Akhbāru'l-Akhyār by Shaikh 'Abdu'l Ḥaqq Muhadith Dehlawi gives a valuable account of the life and doctrines of Jīlānī (Raḥ.'A). It was compiled in 996/1588, but revised and completed after three years. Some of the sources available to Dihlawī are extinct now, which adds to the validity of this work.

Zubdat al-Āthār by the same author is *Talkhiṣ* (precise form) of *Bahjat al-Asrār*.

A certain amount of attention has also been devoted to the life and doctrines of the Shaikh (Raḥ.'A) in Europe. The following books deal with either the Shaikh or his order:

E. De Neven	*Les Khouan. Orders religieux Cherles Musulmāns* de I Algerie 2nd edn., Paris, 1846 (The author's name is not on the title page, but at the end of the dedication).
E. Le Chatelier	*Conferies Musulmanes dans I Hejaz*, Paris, 1982.
L. Rinn	*Marabouts et Khouan*, Algiers, 1884.
Depont ct Coppoani	*Conferies religieuses Musulmanes*, Algiers, 1897.
Carra de Vaux	*Gazali*, Paris, 1902.

Among these authors E. Le Chatealier had a number of works including, among them, a life of Jīlānī (Raḥ.'A), entitled *Tafrīj al-Khātīr fī Manāqib Sayyid 'Abdu'l Qādir al-Jīlānī.* Rinn and Coppoani depended largely on him. Vaux based his statements on the biography of the Shaikh (Raḥ.'A), entitled *Qalā'id al-Jawāhir* by Muhammad Ibn Yahyā al-Tādifī. Besides this,

Ghibṭah al-Nāzir fi Tarjamat al-Shaikh 'Abdu'l Qādir by Asqalānī was published by E.D. Ross.

These French writers, however, deal more with the Qādirīs than their founder.

Some of the earlier mentioned sources on the biography of the Shaikh (Raḥ.'A) which are near contemporary can be studied side by side with Jīlānī's (Raḥ.'A) writings, his sermons compiled under the title of *Fath-i Rubbānī*, his discourses entitled *Futūḥ al-Ghaib, Jila'l-i-Khaṭīr*, his ethico-legal manual entitled *Ghunyāt al-Tālibīn* and his letters compiled in the form of *Maktūbāt-i-Haḍrat-i Shaikh al-Thaqalayn Shaikh Muhy-ud-Dīn Abū Muhammad 'Abdu'l Qādir Jīlānī*. From these sources we can form a correct idea of Jīlānī (Raḥ.'A) and the picture that results is that of a powerful preacher, whose personality and the impact of utterances was capable of stirring congregations to enthusiasm.

Jīlānī (Raḥ.'A) spent 73 years of his life in Baghdad. When he migrated to Baghdad, Caliph Mustazhir Billah Abu'l 'Abbās (487/1094 – 512/1118) was the reigning monarch, after whom, the Shaikh (Raḥ.'A) witnessed the period of four other 'Abbasid Caliphs: al-Mustarshid Billāh (512/1118 – 529/1135), al-Rāshid Billāh (529/1135 – 530/1136), al-Muqtafil' Amrillāh (530/1136 – 555/1160) and al-Mustanjid Billāh (555/1160 – 565/1170).

In order to have right perception of his times (fifth/eleventh–sixth/twelfth centuries) we have primarily relied upon these sources:

Al-Kāmil fi al-Tārīkh of 'Izz ud-Din Abū'l Hussain 'Ali Ibn Muhammad Ibn al-Athīr (d. 630/1232-33) which was brought down to the year AH 628.[2] Interestingly this work was published

2. *Tārīkh al-Kāmil* was edited by C.I. Tornberg from 1851-53, and also published in Cairo in 1301/1883, whereas publication of →

before *Tārīkh ur-Rasūl wa al-Mulūk* of Abū Ja'far Muhammad bin Jarīr al-Tabarī (d. 310/923).

Wafāyāt al-A'yān of Shamas ud-Dīn Ahmad bin Muhammad Ibn-i Khallikān (d. 681/1282).[3]

Another important Arabic source is the famous *Tārīkh*, history of Wali ud-Din Abū Zayd 'Abdur Rahmān Ibn-i Khaldūn (d. 808/1406).[4]

Rāhat us-Sudūr wa Āyat us-Surūr of Abū Bakr Muhammad bin 'Ali al-Rāwandī (d. 599/1202).[5] In the main *Rāhat us-Ṣudūr wa Āyāt us-Surūr* contains the history of the great Saljūqs from the rise of the dynasty early in the fifth century AH down to its fall in 590/1194.

Some ideas of the organization of the state and general conditions of life of this period is given in *Siyāsat Nāma* of Niẓām al-Mulk (d. 485/1092), which was written at the instance of Sulṭān Malik Shāh, to point out the loopholes and aspects of maladministration in the government of Saljūqs. In the same

---

→ Tabari's work was undertaken by a group of orientalists and completed over a period of twenty-two years (CE 1879-1901).

3. The first English edition of the book was published in Paris from CE 1842-71. The author enriches our information with the sources that have not come down to us.

4. The book, generally known as *Muqaddima*, was published at Bulaq in 1284/1867. The author lived in Spain and Africa.

5. This book was edited by Muhammad Iqbal, London, 1921. The author furnishes a fine collection of proverbs and poems while explaining the episodes and events of the period. The author also quotes the verses of Anwarī, Nizāmī and Jamāl ud-Dīn Isfahānī, most of whom were contemporaries of the author.

   The only source of the historical information for the earlier part of the book has been Zahir ud-Din Nishapuri's *Saljūqnāma*, which is now extinct.

way Ghazālī's *Nasīhat al Mulūk* (Counsel for the Kings) also points to the aspects of misgovernment and prescribes the *modus operandi* for an effective and just administration. Both the monographs were, however, addressed to the Saljūq Sulṭāns.

In fact, the accounts of both these political theorists are our basis for discussing the nature of 'Abbasid state and the political ethos of the period.

The Cambridge History of Iran (vol. V), has provided us with thoughtful details about the internal structure of Saljūq administration and the religious developments of the period.

The most valuable source, which deals broadly with the various aspects of life during the period of our study, is the *Venture of Islam* (vol. II), by Marshall G.S. Hodgson.[6]

The Decline of the Saljūqid Empire by M.F. Sonaullah provides some useful material on the internal structure and political institutions of this period.[7]

Turkistan Down to the Mongol Invasion by W. Barthold is not only a political history but also a rich treasure of sources.

Tārīkh-i Salājiqa Wa Khawārizm Shāhān by Abbās Parvīz and *Az Salājiqa Ta Safaviya* by Nusratullah Mashkawtī contain a good deal of substance on the period under review.

Sayyid Husain Nasr's *Ismā'ilī Contribution to Islamic Culture* is a unique monograph about the different and diverse aspects

6. The author, besides dealing with the history of Islamic civilization in the period under review, gives precise account of the *silsilās* (Ṣūfī orders) of the period and discusses in some detail the aspects of the victory of Sunni Orthodoxy during the period.
7. It is originally the author's Ph.D. thesis published by the University of Calcutta in 1938. The author meticulously analyses the factors leading to the downfall of the Saljūqs.

of Isma'ilī activity and opens a broader vista of sources for the reader.

Ṣūfī Orders in Islam by J.P.S. Trimingham, *Classical Ṣūfī Thought* by A.J. Arbery, *A History of Ṣūfism in India* by A.A. Rizvī and *Ṣūfism in Kashmir* by A.Q. Rafīqī and few other works are some of our secondary sources on the development of Ṣūfism and Ṣūfī *silsilā*s (orders).

We have been greatly benefited by the pioneering work of Dr Ghulam Yahya Anjum[8] on the origin and development of Qādiriyya *silsilā* in north India, which was originally a U.G.C. sponsored project under "Young Researchers Career Award Scheme". Two research articles of the same author under the title of "Bar-i Saghīr mein Silsilā Qādiriyya; tarwīj wa Ishā'at" and "Silsilā Qādiriyya Oor is Kay Bani Par Tasānīf Ka Ijmāl-I Jā'izah" published in *Fikr-o Naẓar*,[9] vol. 33, no. 2 and vol. 36, no. 1 respectively, have also proved fruitful during our study. His published works in Urdu entitled: *Hindustan Mein Silsilā Qādiriyya kā Bān-i Koun* and *Qutbu'l Hind Sayyidina 'Abdu'l Wahhāb Jīlānī*, have not been left unnoticed by us.

The following three research articles published in *Journal of Royal Asiatic Society* (*JRAS*) of Great Britain and Ireland that we have come across during our study, notwithstanding the fact that some findings of the contributors of the last two articles need further critical examination, have also benefited us. The articles comprise English translation of the first part of the *Natijatu'l Taḥqīq*[10] translated from the text lithographed

8. The author is a Professor in the Department of Islamic Studies, Jamia Hamdard, Delhi, India.
9. This Journal is published by Idārah Tahqīqāt-i Islāmī, International Islamic University, Islamabad, Pakistan.
10. It was originally written by Abū 'Abdullāh Muhammad al-Dilā'i (d. AH 1089).

at Fez in the year AH 1309 by T.H. Weir,[11] B.D., M.R.A.S.

The second article is entitled "Historical Enquiry Concerning the Origin and Development of Ṣūfism" by R.A. Nicholson, published in *JRAS* in the year 1906.

The third article is entitled "Contributions to the Biography of Shaikh 'Abdu'l Qādir al-Jīlānī after al-Dhahabī" by D.S. Margoliouth published in *JRAS* in the year 1907.

Last, but not least, we would like to mention here that a number of manuscripts of hagiographic nature were consulted in various libraries of India especially those available in the Manuscript Section, Maulana Azad Library, Aligarh Muslim University, Aligarh and manuscript section, Central Library, Jamia Hamdard, Jamia Nagar, New Delhi. The details of this valuable treasure and some of the works cited earlier will, however, be discussed separately in part "B" of chapter 2 of the present work.

In working out the details of our project we had to exploit the scattered references in different sources. Often the silence of sources about some vital aspects of our theme made us to employ hairsplitting efforts to reach to the possible conclusions.

Scheme of Chapterization of the Present Work

The first chapter of this book deals with the "Times of Shaikh 'Abdu'l Qādir Jīlānī (Raḥ.'A)." We have arranged our findings in two subheadings, viz. "Religious Meileu" and "Abbāsid State: An Estimate." Sunnī Revival, Shī'ism, Ismā'ilīs and Ṣūfism constitute the former and our study of Abbasid State comprises (i) Political theorists and their theories, wherein

11. It figures as article VI in *JRAS Year Book* 1903. Weir was Assistant Professor of Hebrew and Semitic Languages at the University of Glasgow.

we have confined ourselves to Nizāmul Mulk Tūsī (d. 485/1092) and Abū Hāmid al-Ghazālī (d. CE 1111), the two highly influential religio-political theorists of the period, and (ii) Pattern of administration which comprises the position and role of *shahna*, the Court, *ra'īs*, the Judiciary, *muhtasib* and *'ulamā.'* Besides this, we have attempted to draw a sketch of the Muslim world on this juncture, at the very outset of this chapter.

The second chapter deals with the "Life and Works of the Shaikh (Raḥ.'A)." An attempt has been made to give details about the location, size and other aspects of manuscripts referred to in this chapter. We have tried to provide a contemporaneous appraisal of the Shaikh's life, here.

The third chapter provides a background study on the emergence of Ṣūfī thought and organization of Ṣūfī *silsilā*s. For the sake of convenience the study has been carried out under two sub-headings, viz., "Origin and Development of *Taṣawwuf*" and "Organization of Ṣūfī Silsilās."

The fourth chapter of this book deals with the "Religio-Sūfic Thought of Shaikh 'Abdu'l Qādir Jīlānī (Raḥ.'A)." We have attempted here, not only to confine ourselves to original utterances, sermons, discourses, *waṣāyah* and *maktūbāt* of the great Ṣūfī, scholar and preacher, but also to interpret the most recurring themes in the vocabulary of Jīlānī (Raḥ.'A), so as to ensure the originality and avoid misinterpretation that would have possibly occurred, otherwise.

The fifth chapter deals with the "Impact of Jīlānī's thought and teachings on the Subcontinent." We have attempted here to bring out the salient features of various Qādiriyya centres that developed subsequently in the subcontinent.

1

Times of Shaikh 'Abdu'l Qādir Jīlānī (Raḥ.'A)

Religious Milieu

The period of Shaikh 'Abdu'l Qādir Jīlānī (Raḥ.'A) marks an important phase of the religious history of Islam. This period is remarkably interesting for the Sunnī revival after a fairly long span of Ismā'ilī domination. It also witnessed the ferment of Shi'i ideas and above all it is the period of the growth of Ṣūfism. We realize that in this period the entire theological system of Islam found its final systematization, and Shi'i-Sunnī conflicts also came to surface and finally, in the twelfth century, the oldest *Ṣūfī silsilās* (orders) were organized. Thus, it was certainly one of the most formative periods in the religio-cultural history of Islam.

To understand the aspects of religion during the period under review, it seems more appropriate to discuss briefly the main religious trends of the period separately.

(I) SUNNĪ REVIVAL[1]

While examining the religious and political history of eleventh and twelfth centuries CE two things strike us. First, the revival was not simply Sunnī, it was traditional too. Certain articulate

1. William Montgomery Watt, *Islamic Surveys*, I, Edinburg, 1962, p. 91; Julian Baldick, *Mystical Islam*, London, 1989, p. 58.

forces of traditionalism are seen reviving in some measure during that period.[2] Secondly, the revival was not to be attributed sharply with the entry of Saljūqs[3] into Baghdad in 447/1055. The revival, in fact, was gaining momentum quite at the beginning of the century.

At the end of fourth/tenth century and the beginning of fifth/eleventh century the Ghaznavid Sulṭān Mahmūd was pursuing a traditionalist Sunnī policy under the Caliph al-Qādir

---

2. G. Maqdīsī, "The Sunnī Revival", *Islamic Civilization*, p. 155; *Cambridge Hist. of Islam*, vol. 28, pp. 570, 599, 602.

3. Saljūqs were a Turkic people from the steppes, a branch of the Ghuzz/Oghuz, who entered military service within the 'Abbasid caliphate and succeeded in seizing control for themselves under their leader Toghrul Beig. Toghrul Beig assumed the title of *sulṭān*, which had never been used before, and this was stamped on his coinage. The dynasty which he founded began in 429/1038 and lasted until 582/1194. An offshoot, the Saljūqs of Rum in Anatolia, existed as a power until shortly before 707/1307.

   Without abolishing either the caliphate or the 'Abbasids, the Sunnī Saljūqs in 447/1055 entered Baghdad and displaced the Shi'ite Buyids who had preceded them as the effective masters of most of the eastern part of the 'Abbasid Empire. Saljūq expansion to the West, extending their influence upon the Byzantine Empire, was one of the causes of the crusade wars. Sulṭān Alp Arsalan and Jalal ad-Dawlah Malik Shah, benefited from the services of the Persian vizier Niẓām al-Mulk Tūsi (d. CE 1092), who achieved fame as one of the most able political figures in Islamic history. After Malik Shah, the Saljūq Empire underwent progressive fragmentation, giving way to other dynasties such as the *Khwarizm Shahis*, originally governors for the Saljūqs. The period of the Great Saljūq Sultanate did, however, provide a stability and political unity to a degree rarely achieved afterwards.

   For detailed chronology of the 'Abbasid caliphate, Buyid suzerainty and Saljūq suzerainty, please see *Appendix B*.

in his newly conquered territories.[4] Under the patronage of the caliph, Sulṭān Mahmūd followed a traditionalist view of religion which was more prominently anti-Shi'i, anti-Mu'tazili and also anti-Ash'ari.[5]

The caliph proclaimed a decree in 408/1017 necessitating the retraction of all prospective officials to Hanafite theology. As a result of this policy the great Hanafi *Qāḍī* Al-Saymari dramatically retracted from the Mu'tazilite philosophy in order to get the post of *qāḍī* in Baghdad.[6] The Ghaznavids were implementing this policy of the caliph[7] from a distance in Khurasan and obviously the Saljūqs had not as yet appeared upon the scene.[8]

Tughril Beg, the first of the great Saljūqs ordered the public cursing of al-Ash'ari from the pulpits of Khurasan. We also find him exiling the great Ash'ari *'ulamā'* from the province.[9] This was the deliberate policy of Turkish Sunnī *sulṭān* which he pursued during the decade after his triumphant entry into Baghdad and after assuming the title of *sulṭān* and "Right Arm" of the Sunnī caliph.[10] The anti-Ash'ari policy of Tughril

---

4. Ibn ul Jawzi, *Al-Muntazam fi-Tarikh al-Umam*, ed. Krenkow, 6 vols., Hyderabad: Dairatul-Ma'arif Press, 1357-59/1938-40, vol. III, pp.38-40.
5. Maqdisi, op. cit., p. 156; see also W.M. Watt, op. cit., pp. 91-92.
6. Ibid., cf. W.M. Watt, op. cit., p. 106.
7. Maqdisi calls it a "traditionalist Sunnī Revival." In his opinion it was a religious revival in which the forces of traditionalism fought against the forces of rationalism of all shades (Maqdisi, op. cit., p. 157).
8. Watt, op. cit., p. 110.
9. Ibid.
10. Rāwandi, *Rāhat al-Ṣudūr wa-Āyāt al-Surūr*, ed. M. Iqbal, London, 1921, p. 105.

Beg was well felt and implemented from 445/1053–455/1063 till the death of the *sulṭān*. Interestingly, the total shift in the anti-Ash'ari policy of Saljūqs is witnessed immediately after the death of Tughril Beg and his *waẓīr* 'Amid ul-Mulk Al-Kundūri. With the accession of Sulṭān Alp Arsalān to the Sultanate and that of Niẓām al-Mulk to the *Wazīrate*, the exiled Ash'ari *'ulamā'* were welcomed back from exile and the victimization of Ash'aris came to an end.[11] Even Mu'tazilites were also tolerated and accommodated.[12] The tolerant policy towards the alienated sects — Ash'arites and Mu'tazilites — was the result of Niẓām al-Mulk's political foresight and administrative wisdom. His tolerant policy was dictated primarily by political expediency.[13]

Both Tughril Beg and Kundūri were Hanafis who supported Hanafi *'ulamā'* who happened to be Mu'tazilites. Niẓām al-Mulk, on the other hand, was Shaf'ei, who supported Shaf'ei *'ulamā'* who happened to be Ash'ari. But at the same time he did not alienate the M'utazilites too. Instead, he befriended and bestowed financial support on them.[14]

Qazvīnī, in his famous book *Kitāb un-Naqd*, which is a Shi'a polemic work of the first half of the twelfth century, observes that the people of Khurasan, Transoxiana and a part of Iraq were Hanafi and Mu'tazilite in theology.[15] A later work *Tabsīrāt*

11. Watt, loc. cit. (the Exiled Ashari-Shafi'i leaders, Imām ul-Haramayn al Juwayni returned from exile to assume that post of professorship at Niẓāmaiya).
12. Maqdisi, op. cit., p. 157.
13. Ibid.
14. Ibid.
15. *Cambridge History of Iran*, p. 283.

    The author has given a complete sectarian geography of Central Asia and Iran.

ul 'Awām written during the beginning of the thirteenth century, shows us the division of the Saljūq domain on religious basis.[16] The author of the book has mentioned the following six Sunnī sub divisions:

1. Hanafi: Theologically divided into Mu'tazilite, Najjariya, Karāmiya, Murjia and Jabriya. The people of Khwārizm are Hanafi-Mu'tazilite, the people of Bukhāra and the "Peasants" of Kāshān are Hanafi-Najjari. In Ghūr and Sind there are Karanis, whereas the Hanafis of Khurasan, Transoxiana and Farghna are Jabri, as are the Turks,

2. Shāf'ī: Theologically divided into six groups: Mushbbiha (anthropomorphists), Salafis, Kharijis, Mu'tazilites, Ash'arites and Yazīdīs,

3. Mālikī: Theologically divided into Mu'tazilites and Ash'arites,

4. Hanbalī, 5. Thawrīs, and 6. Dā'ūdīs

This period witnessed frequent religious debates and discussions. These debates sometimes ended in massacres. In Nishāpur after the terrible onslaught of the Ghuzz (CE 1154), every night one sect would assault a quarter of the town inhabited by members of another sect. They would resort to loot, arson and burning.[17]

Similar things happened in Shiraz between Hanafis and Shaf'eis, in Rayy between both of them and the Shi'is and between all of them and Ismā'ilīs.[18]

Ideologically, the *Sunnīs* tended to assimilate all forms of

16. *Cambridge History of Iran*, p. 284.

17. Rāwandī, op. cit., p. 182.

18. *Cambridge History of Iran*, p. 285.

Shi'i philosophy. "Shi'i ideology is the corridor leading to heresy," writes an ex-Shi'i convert to *Sunnī* ideology before CE 1161 in his anti-Shi'i book *B'adu Fadaih al Rawāfiḍ*.[19] The same author says that the Shi'is are Zoroastrians under Muslim garb. The author also accuses the Shi'is of propagandizing especially in the lower classes and amongst ignorant artisans and that they are *dahriyya* (materialists).[20]

The revival of Sunnism can be best understood by peeping into the expositions of Ghazālī (d. 1111 CE). He is one of the best representatives of Central Asian Sunnī ideology that has remained for centuries the religious milieu in which the greatest Iranian geniuses, literary and otherwise, have been bred.[21] It is a fact that along with his Sunnī philosophy, Ghazālī, like his master Juwayni, became the pillar of the state religion, at a troubled time in its history.[22] Ghazālī is, in a way, the résumé and practical end of the Sunnī philosophy. After him Sunnīs did not produce much that is significant in the theological field.[23] Thus, Ghazālī's radical mistrust of human reason, his consequent condemnation of philosophy and his intellectual aristocratism (he discouraged the common people from studying theology, saying that they must only believe)[24] strengthened the trends of orthodox Sunnī thought.[25] Ghazālī

---

19. *Cambridge History of Iran*, p. 286.
20. Ibid.
21. Ibid.
22. Abū ẓāmid al-Ghazālī, *Naṣīḥat al'Mulūk*, tr. F.R.C. Bagley, Oxford, 1964, p. 34.
23. *Cambridge History of Iran*, p. 286.
24. Ghazālī was of the opinion that use of intellect (*ijtihad*) in religious and legal issues should be reserved only in qualified persons. (*Naṣīḥat al-Mulūk*, op. cit., p. 37).
25. *Cambridge History of Iran*, Ghazālī, ibid.

also strived hard to introduce a moderate mysticism into orthodoxy. He wished to make jurisprudence mystical and mysticism juridical. In this way the conviction of Ghazālī and the moderate Ṣūfīs was compatible with orthodox Sunnīte belief and respect for Islamic law. Indeed, Ghazālī himself did more than any other writer to reinforce the intellectual content of Sunnīte dogma.[26]

A more trusted testimony to the Sunnī revival is the final destruction of Mu'tazilism and the triumph of Ash'arism during the twelfth and thirteenth centuries. The most famous figure of this movement was Juwayni (d. 1085), the master of Ghazālī, known as *Imām al Haramayn*. He was the greatest Shāf'ei-Ash'ari theologian of Khurasan during this period.[27] Another Shāf'ei-Ash'ari scholar of the period was al-Shahristani (d. 1153), who served Sulṭān Sanjar and is chiefly famous as the author of the famous manual *Al-Milal wal Nihal*. He lived in Khurasan and Khawārizm.[28]

The growing influence of the orthodox Ash'arite School brought with it, of course, a decline in the speculative science. Ghazālī's *Tuḥafat al Falāsafa* (Destructum Philosophorum) is the only most authoritative example of this attitude.[29]

The importance of the Sunnī revival lies in the fact that Sunnī religious learning was imparted in great educational institutions, which might be considered to be amongst the first universities of the civilized world. These institutions were founded and aided by the famous Saljūq *Wazīr*, Niẓām al-Mulk Ṭūsī — hence called the Niẓāmiyās. These institutions were

26. *Cambridge History of Iran*, Ghazālī.
27. *Cambridge History of Iran*, p. 287.
28. Ibid.
29. Ibid.

like colleges, with scholarships, good salaries for the professors and a traditional and well-organized curriculum. Prominent among these were the Niẓāmiyas of Baghdad and Nishāpūr.[30]

In fact, the Niẓāmiyas, with Shāf'eite professors, represented the success of the resurgence of the dogmatic theological movement, known by the name of Ash'arism.[31] In the opinion of Goldziher, who has held in high esteem the services of Niẓāmiyas in the history of Muslim educational thought,

> For a long time it was not possible for (the Ash'arites) to teach theology in public. It was until the middle of eleventh century, when the *Wazīr* of the Saljūqids, Niẓām al-Mulk, created public chairs in the great schools founded by him in Nishāpūr and Baghdad for the new theological doctrine, that the Ash'arite dogmatic theology could be taught officially and could be admitted into the system of orthodox theology. It is therefore, here that the victory of the Ash'arite school was decided in its struggle against Mu'tazilism on the one hand, and intransigent orthodoxy (Hanbalism) on the other. The era in which these institutions flourished is therefore important, not only in the history of education, but also in that of Muslim dogmatic theology (Sunnī thought).[32]

Ash'arism is claimed to have won its victory in Baghdad in the middle of eleventh century and the credit for this victory is assigned to Niẓāmiya colleges. Niẓām al-Mulk and Ghazālī whose genius, as professor of theology, made possible the acceptance by Muslim orthodoxy of not only Ṣūfī mysticism, but Ash'arism was also accepted as the official theology of

30. *Cambridge History of Iran*, p. 289
31. G. Makkdisi, "Muslim Institutions of Learning in the Eleventh Century Baghdad", *BSOAS*, vol. 24, 1961, pp. 2-3.
32. Ibid.

Islam at this period.[33] Thus, we are reasonably sure that the *madrasah* (Niẓāmiya) symbolized the victory of orthodox Sunnī theology over speculative and natural philosophy.[34]

(II) THE SHĪ'AS

The *Shi'a* movement began as a political protest against the conferring of the *imāmate* or leadership of Islam on men like Haḍrat Abū-Bakr, 'Umar and 'Uthmān (Raḍ.A), who were not descendants of the Prophet (SAW).[35] Soon after the demise of the Prophet (SAW) there arose a difference among the Muslims as to who should succeed the Prophet (SAW) as leader of the *ummah*. Then the question of *imāmate* formed the principal point of difference between those who believed that it was the right of Prophet's (SAW) family (*ahl ul-Bayt*) and those who believed that it belonged to *ummah* as a whole. Those who supported the cause of the Prophet's (SAW) family were called *al-sh'iat-li-ahlil-Bayt* (adherents of the people of the house). Since Haḍrat 'Ali (Raḍ.A) was the most prominent figure among the family of the Prophet (SAW) he became the rallying point of the supporters of the said cause, and the latter came to be known as *Sh'ia-tu'Ali* hence Shi'a or Shi'is.

Before becoming the official religion of Safavids of Iran in sixteenth century, Shi'is had resisted, at a number of places, the onslaught of Saljūqs. Therefore, it is difficult to assign a well-defined geographical area to them. They continued to flourish in various areas of Saljūq realm with its numerous sub-groups. It is, however, a reality that during the period of

---

33. G. Makkdisi, "Muslim Institutions of Learning in the Eleventh Century Baghdad", *BSOAS*, vol. 24, 1961, pp.2-3.
34. Ibid.
35. A.L. Tabawi, "Origin and Character of Madarsa", *BSOAS*, vol. 25, 1962, pp. 228.

our study it passed through many phases of tough antagonism, which, at times, varied in nature. Of numerous Shi'i groups, only following four were however, prominent:

1. *Nāṣirīs*, 2. *Zaydīs*, 3. *Imāmīs* (twelvers), and 4. *Ismā'ilīs*.

Nāṣirīs

A name given in the twelfth century to those extremists who attribute to 'Ali divine or quasi-divine powers.[36] But all other Shi'i sects considered them heretic and *kāfir* (infidels).[37]

Zaydīs

They were the followers of Zayd, grandson of Al-Hussain, whom they regarded as the founder of their sect. Of all Shi'i sects they are nearest to Sunnīs in ideology and in some respects the most tolerant. Contrary to other Shi'ite groups the Zaydīs believe in no hidden *imām*. They do not practise *muta'* (temporary marriage) and allow no *taqiyyah* (dissimulation).[38]

Theologically, the Zaydīs were Mu'tazila and in jurisprudence they were practically identical with the Sunnīs in as much as they considered *qiyās* (analogical deduction/ reasoning), *roy* (arbitrary opinion), *ijtihād* (independent judgement) and *istiḥsān* (preference) to be the sources of *Shari'a*. They declared all those as *kāfirs* (infidels) who did not accept Zayd as the true successor of 'Ali the son of Imām Hussain.[39]

---

36. Shahristani, *Al-Milal wan-Nihal*, ed. Cureton, London, 1842-46, pp. 143-45.
37. Ibid.
38. Hitti, op. cit., p. 449.
39. *Cambridge History of Iran*, op. cit., p. 290.

During this period Zaydīs were still strong in the regions of Daylam, Gīlān, Tabaristan and Gurgan. In these areas the Zaydīs recited the *khuṭbah* (Friday sermon) in the name of their *imāms* and struck coins in their name.[40]

Imāmīs

Apart from the Ismā'ilīs, the strongest Shi'ite group of this period was *Ithna Ash'ariya* (Twelvers, as the Western orientalists call them).

The orthodox Shi'ites (Ithna Ash'ariya) believed that the *imāmate* had descended from Prophet Muhammad (SAW) to

1. Ali

↓ ↓ ↓

2.Hasan

3. Hussain (d. 61/680)
↓
4. Zain-ul-'Abidin (d. *c*. 94/712)
↓
5. Mohmad Baqir (d. 113/731)
↓
6. J'afar Sadiq (d. 148/765)
↓
7. Musa Kazim (d. 183/799)
↓
8. 'Ali Rida (d. 202/818)
↓
9. Mohammad Taqi (d. 220/835)
↓
10. 'Ali Naqi (d. 254/865)
↓
11. Hasan Askari (d. 260/874)
↓
12. Mahdi (disappeared in 260/874)

40. *Cambridge History of Iran*, op. cit., p. 290.

Haḍrat Ali and his descendants according to the genealogy given below:

According to Shi'ite traditions, the twelfth *imām,* namely Mahdī, was born in Samarra in 255/868 or 256/869. At the time of death of his father he was either four or five years of age. He was designated as *imām* a few days before the death of his father and very soon after his death he disappeared or went into concealment which consists of two periods, short (*sughrā*) and long (*kubrā*).

The political theories of the Ithna Ash'ariya Shi'ites depend on three fundamental precepts, namely, (i) the divine right of the descendants of Haḍrat Ali to succeed to the *imāmate,* (ii) the sinlessness of all the *imām*s, and (iii) the return of Mahdī, the twelfth *imām.*

However, in spite of the anti-Shi'i policies of the first two Saljūq rulers, Shi'a centres were flourishing in Iran as elsewhere during this period.[41] Shi'is had their own libraries, *madāris* and *masājid* and even succeeded in penetrating into court life.[42] Thus, Hibatullah Muhammad bin 'Ali (known as Ibn al-Muttalib) was a minister of Caliph al-Mustazhir, S'ad ul-Mulk Avji was *Wazīr* to Sulṭān Muhammad bin Malikshah[43] and Sharf-ud-din Anushirvan Khalid Kāshānī was *Wazīr* both to Caliph al-Mustarshid and Sulṭān Muhammad bin Malik Shah.[44] The extent of Shi'a influence and their penetration into

41. *Cambridge History of Iran,* p. 292. It may be noted that after the period of first two Saljūq rulers Tughril Beg and Alp Arsalan, the Shi'ite enjoyed a relatively better religious freedom. (See: *Siyāsat-Nāma,* pp. 164-65.)

42. *Cambridge History of Iran,* p. 292, *Siyāsat Nāma,* p. 165.

43. Rāwandi, op. cit., p. 152.

44. Rāwandi, op. cit., p. 204; Abbas Parviz, *Tarikhi-Salajiqa wa Khwarazm Shahan,* Tehran, 1930, p. 447.

official circles can be gauged by yet another fact that orthodox Sunnīs feared the alliance between the Saljūq ruling class and the Shi'is. The author of *Faḍaih al-Rawāfiḍ* expresses this fear in these words, "now there is no *sarāi* of Turks that has not at least ten or fifteen *rawāfiḍ*,[45] and many of them are employed as *dābir*s in the *diwān*s. The Shi'i author of *Kitāb un-Naqd*[46] even has words in praise of the Turks who sometimes used to protect the Shi'a in the period following the death of Niẓām al-Mulk and Malikshah.

Shi'a influence was particularly strong in Khawārizm, which happened to be an old stronghold of Shi'ias. The Khawārizm Shah Muhammad, at the beginning of thirteenth century, is reported to have proposed to declare the Abbāsids unworthy of the caliphate and Hussainis ('Alids) legitimate heirs of the caliphate.[47]

Among the features of the methodology for spreading their beliefs and influences the Shī'a, during the post Niẓām al-Mulk period, took recourse to *manāqibis* or *manāqib khwāns*.[48] The *manāqibis* are said to have existed in Iraq even during the Buyid period but due to the fear of persecution by early Saljūqs they kept their activities secret and often migrated from place

---

45. One fails to understand the apathy of the medieval author to distinguish between extremist sects like Ismā'ilīs and the Shi'a. The term "Rawāfid" to be used for Shi'a is, however, neither proper nor historically correct.

46. Syed Murtada Razvi, ed. A. Iqbal, Tehran, 1313/1934; cf. *Cambridge History of Iran*, p. 292.

47. Juwayni, *Tarikh-i-Jahān Gusha*, tr. J.A. Boyle, Manchester, 1958, vol. II, pp. 96-97.

48. *Manāqib* means virtues and *manāqib khwān* is a singer who extolls the virtues of a person.

    Also, see, *Cambridge History of Iran*, vol. V, p. 293.

to place.[49] But after the death of Malik Shah, the *manāqib khwāns* used to sing *qaṣidās* (panegyric) in praise of the *Shī'a imām* because he had attacked the Sunnī usurpers. These *qaṣidās* also contained doctrinal and theological elements. In their fantastic tales the *manāqib khwāns* extolled the military exploits of Haḍrat 'Ali and his paladins.[50]

In order to counterbalance the *manāqib khwāns*, the Sunnīs employed *faḍā'il khwāns* (also means singers of virtues), who exalted the superior virtues of Caliph Abū Bakr and 'Umar.

It is also during the period under review that *tāẓiyās* (not in the modern sense of theatrical plays) were revived. These mourning ceremonies on the martyrdom of Hussain at Karbalā seem to have started or developed first under the Saljūqs. They were sometimes practised by the Sunnīs too, and even in strong Sunnī towns, like Hamadān.[51] According to some religious literature of the period the prominent Shi'a centres during this period were Kāshān, Tafrīsh, Aveh, Qum, Ray, Qazvīn, Mazandarān, Nishāpūr and Sabzavār. The famous Shamsud-Din Laghari has been quoted in *Rāḥat us-Ṣudūr* testifying the same fact.[52]

The important Shi'a *madāris* of this period were in Rayy, Khurasan and Sabzavar. Some of these *madāris* had 200 to 400 students.[53] In Kāshān these *madāris* were called Safawiya, the Najdiya, the Sharafiya, etc. and had learned masters like *Imām* Zia ud-din Abul Rida Fadl-ullah bin 'Ali al-Hussain, on their staff.

---

49. *Cambridge History of Iran*, p. 293.
50. Ibid., p. 293.
51. Ibid., p.294.
52. Rāwandi, op. cit., p. 495.
53. *Cambridge History of Iran*, p. 294.

The basis of a complete Shi'a theology was laid down during this period, which produced only in the next century Nasir-ud-din Ṭūsī the greatest of all Shi'a theologians.[54]

Thus, as pointed out earlier, the later twelfth century CE provided a lease to the Shi'as and their protagonists. The writings of Shi'a authors in various disciplines of religious and philosophical thought bear a testimony to this. Amongst such polemical works mention can be made of a work of Sayyid Murtaḍā (d. CE 1045) written against *Al Mughni fil Imāma* by the Qāḍī Abdul-Jabbār al Mu'tazili of Hamadān (d. CE 1023). Another polemical writer was Abūl-Qāsim Hussain bin Muhammad of Isfahān known as Rāghib Isfahāni (d. CE 1108). The famous *Kitāb un-Naqd* was also composed around CE 1165. This period produced a number of those compositions, partly heresiographic and polemical, partly theological and historical, which could be defined as fore-runners of our modern handbooks of comparative religion.[55] The oldest one in Persian was written in CE 1092 by a Shi'i, Abul Ma'ali Muhammad Ubaidullah with the title *Bayan ul-adyān* (An explanation of Religions).[56] During the earlier period of seventh century AH was produced the *Tabsīrat ul 'Awām* by Sayyid Murtaḍā Dā'i Hussaini of Rayy, also a sort of encyclopaedia of religions containing useful data. The book comprises twenty-one chapters."[57]

Ismā'ilīs

After the death of *Imām* J'afar al-Ṣādiq, the body of his followers who remained faithful to the line of his descendants through his elder son and designated heir, *Imām* Ismā'il, came to be

54. *Cambridge History of Iran*, p. 295.
55. Ibid.
56. *Cambridge History of Iran*, p. 295; Abbas Parvez, op. cit., p. 422.
57. Abbas, op. cit., p. 424.

known as Ismā'ilīs.[58] Ismā'il predeceased his father. But Ismā'ilīs declared him not to be dead but hidden, and recognized him as the seventh *imām*, being in consequence known as seveners.[59]

According to the Ismā'ilī sources the next four *i'ima* who succeeded Ismā'il were hidden or concealed and taught their message to people through their agents. These *imāms* were expected to reappear to inaugurate the reign of justice and truth.[60] The later Ismā'ilī sources speak of this period as constituting a *dawr us-satr* (period of concealment). During this period the *i'ima* settled at Salamiya in Syria, but their identity and whereabouts were known only to a few trusted disciples.[61] They continued to engage themselves in creating a remarkable network of emissaries (agents) who came to be known as *dā'is*.[62]

---

58. Abbas Parvez, op. cit., pp. 172–204. Also see M. Hodgson, *The Order of Assasins*, Hague, 1995, pp. 22 ff.; Bernard Lewis, *The Origins of Ismā'ilīsm*, Cambridge, 1949, pp. 1-23 and *History of the Assians*, London, 1967, pp. 1-20; W. Ivano, *A Brief Survey of the Evolution of Ismā'ilīsm*, London, 1952, pp. 1 ff; *Cambridge History of Iran*, vol. IV, ed. R.N. Prye, Cambridge, 1975, pp. 520-23; *Encyclopaedia of Islam, Art,* Ismā'ilīa?

59. M.G. Hodgson; *The Order of the Assassins; the Struggle of the Early Nizari Ismā'ilīs against the Islamic World*, The Hague, 1955, p. 256.

60. *Cambridge History of Iran*, p. 425; S.H. Nasr, ibid., pp. 213-15; Saunders, op. cit., p.127.

61. S.H. Nasr, *Three Muslim Sages*, Cambridge, 1964, pp. 212-13.

62. *Dā'is* (propagandists) formed a trained hierarchy; each *da'i* who commonly distinguished himself as a merchant or artisan, was assigned a particular territory where he sought to increase likely converts and initiated those who joined the movement step by step into its secret doctrines and ritual.

    A *da'i* was carefully selected and was expected to subject himself to a rigorous training and discipline. The *da'i* in Ismā'ilī circles →

The Ismā'ilī *d'awah* (call) was steadily gaining momentum, and consolidation of its influence was being realized chiefly in Iran, India and Transoxiana. These regions provided material and moral support to the Ismā'ilī sentiments, which were practically manifested in Egypt where the ruling Fāṭimīd dynasty was established.[63]

But in the eleventh century, the Ismā'ilīs suffered a number of severe political and military setbacks. The force of Mahmūd of Ghazna, who was fiercely anti-Ismā'ilī caused considerable change in Sindh, where a large number of Ismā'ilīs were brutally massacred.[64]

Around the middle of the eleventh century, Africa too was lost to the Fāṭimīds as a result of a local rebellion in favour of the 'Abbāsids, which was once again accompanied by the massacre of several Ismā'ilī communities in the area.[65] But, still due to the untiring efforts of Dā'i 'Ali bin Muhammad al-Sulayhi, sufficient support and allegiance was secured in Yemen. Similar attempts were made to re-establish control amongst the communities as had survived the massacre carried out by Mahmūd. *Dā'is* also went out to Gujarat and along the western coast of India. In the upper Oxus region, the eminent *dā'i* Nasiri-i-Khusraw carried out a sustained exercise of preaching the Isma'ilı faith.

→ was expected not only to lead an ethically exemplary life, but also to be in possession of a keen knowledge of the highest intellectual sciences of the day. Thus, the *da'i* had not only to summon the people to allegiance to the rightful *imām*, but also to promote the social, moral and spiritual welfare of the *imām*'s followers. They attempted to introduce a religious reform precisely in opposition to the whole pattern of Sunnah.

63. S.H. Nasr, op. cit., p. 235.

64. Ibid.

65. S.H. Nasr, op. cit., p. 235.

In Iran and Transoxiana the *d'awah* was carried out under cover particularly after the rise of Saljūqs who were bent upon exterminating the Ismā'ilī supremacy.[66] However, the Ismā'ilī influence continued to grow in spite of the anti-Ismā'ilī policies of the Saljūqs. Ismā'ilīs seem to have been numerous in towns in all parts of the Saljūq kingdom. Many are reported to have been craftsmen and some were merchants.[67]

With the increasing Saljūq power the Ismā'ilīs, however, found themselves in an increasing hostile environment, which prevailed, not only in the political and military sphere but also at intellectual level. The most well-known attempt to combat Ismā'ilīs through the articulation of a rival theology and *Sharī'ah* was exemplified in one of the works of al-Ghazālī (d. CE 1111), which was undertaken at the behest of *Wazīr* Niẓām al-Mulk.[68] The Ismā'ilīs attempted to introduce a religious reform precisely in opposition to the whole pattern of *Sunnīs*.[69] During the eleventh century the Ismā'ilīs of the Saljūq lands were preparing active insurrections on an unprecedented pattern. They are said to have killed a *mu'adhin* at Saveh lest he should leak out their secrets. They were looking to multiplicity of risings everywhere at once, to overwhelm the established social structure from within.[70]

---

66. *Cambridge History of Iran*, p. 427.
67. Ibid; Hodgson, *The Venture of Islam*, Chicago, 1974, p. 54.
68. See G. Maqdisi, *The Sunnī Revival*, pp. 155-68. For more details see: Henry Corbin, "The Ismā'ilī Response to The Polemic of Ghazālī", in S.H. Nasr, op. cit., pp. 69 ff.
69. Hodgson, ibid. They were resisting the *Shar'ia* which was taught in the rapidly multiplying Sunnī madrasahs. (*Cambridge History of Iran*, ibid)?
70. *Cambridge History of Iran*, p. 427.

The Ismā'ilīs extended their power by striking up alliances with local princes or *amīrs*, by persuading the people to come into the fold of their *d'awah* and by resorting to military action.[71]

The Ismā'ilīs changed their political and military strategy in obtaining their goal. They followed a policy of dealing with the enemy on a piecemeal basis, each campaign being aimed at a selected local target and the consolidation of Ismā'ilī power in that specific area. All the Ismā'ilī settlements showed a remarkable internal cohesiveness, and their campaigns as a result were characterized by great solidarity and discipline on the part of the adherents of faith. Alamūt was the nerve centre wherefrom all directives, administrative as well as strategic, were issued. If a particular settlement fell prey to the hostile attacks the other remaining strongholds were ready to give shelter to the inhabitants of the former settlement.[72]

To eliminate their enemies and to achieve military and political objectives, the Ismā'ilīs resorted to an important auxiliary technique — the assassination. They made a frank policy of it, even insinuating their men among a potential enemy's servants in advance.[73] After assassinating *Wazīr* Niẓām al-Mulk, they murdered, all of a sudden, 'Abd ur-Rehmān Sumayrami, the *Wazīr* of the mother of Sulṭān Berkyaruk in the month of *Safar* 490/1097.[74] Towards the end of *Ramaḍān*

---

71. Abbas Parvez, op. cit., p. 180; S.H. Nasr, op. cit., p. 248; for details of Ismā'ilī organization see M. Hodgson, *The Order of Assasins*, op. cit., pp. 45, 64 and 69.

72. S.H. Nasr, op. cit., p. 248; For more details of Ismā'ilī conquests of Towns and fortresses and their rule thereof; see Abbas Parvez, op. cit., pp. 189-90 ff.

73. Hodgson, op. cit., p. 60.

74. Ibn al-Athir, *al-Kāmil fi-'l Tārīkh*, ed. Tornberg, Leiden, 1851-76, p. 112.

493/1100 two *fidais* assassinated Amir Bulkabak Sarmaz, the *Shahna* of Isfahan, in the palace of Sulṭān Muhammad al-Isfahān, although the victim always used to wear a coat of mail and was never without a large number of bodyguards.[75] In the year 499/1105-6 Abūl-ala Sa'id Abū Muhammad, *Qāḍī* of Nishāpūr was murdered by an Ismā'īlī *fidāi* in the *jam'ia masjid* of Isfahān.[76] Abūl Muzzafar al-Khajandi was murdered by an 'Alid *bāṭinī* at Rayy, as soon as he left the chair after preaching a sermon in 497/1103.[77] Ibn al-Athir mentions the murder of Fakhr al-Mulk, the eldest son of Niẓām al-Mulk,[78] by an Ismā'īlī in 500/1105.[79]

Having got encouraged by these assassinations the *fidāis* created a havoc and rumpus by killing, all over the empire, a large number of *'ulamā'* and *fuqahā* (theologians) and those who opposed them.

In 494/1101 Berkyaruk (in western Iran) and Sanjar (in Khurasan), made an agreement against Ismā'īlīs who were considered a general threat to Saljūq power.[80] The main result of this agreement of reconciliation was a grand massacre of suspected Ismā'īlīs at Isfahān, Baghdad and elsewhere. Army officers were especially affected and several of them fled.[81]

---

75. Ibn al-Athīr, Rāwandī, op. cit., p. 141.
76. Ibn al-Athīr, op. cit., p.163
77. Ibid., p. 153.
78. He was the *Wazīr* of Sulṭān Berkyaruk and later on that of Sulṭān Sanjar. Ibid., p. 174.
79. Ibid., p. 175.
80. It may be noted that Berkyaruk was earlier accused of having been in league with the Ismā'īlīs which later proved false, since he was himself attempted by Ismā'īlīs (Rāwandi, op. cit., p. 143).
81. Rāwandī, op. cit., p. 143.

Sanjar sent an expedition against the Ismā'ilīs of Tabas in Kuhistān. Three years later he sent another, which wrecked Tabas and destroyed as much as possible.[82] The second expedition as a *jihad* (holy war) was joined by many *Sunnī* volunteers, in addition to the regular troops, and the Ismā'ilī captives, as apostates were enslaved.[83]

(III) ṢŪFISM

We propose to discuss the origin and development of Ṣūfism and organization of Ṣūfī *silsilās* (orders) in chapter 3. So, we shall be confining ourselves to some aspects of Ṣūfism during eleventh and twelfth centuries CE only.

The socio-political life during eleventh and twelfth centuries CE bears deep imprints of Ṣūfī ethos. Ṣūfism, too, seems to have found the great patrons and sincere protectors among Saljūq administrators, princes and powerful personalities during the period of our study. This perhaps was the main cause of the unceasing development of Ṣūfism in this period. Ṣūfīs during this period were fairly free to teach their doctrines and carry on their practices.[84]

Before the period of our study Ṣūfism had undergone considerable developments and modifications, as the Muslims had long been in contact with people of other races and cultures

82. Rāwandi, op. cit., p. 143.

83. Ibid.

84. *Cambridge History of Iran*, p. 300. One of the greatest patrons of Ṣūfīs in Saljūq era was the great *Wazīr* Niẓām al-Mulk Tūsi himself. Tūsi had himself been in his youth a pupil of the famous Ṣūfī Sa'id Abul Khair, and about that saint, he is said to have remarked: "All that I have, I owe to Sheikh Abu Sa'id Tūsi founded many *khānqāhs* and gave much money to the embryonic Ṣūfī organism of his age."

in the course of their history. Again, with the coming of Saljūqs many intellectual and political transformations took place, which changed completely the direction of the development of philosophy, the science and the *kalām*.[85]

A new trend of pacification and assimilation between Ṣūfism and *Sharī'ah* came to be realized afresh during this period. In fact, this period witnessed a broad measure of agreement on the meaning of Ṣūfism and the details of the Ṣūfī experience and theory.[86]

The great Ṣūfī teachers of the time came to the rescue of Islam, which was in dire need of reform and revival. These teachers chose to reform the faith from within by uniting the fragmented religious thoughts.[87] The last obstacle in the path of assimilation was set aside by the Himalayan efforts of Ghazālī, the great theologian, Ṣūfī and jurist who demolished and rejected the philosophers and philosophizing Ismā'ilīs and completed a reconciliation between orthodoxy and Ṣūfism which immensely fortified Islam against the challenges that were soon to threaten even the very existence of Islam.[88] Some of the greatest impulses were given to a re-orientation of the piety of Islam on the basis of Ṣūfism. The orientation of Muslim piety to historical consideration had gradually become less intense with the end of the high Caliphal age.[89] At the same

---

85. *Cambridge History of Iran*, p. 463.
86. *Cambridge History of Iran*, p. 614.
87. Ibid.
88. Ibid.; cf. Hodgson, op. cit., p. 201. For details of Ghazālī's role in reconciling *Shari'a* and *taṣawwuf*, see Zarin Kub, *Justuju dar Tasawwuf-i-Iran*, pp. 85 ff.
89. R.S. Bhatnager. *Dimensions of Classical Ṣūfī Thought*, Delhi, 1984, pp. 191-94.

time the less temporarily insistent pattern of Ṣūfism gained increasing respect. The time of formation of the international society was a formative age for a new popular Ṣūfism also.[90]

Thus, in a period of the transposition of intellectual life into the middle period forms, Ṣūfism was being prepared to play a larger role, both social and intellectual, than it had played in high Caliphal times and it was ready for whatever tasks might be required of it.[91]

The beginning of sixth/twelfth century witnessed the development of an institution, which thereafter dominated the Ṣūfī movement and mediated its mass appeal. The organized *silsilās*[92] of Ṣūfism were founded and some important aspects of *tarīqat* ritual were introduced.[93] Doubtless, the Ṣūfī orders had been existing for a pretty long period but the organizational history of these orders is found only after the emergence of Saljūqs to power. Massignon is of the opinion that the initiation (*ijāza*) ritual of the Ṣūfī brotherhoods/ fraternities (*ikhwān*) was first introduced in the twelfth century.[94] It is, in fact, not the perceptive preaching alone that won for Ṣūfism its leading role but the institutional form that it took.[95] This popular appeal of Ṣūfism in this period and its social role in the earlier middle period were most enduringly

---

90. Hodgson, op. cit., p. 203.
91. Ibid., pp. 201-3.
92. *Cambridge History of Islam*, op. cit., p. 620; Hodgson, op. cit., p. 211; cf. Baldic Julian, *Mystical Islam*, London, 1989. "The Emergence of Brotherhood", pp. 72 ff; and A.A. Rizvi, *A History of Sufism in India*, vol. I, Delhi, 1978, pp. 78-79, 97.
93. *Cambridge History of Iran*, op. cit., p. 296.
94. See Massignon's article "Tariqa" in *Encyclopaedia of Islam*.
95. Hodgson, op. cit., p. 209.

based on a particular form of the Ṣūfī ministry (*pīri murīdī*), the relationship of the teacher (*pīr*) and disciples (*murīd*).[96]

With the introduction of *pīri-murīdī* chain the convents (*ribāṭs/khānqāhs*) were founded and endowed, where a celebrated saint would reside with a group of his followers, who studied under him and worshipped with him for a shorter or a longer period. Initiation (*ijāza*) into the Ṣūfī mysteries was marked by the investiture of a special dress (*khirqa*) symbolizing his acceptance of and entry into a tradition of divine service mounting back stage by stage to the Prophet Muhammad (SAW).[97] The *ijāẓat nāma* was also issued by the *pīr* to his *murīd shāgird*) attesting the true spiritual descent.[98]

At first there was a certain subordination of *pīrs* and *khānqāhs* at a distance of the headquarters of the head of the order — usually at the founder's tomb. In this way the several *silsilās* formed a flexible interlocking network of authorities.

The line of Ṣūfī *ṭariqās* at once deepened the moral resources and tied them up into a system of universal brotherhood that was the trait of high Caliphal times. The Ṣūfism supplemented the *sharī'ah* as a principle of unity and order, offering the Muslims a sense of spiritual unity. They developed a picture of the world, which united the whole *dār-ul-Islam*, and even the lands of the infidels (*dār-ul-Harb*) under a comprehensive spiritual hierarchy of *pīrs*, which was all the more effective.[99] The individual *khānqāhs* and saints' tombs to which the faithful could come for spiritual guidance and consolation from pious men were part of an inclusive holy order not merely the order

96. Hodgson, op. cit., p. 209.
97. For more details, see Hodgson, op. cit., p. 210.
98. *Cambridge History of Islam*, loc. cit.
99. *Cambridge History of Iran*, op. cit., p. 221.

of a given *ṭariqāh*, but of God's chosen men throughout the world.[100]

The four main orders, which flourished during this period are: The Chistī order, the Qādirī order, the Suhrawardī order and the Naqshbandī order.

The Chistī Order

The Chistī order owes its origin to Khaja Abu Iṣḥāq Shāmī Chistī (d. CE 966).[101] He was a descendant of the Prophet Muhammad (SAW). The Chistī community, originating at Chisht in Khurāsan, specialized in the use of *samā'* in their exercises. The wandering *dervishes* of this order, who were also known as *Chist* or *Chisht*, would enter a town and play a rousing air with flute and drum to gather people around them before reciting a tale or legend of initiatory significance.[102] Like other Ṣūfī orders, the specialized methodologies of the Chistīs soon became crystallized into a simplified love for *samā'*.[103]

The following four saints, are regarded as spiritual descendants of Abū isḥāq Shāmī Chistī (R.'A.)

(i) Khawāja Abū Ahmad (d. CE 966), vicegernt to Abū Ishāq, became an *abdāl*,[104]

(ii) Khawāja Abū Muhammad (d. CE 1020) son and successor of Abū Ahmad,

(iii) Khawāja Abū Yūsuf (d. CE 1067), Vicegerent of Abū Muhammad, and

100. *Cambridge History of Iran*, op. cit., p. 221.

101. Idries Shah, *The Way of the Ṣūfī*, London, 1982, p. 127; T.C. Rastogi, *Islamic Mysticism*, New Delhi, 1982, p. 114.

102. Idries Shah, loc. cit.; see also Rastogi, op. cit., p. 13.

103. Ibid.

104. *Abdāl* is a saint of distinctive qualities.

(iv) K͟hawāja Mawdūd (d. CE 1133), son and successor of Abū Yūsuf.[105]

Other branches emanating from the town of Chist in modern Afghanistan did not survive for long in the Perso-Islamic world.[106] Instead, this order flourished in the Indian subcontinent. Thus, one may conveniently say that the Chistī order of Ṣūfism is essentially an Indian one.[107] Some of the disciples of K͟hwāja Mawdūd dispersed insignificantly as wandering *dervishes*.

The emergence of Gurids in tenth century proved less favourable to the peaceful existence of the followers of this order.[108] It was in these circumstances that K͟hawāja Mu'inud-din Chistī, one of the greatest Ṣūfīs of the Middle Ages, decided to settle in the east at Ajmer, on the borders of the Ghurid Empire.[109] The order was spread by his followers, K͟hawāja Qutub ud-din Bakhtiyar Kākī, K͟hawāja Farīd ud-dīn Gunj S͟hakar, Makhdum Alau-ud-din Ali Ahmad Ṣābir, K͟hawāja Niẓām ud-din Auliya and K͟hawāja Nassīr ud-din Mahmūd. The followers of this *ṭariqāh* believe in audible method of performing prayers and regarded *samā'* (Ṣūfī audition) as the food of soul.

The Qādirī Order

Qādirī order of Ṣūfism was organized by the founder 'Abdu'l Qādir of Gilan[110] who was born at Nif, in Gilan district, to the

105. Rastogi, op. cit., p. 11; *Cambridge History of Iran*, op. cit., p. 297.
106. Rizvi, op. cit., p. 114.
107. Ibid.
108. Ibid., p. 115.
109. Ibid.
110. A detailed account of his life is given in the next chapter.

south of the Caspian Sea, in CE 1077. He died in Baghdad in CE 1166.[111]

Abdul Qādir became the most widely revered of all Ṣūfī *pīrs* as a preacher to the population. He set out for Baghdad in his teen age to acquire more knowledge of religion. In Baghdad he selected a pious man as his spiritual guide who was a syrup vendor by trade and who was extraordinarily severe in disciplining him. After completing his studies he would often stay the whole night in worship or sometimes he went off wandering in desert areas. He continued a long course of spiritual austerities first at a town in Khuzistan and then back in Baghdad.[112]

After achieving the spiritual maturity he set out to teach the people. He was provided a *madrasah* (college) where he lectured on all the standard subjects like *Qur'ān, Ḥadīth, Fiqh* Jurisprudence, etc. Now, he got married and from his, four wives had a total of forty-nine children, among them four of his sons became known as religious scholars of some repute.

As a teacher and especially as a public preacher, Jīlānī (R.'A.) became extraordinarily popular in Baghdad. His *madrasah* (college) had soon to be extended and he took to preaching sessions on Friday and Wednesday morning in the mass prayer grounds (*'Idgāh/Muṣṣala*) outside the city, for there was no other place big enough to hold the crowds.[113] Every visitor to Baghdad made it a point to hear him.[114]

Jīlānī (R.'A.) is said to have converted a number of persons

---

111. Hodgson, op. cit., p. 207, Shah, op. cit., p. 138.
112. Hodgson, loc. cit. See also M.M. Sharief, *History of Muslim Philosophy*, vol. I, Delhi, 1993, pp. 349-51.
113. Hodgson, op. cit., p. 208. cf. Sharief, loc. cit.
114. Hodgson, op. cit., p. 287.

to Islam, and to have won many Muslim sinners to repentance. The writings, prayers and sermons of Jīlānī (R.'A.) have been preserved in his most celebrated books, *al-Ghuniyā li-Ṭālib-i-tāriq il-haqq, Futūḥ al-Ghaib, Fatḥi Rubbāni* and *Jilal al-Khaṭīr*.

The followers of this order practise both *dhikr-i-khafi* (silent recollection) as well as *dhikr-i-jali* (vocal recollection) of the divine names of God. They wear a white turban with white rose. The rose is a symbol of the unity of *sharī'ah* (religious law), *ṭariqāh* (divine journey) and *ma'rifat* (gnosis) whereas its whiteness indicates complete surrender of the followers of the path to spiritual guide. Members of this *silsilā* (order) lay emphasis on the realization of moral attributes like charity.

The Qādirī order found followers in numerous parts of the Islamic world and was especially powerful in India, where its influence is widespread to the present day. A determining factor in the success of this and other similar orders was their faithful adherence to the religious laws and practices of orthodoxy, and their strong condemnation of antinomianism and incarnationist tendencies. The teachings of 'Abdu'l Qādir Jīlānī (Raḥ.'A) are firmly based on the *Qu'rān* and Traditions. The religious exercises it recommends are in conformity with the Sharī'ah.

The Suhrawardī Order

The Suhrawardī order, originally founded by Abū Najib Suhrawardī, was popularized by Shihāb-ud-din Suhrawardī (539-632/1144-1234). Shihāb ud-din was born at a time when the fate of the whole Muslim world was hanging in the balance. The last king of the Saljūqs, Sulṭān Sanjar, died in 552/1157 and it was immediately followed by the rampant devastations of Chengiz Khan which started in 615/1218. The insecurity, fear, massacre, loot, arson and other evils must have certainly influenced the mind of Shihāb-ud-din. That is why a note is often met within his work *'Awārif ul-Ma'ārif* in which he expresses with a sad heart the decline in moral character of his contemporaries. He passed the major part of his life in Baghdad where he now lies buried. His *'Awārif ul-Ma'ārif* is a standard treatise on mysticism and is extensively studied in all mystic circles.[115]

India, Persia and Africa have all been influenced in their mystical activity by the methods and personages of the order. The instructional material of the order is to be undertaken very carefully and a disciple must eventually undergo all the instructional devices. Without them, it is believed, there is a possibility that the student may simply develop altered states of mind, which render him unfit for ordinary life.

The Suhrawardī order was brought to India by a number of the disciples of Shaikh Shihāb-ud-din Suhrawardī, who migrated from Iran and Transoxiana. The most prominent among those who introduced this order in India was Shaikh Bahāu'd-Dīn Zakariyya.[116] Subsequently, the order widely spread in the Punjab and Sindh.

The Ṣūfīs of this order believe in *sharī'ah* and theological form of Ṣūfism. The *silsilā* a further branched out into a number of sub-sections.[117]

The Naqshbandī Order

The Naqshbandiya *silsilā* was established and popularized by Muhammad Bahā'ud-din Naqshband (d. CE 1389).[118] According

115. Sharief, op. cit., p. 354.
116. Rizvi, op. cit., p. 190.
117. For a detailed account about the order see Rizvi, op. cit., pp. 190-91 and Sharief, op. cit., pp. 350-51.
118. Sardar Iqbal 'Ali Shah, *Islamic Ṣūfism*, op. cit., p. 155.

to Turkish work of antiquity entitled *Rashahat 'Ain al Hayāt* (drops from the Fountain of Life) K͟hawāja Bahā'ud-din propounded such spiritual doctrines which distinguish it from other cults.[119] Some sources say that Naqshband was his surname, and that he was the author of a work called *maqāmāt* (stations) and another one written under his own name as the prayers of Baha.

The order, also known as the school of *khawājgān* (masters) rose in Central Asia and greatly influenced the development of mystic tendencies in Indian and Turkish empires.[120] The order gave rise to many special schools, which adopted individual names, and many authorities regard this as the earliest of all the mystical chains of transmission.[121] In India, this order spread through Bāqi Billah Berang (d. CE 1633). The followers of this order are orthodox Ṣūfīs who firmly believe in Islamic traditions. They discard *samā'* (Ṣūfī audition) and accept *d͟hikr-i-k͟hafi* or silent recollection of God. They lay emphasis on the obedience of the "Shaykh" who illuminates the soul to attain *mā'rifat* (gnosis). The main ceremonies of this *ṭariqāh* are regular recitation of prayers and organization of weekly assemblies of the members of the order.

The followers of this order have not identified themselves with any particular dress and they have carried on their pious activities quite unassumingly, therefore it is slightly difficult to identify its members because the *k͟hawājgan* have worked entirely within the social framework of the culture in which they lived and in the areas like Central Asia and West Asia they are known mainly as Muslim pietists.[122]

119. Sardar Iqbal Ali Shah, *Islamic Ṣūfism*, Delhi, 1979, p. 97.

120. Shah, op. cit., p. 155; Rizvi., op. cit., p. 95.

121. Ibid.

122. Shah, op. cit., p. 155.

There are eleven principles which are strictly followed by the members of this *ṣilsilā*. These are:

1. *Hōsh dar dam* (consciousness in breathing): This means that the follower of the path should remain aware about the remembrance of Allāh, while he inhales or exhales.
2. *Naẓar bar qadam* (watching over the steps): It implies that the aspirant has to keep a watch over his footsteps on the mystic path. He should concentrate upon his outward as well as inward behaviour in a balanced way.
3. *Safar dar waṭan* (inward journey): This means that the *sālik* (seeker of the path) should concentrate on his inner life, renouncing the transient.
4. *Khalwat dar Anjuman* (retirement in gathering): It means that the seeker of Allāh has to adopt an attitude of loneliness in the midst of his fellow men.
5. *Yād kard* (recollection): This signifies that the pilgrim should remember Allāh and recollect His names every time.
6. *Bāz gasht* (restraining thought): It means that the aspirant has to control his thoughts. If his heart is engaged with anything else he should return to Allāh.
7. *Nigāh dāsht* (watching thought): This principle means that the follower of the mystic path should keep an eye over his spiritual attitude and should not allow any evil thought to enter his mind.
8. *Yād dāsht* (enduring recollection): This means that the servant of Allāh has to concentrate upon Him unceasingly.
9. *Wuqūf-i-zamāni* (a pause for duties): It means that the seeker of God should settle down for the assessment of his spiritual duties on his way to Allāh.

10. *Wuqūf-i-'adadi* (a pause for performing recitation): It signifies that the pilgrim needs an intermission while performing the recitation of divine names.
11. *Wuqūf-i-qalbi* (pause for experiencing God's presence): This means that the seeker after Allāh has to pause for some time for the realization of his fellowship with Allah in his heart.[123]

Another important Ṣūfī order of the epoch was known after its founder Ahmad bin 'Umaru'l-Khayūqī, popularly called Najmu'd-Dīn Kubrā, who was martyred in CE 1221 during the invasion of his native country Khawārizm by the Mongols.[124]

A number of branches of his order, the Kubrawiyya spread to Baghdad, Khurasan and India. The two branches of this order that spread in India are known as Fridausiya and Hamadāniya, whereas its branches that spread in Baghdad and Khurasan are known as Nuriya and Rukniya.[125] He is also known as *shaikh-i-walī tarash* (the carver of saints), because of the great number of Ṣūfīs who surrounded him as disciples and followed his teachings.[126]

Apart from various works which Kubrā wrote in Arabic and Persian special mention can be made of *Al-uṣūl al-'Ashra* (in Arabic). In this book the author makes mention of the ten guiding principles of Ṣūfism: repentance, renunciation, trust in Allāh, resignation, the final stage (*riḍa*), etc.[127] Another of

---

123. For details, see Rizvi, op. cit., pp. 95-97.
124. *Cambridge History of Iran*, op. cit., p. 298; Rizvi, op. cit., p. 93.
125. Rizvi, op. cit., p. 93.
126. Ibid.
127. Rizvi, op. cit., p. 93.

his Persian books, the *Ṣifat ul-Ādāb,* contains rules of Ṣūfism. Yet again his famous *Minhāj us-sālikīn* (an open road for traveller on the Ṣūfī path) is a celebrated manual on the principles of Ṣūfism.[128]

Other Orders

Apart from the orders mentioned above there were many others too, which either could not make their identity prominent, or were known only as sub-orders. Some of them are *Yasaviya, Rifa'iya* and *Madyaniya.* These came into existence in the twelfth century CE. The *Yasaviya* order, established by Ahmad al-Yasavi (d. CE 1166), became popular in Turkistan. The *Rifa'iya* order was founded by the great theologist Ahmad Ibn Rifa'i (d. CE 1182). It was mainly followed by the dervishes of Turkey, Egypt and Syria. The *Madyaniya* order was founded by Abū Madyan (d. CE 1197). This order was further expanded into some main branches, viz. *Shadhiliya* (by Abūl Hasan Shadhili d. CE 1258), *Wafaiya* (by Ali Wafa d. CE 1404), *'Arusiya* (by Ahmad bin al-'Arus d. CE 1463), and *K͟hawāṭīriya* (by Sa'id ibn Yūsuf, d. CE 1702).

There are many other prominent Ṣūfī orders, which were founded after the period of our study. Prominent among them are *Qalandariyya, Mawlaviya* (established by Jalal ud-din Rumi d. CE 1273) and flourished especially in Turkey). In addition to these, *Bektashiya, Jalaliya* and *Khalwatiya* are the main Ṣūfī orders of the fourteenth century.

Abbāsid State: An Estimate

POLITICAL THEORISTS AND THEIR THEORIES

The polity and the administrative system during the period

---

128. Ibid.

of our study, i.e. eleventh and twelfth centuries CE cannot be studied in isolation. It can largely be regarded as representing or corresponding to the early middle ages. In fact, the administrative system of this period is a part of that unbroken thread of socio-political history, which, in spite of its Arab ethos grew out of the heritage of thought represented by the Semitic civilizations of the past.[129] This system owed much to a long administrative tradition that stretched back to pre-Islamic times.[130] Thus, behind this period is a long continuity of administrative practice. However, the old institutions gained a new meaning; developments, which had begun in the period, crystallized and new elements of worth were added to the Persian heritage.[131] Old institutions such as *Iqtā* and the *madāris* were given a new content and a new institution, the *atabgate* emerged. The details of this administrative system, which set the pattern for succeeding centuries, were worked out by the officials of the bureaucracy[132] and the religious institutions.[133]

---

129. Bashir-ud-din, "The political Theory of Islam", *Islamic Culture,* October 1934, p. 587.

130. A.K.S. Lambton, "Aspects of Saljūq-Ghuzz Settlement", *Islamic Civilization*, ed. D.S. Richard, p. 105.

131. *Cambridge History of Iran*, vol. V, p. 203. cf. M.G.S. Hodgson, *The Venture of Islam,* Chicago, 1974, vol. II, p. 10.

132. The administrative measures of the famous Saljūq Wazīr Niẓām al-Mulk Tūsi as put forth in his *Siyāsat Nāma* is a testimony to this.

133. For example, Māwardī (d. 430/1058) author of *Al-Ahkām us-Sulṭāniyyah*, the greatest theoretical exposition of Islamic constitutional law, writing during the Buyid period made an attempt to legalize what was in effect an usurpation of the power of the caliph. In the same way Ghazālī (d. 505/1111) who in his *Naṣīḥat al-Mulūk* envisaged a new association between the caliph and the *sulṭān* and assured co-operation among them.

The theoretical basis of the state's administrative system was derived from two main sources: the Islamic theory of state and the old Persian theory. Even Al-Ghazālī, who is generally considered the most important religio-political thinker of medieval Islam, views the Muslim civilization of this period as a Perso-Islamic synthesis.[134] After Al-Māwardī,[135] Ghazālī worked out a new relationship between the caliph and the *sulṭān*.[136] Similarly the old Persian theory of state was expressed by Niẓām al-Mulk largely in terms of political expediency.[137]

It is impossible to study the administrative system of the Abbāsids without examining political theories and ideas of both Niẓām al-Mulk Ṭūsī (CE 1017-92) and Abū Ḥāmid al-Ghazālī (CE 1058-1111), whose thought had profound effect on the political as well as the administrative system of this period.

Khawāja Abū Ali Hassan Ibn Ishāq was born at Nūqān a village of Ṭūs (modern Mashhad) in Persia in 408/1017. Hassan's father was a taxation officer or revenue agent. He learnt holy *Qur'ān* by heart by the age of eleven and exhibited his administrative talent even at his *madrasah* organizing the students in groups for better instructions.[138] Ṭūsī studied at Baghdad and Nishāpūr, the established centres of learning

134. Ghazālī, *Naṣīḥat al-Mulūk*, tr. F.R.C. Bagley, Oxford, New York, Toronto, 1964, p. XVI.

135. M.G.S. Hodgson, *The Order of Assassins*, The Hague, 1955, p. 55.

136. A.K.S. Lambton, *State and Government in Medieval Islam*, Oxford, 1981, p. 106.

137. Ibid.

138. Ilyas Ahmad, "The Political Theory of Niẓām al Mulk Tūsi", *Iqbal*, July, 1961. p. 65.

and academic excellence. At Nishāpūr, Khawāja Hassan studied under the guidance of famous scholar Imām Muwāfiq.[139] Later on, after studying *Qur'ān, Ḥadīth* and *Fiqh*, he went to Bukhāra where he acquired excellence in the arts and sciences of his times.[140] He also travelled to Kabul, Bulkh and Ghaznī. He entered into the service of Abdur Rashid (son of Sulṭān Mahmūd of Ghazni) and thus became familiar with *Kitābat* (secretaryship) and work of the court.[141] From the Ghaznavid court, the Khawāja left for Merv, which was then under the Saljūq Sulṭān Chagri Beg. The latter, being much impressed by the ability of the Khawāja appointed him as the *kātib* and *muḥāsib* of the prince Alp Arsalān as well as his *mudabbir, mushīr* and *atālīq* (secretary and tutor).[142] In this way Khawāja rose to the position of the prime minister of Sulṭān Alp Arsalān and later that of Sulṭān Malikshah. He is unanimously called as the prime minister of the realm of Saljūqs and one of the greatest *wuzarā'* the East has ever produced.[143]

---

139. Ilyas Ahmad, ibid. Umar Khayyam and Hasan-i-Sabbah too had studied under him.

140. Ibid, p. 66.

141. Ibid.

142. Ibid.

143. P.K. Hitti, *History of the Arabs*, London, 1970, p. 477; cf. Browne, *A Literary History of Persia*, vol. II, op. cit., p. 175.

Rizvan Ali Rizivi, "Political and Administrative Measures of Niẓām al-Mulk Tūsi", *Islamic Studies*, vol. 19, pp. 111-12.

Faizul Hasan Faizi, "A Peep into the Wasaya of Niẓām al-Mulk", *Islamic Culture*, vol. 20, 1946, pp. 392-94;

Harun Khan Sherwani, "Some Precursors of Niẓām ul Mulk Tūsi", *Islamic Culture*, Jan, 1934, pp. 15-16;

Harold Bowen, "Early Saljūqid Wuzarā'", *BSOAS*, vol. 20, 1957, pp. 110-17.

In CE 1063 Khawāja Hassan became the prime minister and continued to hold this position till CE 1091, when he was dismissed because of court intrigue and was later assassinated by a *fidāi* (an agent of the *bāṭiniyya*) on 10th Ramaḍān 485/1092.[144]

As prime minister, Niẓām al-Mulk directed his policy primarily through the great *dīwān* or administrative office (*Diwān-i-Waẓīr, Diwān-i-Sulṭān*), the executive centre of the state over which he presided.[145] Niẓām al-Mulk moulded the administration of the empire largely to his own liking and filled the bureaucracy, whose five-part division obviously followed that of the Ghaznavids, with officials who were either from his own family or were his proteges and supporters.[146] He also tried to buttress the structure of the Saljūq empire, and to counter the splendour and prestige of the Fāṭimīd caliphate in Cairo, by encouraging the progress of the Sunnī revival in Iraq and Iran. In order to counter the Mu'tazilite thought and Fāṭimid institutions for training Ismā'ilī *da'ī*s or propagandists, Niẓām al-Mulk desired to speed up the provision of educational institutions within the Eastern Islamic world. As a result, he encouraged the introduction of a network of colleges and *madāri*s throughout the empire known as the Niẓāmiyas in his honour.[147] The best known among them was the Niẓāmiya University at Baghdad and *madāri*s at Bulk, Herāt, Merv, Amūl, Isfahān, Baṣrah and Mosul. In addition to this, Niẓām al-Mulk's administrative policies throughout the Empire required the training of reliable personnel as secretaries and officials. However, not only was *madrasah*

144. Rāwandi, *Rahat al-Sadur wa-Ayat al-Surur*, ed. M. Iqbal, G.M.S., n.s II, London, 1921, p. 117.

145. *Cambridge History of Iran*, pp. 68-77.

146. Rāwandī, op. cit., p. 132.

147. Rāwandī, op. cit., p. 214.

education free, as of course it was in other educational institutions, but generous living allowances were provided to students at Niẓāmiyas.[148] Niẓām al-Mulk regarded the appointment of suitable scholars to teach at his Niẓāmiyas as a personal responsibility. After opening the Baghdad Niẓāmiya in 459/1067, he took considerable pains to secure for it the scholar Abū Isṇāq al-Shīrāzī, and later in 484/1091, he invited one of the greatest mystics and theologians of his time, Abū Ḥāmid al-Ghazālī to lecture there on the occasion of Malik Shah's first visit to Baghdad in 479/1081.[149]

In spite of being occupied with the state administration he established educational institutions, hospitals, *masājid* and palaces covering the Empire with roads and canals to facilitate the traffic and fertilize the soil.

Niẓām al-Mulk was not only a great administrator but also an eminent scholar who wrote *Siyāsat Nāma* or *Siyar al-Mulūk*, a work on administration and governence, which presents an enduring monument of his genius and potential.[150] The work was composed at the behest of Sulṭān Malik Shah.[151] It is said that Malik Shah wanted scholars, at his court,

---

148. George Maqdīsī, "Muslim Institutions of Learning in Eleventh Century Baghdad", *Bulletin of the School of Oriental and African Studies* (*BSOAS*), vol. XXIV, 1961, p. 1. Cf. A.L. Tibawi, "Origin and Character of Al-Madrasa", *BSOAS*, vol. XXV, 1962, pp. 218-38; see also G. Gibert, "Institutionalization of Muslim Scholarship", *Studia Islamica*, vol. LII, 1980, pp. 105 ff.

149. Ibn al-Athīr, *'Al-Kāmili-'l Tārīkh*, ed. C. J. Tornberg, vol. X, p. 104; Montgomery Watt, *Muslim Intellectual: A Study of al-Ghazālī*, Edinburgh, 1963, pp. 22-23.

150. Abd al Razzaq, *Niẓām al-Mulk Ṭūsī*, Nafees Academy, Karachi, 1968, pp. 50-55.

151. Niẓām al Mulk Ṭūsī, *Siyāsat Nāma*, tr. Hubert Darke, London, 1960, pp. 1-2; Ilyas Ahmad, op. cit., p. 72.

including Niẓām al-Mulk, Sharf al-Mulk, Taj al-Mulk and Majid al-Mulk to examine the state of affairs of his reign and realm and to find out any evil or defects at his court assemblies (*majālis*) and *dīwān*, so that the affairs of *Din-o-Dunya* (spiritual and temporal affairs) could be set right.

All these scholars submitted their monographs to Malik Shah but the work of Niẓām al-Mulk was approved and made as the working constitution, *Dastūr ul-'Amal*, of his reign.[152]

The *Siyāsat Nāma* deals not only with the duties of the king and his ministers but also with all the details of the court and different departments of administration, such as revenue, military and civil affairs. All the ideas and formulations have been reasoned out on the basis of the *Qur'ān*, *Ḥadīth*, *Fiqh* and history.[153]

In order to detect heresy, the author calls for the re-establishment of a state intelligence service,[154] and for holding of royal audiences regularly. Both were traditional *Sāsānian* and Muslim practices, but the Sulṭān Alp Arsalān had renounced the former on the ground that spying was unchivalrous, and the latter had evidently fallen into neglect.[155]

Niẓām al-Mulk exhibits statesmanship and lays great stress on promoting justice, orthodox religion and the stability and prosperity of the kingdom.[156] He begins his treatise, *Siyāsat Nāma*, on the art of government with a historical setting that in all ages Allāh has bestowed royal dignity on a king for the

152. Niẓām al-Mulk, op. cit., p. 2; Ilyas Ahmad, op. cit., p. 72.

153. Ibid.

154. Traditionally this was a function of postal officials, *Encyclopedia of Islam*, 2nd edn., art, *Barīd*.

155. Ghazālī, *Naṣīḥat al-Mulūk*, p. 14; *Cambridge History of Iran*, p. 76.

156. Ghazālī, op. cit., p. 15.

care and welfare of his people so that, after Allāh, the king on the earth was to see that His commandments and directives were carried out and the justice was maintained.[157]

Niẓām al-Mulk speaks of the "divine right" of a king, but at the same time he has tried to put (moral) checks on the authority of the king. "The king," he says, "should not act against the *sharī'ah* and should always keep before his mind the 'day of Judgement' when he will have to render account before Allāh."[158]

The duty of the king according to Ṭūsī, is to ensure that divine laws and commandments are not violated. The ruler should always seek the pleasure of Allāh by maintaining justice so that he may earn good name not only in this world but get salvation in the *ākhira* too.[159]

According to Ṭūsī a Muslim ruler has the following duties:

(i) He should maintain peace and order, put down disorder and anarchy, punish the criminals in proportion to their crime and establish justice.[160]

(ii) He should apply his wisdom and knowledge for the welfare of the people and should appoint proper officers to proper positions in accordance with their ability and worth and that these officers should, apart from regulating the affairs of religion, serve the people in the real spirit.[161] If the negligent and oppressive officers won't mend their ways, they should be

157. Niẓām al-Mulk, op. cit., p. 9.

158. Ibid., p. 12.

159. Niẓām al-Mulk, op. cit., pp. 142-43.

160. Ibid., p. 143.

161. Niẓām al-Mulk, op. cit., p. 125.

replaced by others.[162] In order to deliver efficient administration, no officer should be given the charge of two duties. Nor should one post be given to two officers for, they will shift the responsibility to one another.[163]

(iii) The king should also adopt welfare measures by constructing canals and bridges and by the improvement of agricultural lands and villages.[164] Ṭūsī expects the king to make his state a "service state" instead of making it a "police state."

(iv) The king should himself listen to the complaints and grievances of the people, twice a week, by allowing them direct access to himself so that the chance of tyranny may vanish and real justice can be established.[165]

(v) The king should always consult the wise and learned men who are experienced in affairs, for the Prophet (SAW) also held consultations.[166]

(vi) The king should keep strict vigil over his *Wuzarā*[167] and officers for, it is their efficiency which ultimately guarantees the welfare of the people and for this purpose the king should appoint informants and spies if necessary.[168]

Ṭūsī had himself been one of the greatest chief ministers

162. Ibid., p. 144.
163. Ibid., p. 163.
164. Ibid., p. 143.
165. Ibid.
166. Ibid., pp. 14, 121, 247.
167. Ibid., p. 95
168. Niẓām al-Mulk, op. cit., pp. 49, 78.

of medieval times, and he had a comprehensive assessment and experience of sharing the responsibilities and difficulties of the institution. In *Siyāsat Nāma* he, therefore, provides us the stories of the oppressions and tyrannies of ministers and the subsequent treatment meted out to them by their masters (rulers). Therefore, he suggests that;

(i) A minister should never be corrupt or unjust, for his subordinates will also resort to the same malpractice and injustice.

(ii) His work and conduct should be in accordance with the thinking of his ruler.

(iii) He should be a man of strong religious conviction and preferably, he should belong to a line of *wuzrā*.

(iv) The *Waẓīr* should be ready to give any sacrifice for his king.

(v) All renowned prophets and kings had good, pious and conscientious *wuzrā* and this great office should always be given to the most worthy men.

Ṭūsī opines that a king should see that the judges (*qāḍīs*) appointed by the state are learned, pious and honest. Those who are corrupt and dishonest should be dismissed and replaced by others.[169] In order to check even the least chances of bribery and corruption in the judiciary, Ṭūsī emphasizes that the judges should be paid a handsome salary so that lack of money may not force them to resort to illegal practices of earning money.[170]

Niẓām al-Mulk makes it obligatory for the king to give judgement in person and hear the arguments of the contesting

169. Ibid., pp. 25, 43, 49.

170. Niẓām al-Mulk, op. cit., p. 43.

parties. If the king is not in a position to converse in Arabic language and has not learned well the precepts of *Qur'ān* and *Ḥadīth*, on account of being a Turkish or Persian, then he needs a deputy through whom he may perform his function. "It is the judges who are king's deputies, therefore, the king should strengthen their hands. Besides, their reputation and dignity must be above reproach because they are the lieutenants of the caliph and bear his Standard."[171]

Ṭūsī is equally concerned about the religious life of the people and puts forth that a king should see to it that people perform their religious obligations (*farā'iḍ*) with full zeal and regularity. For this purpose, he expects the king to ensure that those at the helm of religious institutions *'ulamā'* are pious and learned and are held in high esteem and are provided their living allowances from the state exchequer (*baitul-māl*).[172] The king should listen once or thrice a week to the *'ulamā'* who may relate to him extracts from *Qur'ān* and *Ḥadith* so that he obtains enlightenment about the affairs of *dīn* and *duniyā*. Only those should be appointed as *i'ima* of *masājid* who are pious and learned in religion.[173]

The landlords, when they are given the charge of a fief or *jāgīr*, should be very careful in collecting the taxes from the peasants. Ṭūsī puts forth that "tax collectors must be instructed to deal honourably with their fellow beings and to take only the due amount of revenue, that too with civility and courtesy, and not to demand anything from them until the time comes for them to pay."[174] Ṭūsī is abreast of the fact that if the peasants

171. Ibid., p. 62.

172. Ibid., p. 62.

173. Ibid., p. 46.

174. Niẓām al-Mulk, op. cit., p. 67.

are demanded to pay the tax before the due time, "they will be compelled and obliged to sell their crops for half (of that what they would be worth when they ripen), whereby they are driven to extremities and have to emigrate."[175] Ṭūsī expects the officers of the state to give all co-operation and help to the peasants by providing them with the tools of agriculture.

Niẓām al-Mulk seems to have been convinced about the need of a high network of intelligence and espionage which must not spare even the *Wuzarā'* and other confidants of the king. This network of intelligence should ensure that the *Waẓīr* is conducting the affairs well, to the benefit of common people.[176]

Like an ideal political theorist, Ṭūsī gives due place to the religious institutions of the state and takes their care in the most reasonable way. He considers the *masājid* as the real fountainhead of the socio-political and religio-cultural ethos. That is why he emphasizes that *i'ima*s of *masājid* and preachers must be men of piety and that the knowledge of the *Qur'ān*, for the position of *imām* in the society, is very essential.[177]

Regarding the prices of the commodities in the market and legitimacy of scales, weights and measures, Ṭūsī writes; "In every city an inspector must be appointed whose duty it should be to check scales and prices and to see that the business is carried on in an orderly and upright manner. He must take proper care with regard to goods, which are brought from outlying districts and sold in the bāzārs to ensure that there is no fraud or dishonesty, that weights are kept true, and that moral and religious principles are observed."[178]

175. Ibid.
176. Ibid., pp. 46-47.
177. Ibid., op. cit., p. 46.
178. Niẓām al-Mulk, op. cit., pp. 46-47.

Again, to ensure that the people observe their religious duties with punctuality and responsibility and to look into the performance of judges, prefects of police, inspectors of weights and measures, and the conduct of tax collectors, Ṭūsī recommends that every city be given in the charge of an inspector general (*muḥtasib*) who would accordingly submit his report to the king about the performance of the above-mentioned agencies.[179]

To keep the king informed about the conditions of masses and about the evil designs of commanders, Ṭūsī recommends that spies must constantly go out to the limits of the kingdom in the guise of merchants, travellers, Ṣūfīs and pedlars and submit reports of everything they observe so that no matters of any kind remain concealed and if anything (untoward) happens it could in due course be remedied.[180]

In order to avert any chance of rebellion from the subjects, nationalities/provincial governors, Ṭūsī is of the opinion that their rulers should regularly keep one of their brothers or sons as resident at the king's court.[181]

Besides this at least 500 men of those ethnic groups should be kept (as hostages) at the court. They can be shifted at the end of the year only after an equal number of their relievers reach the king's court. "In this way no one will be able to rebel against the king because of the hostages."[182]

Ṭūsī puts forth a definite method for submitting the request and petitions of the soldiers, servants and retainers. He holds

---

179. Ibid., pp. 49, 66-67.
180. Ibid., p. 73.
181. Ibid., p. 104.
182. Niẓām al-Mulk, op. cit.

that every request of a soldier must be passed on through proper channel (through troop leaders) and superior officers, so that if a favourable answer is given it will be received from their hands.[183] With this, he feels, the respect of the officer will be maintained and the subordinates also would be disciplined. Regarding the initiating of disciplinary action against any member of a troop who is insolent to his superior officer or fails to give him due respect and oversteps his bounds, he must be punished so that the proper distinction between the superiors and subordinates is maintained.[184]

Ṭūsī was against the interference of queens in the affairs of the state. In his opinion, women by dint of their over-emotional nature are easily exploited by the vested interests at the court and if their (queens') wishes are obeyed, it would lead to chaos and utter imbalance in the state machinery. He feels that women are not accustomed and exposed to the vicissitudes of practical life; therefore their commands cannot bear any positive and healthy results.[185] He further says, "in all ages nothing but disgrace, infamy, discord and corruption have resulted when kings have been dominated by their wives."[186]

After dealing with the delicate and intricate affairs of the state administration and with the pattern of holding *darbār* (court), Ṭūsī turns towards the financial aspects of the state. He says that each *'āmil* (governor) should keep a record of the income and expenditure and if he fails to keep the account, he should compensate the deficit from his own pocket. The

---

183. Ibid., p. 124.
184. Ibid., pp. 124-25.
185. Niẓām al-Mulk, op. cit., p. 185.
186. Ibid.

king should neither be a miser nor extravagant, he should rather adopt a moderate policy in spending the money.[187]

The salaries of the soldiers and all officials should be paid in cash and as far as possible the king should himself pay them so that this personal touch may enliven people's allegiances and affection for their king.

In his *Siyāsat Nāma*, Ṭūsī has devoted seven chapters (41-47) to highlight the activities of heretics and has denounced the role of heretic sects especially that of Ismā'ilīs and Bāṭinīs.[188]

In his concluding chapter Ṭūsī has put forth the guidelines about the treasuries and the procedures and arrangements for looking after them.[189] He once again comments on the subject of dealing with the complaints, giving answers and dispensing justice.[190]

Abu Ḥāmid al-Ghazālī (450/1058 – 505/1111) born in Khurasan near Ṭūs, lost his father at an early age, but through the care of his guardian received good education from scholars and theologians at Tus and Gurgan. In or about 473/1080 he entered the *madrasah* Niẓāmiyah at Nishāpār which had been entrusted by Niẓām al-Mulk to the direction of Abul M'ali abd al-Malik al-Juwayni, the leading *Shaf'ite* theologian of the day. Ghazālī spent five working years under Juwayni at Nishāpūr. After Juwayni's death he went to Niẓām al-Mulk' camp[191] and

---

187. Niẓām al-Mulk, op. cit., pp. 250-51.

188. Ibid., p. 193.

189. Ibid., p. 246.

190. Niẓām al-Mulk, op. cit., p. 247.

191. According to D.B. Macdonald, art. "Ghazālī" in *Shorter E.I.*, he spent the next years in Niẓām al-Mulk's retinue of canonists and theologians, but he may have remained in the Niẓāmiyah at Nishāpūr.

in 484/1091 the latter appointed him to professorship in the Niẓāmiyah at Baghdad. Students flocked to attend his lectures and honours were heaped upon him.

As an Asha'rite[192] and a trained theologian, G͟hazālī regarded the *'aql* (intelligence, sometimes translated "reason") as God's highest gift to man. He was opposed to *naql* (copying) whether in its Bāṭinite form of blind obedience to an authoritative teacher or in the form of rigid adherence to custom and *taqlīd* (precedent) as practised by Hanbalites and some other Sunnīs. He favoured the use of *'aql* (intelligence) in support of religion. He objected, however, to the attempts of philosophers to find intellectual proofs of the existence of Allāh and the reality of *nabūwat* (Prophethood) and *wahy* (Revelation) and to the attempts of Bāṭinites to prove the logical necessity of there being an authoritative teacher.[193]

G͟hazālī wrote numerous works on legal and other subjects including his *Mustazhiri, Maqāsid al-Falāsafah* (aims of philosophers), *Tahafat al-Falāsafa* and *Al-Iqtisād fil I'tiqād*. With all his academic engagements, together with responsibility for teaching 300 students and at attending various official duties, G͟hazālī was greatly overburdened. In *Rajab* 488/July 1095 he suffered a nervous breakdown and spiritual crisis. Realizing that his best work has been motivated by desire for influence and recognition, he was assailed by doubts. He became sceptical about everything not only about reason but about the evidence of the senses and for two months he was without the religious faith.[194] He resolved "after being answered by Allāh in his prayer" to follow the Ṣūfī path, and after giving

192. The followers of Abul Hasan al-'Ash'ari, the tenth-century theologian (died in CE 935).

193. *Naṣīḥat al-Mulūk*, p. 34.

194. Al-G͟hazālī, op. cit., p. 135.

away his wealth except enough for his children and his own subsistence, left Baghdad in *Dhul-Q'adah* 488/December 1095, secretly in the guise of a *dervish* for fear lest his friends or the caliph al-Mustazhir might restrain him.[195] For two years he lived a retired life in Syria, studying and practising spiritual purification as taught by the Ṣūfīs. Then he made his pilgrimage to Makkah, visited Madīnah and returned to Damascus. During these years he worked on his great treatise regarding revivification of the "sciences of religion" under the title *Iḥyā al-'Ulūm al-Dīn*. He spent some time at Baghdad without resuming his official position and finally reached Ṭūs in 493/1099.[196]

Ghazālī, in *Dhul-Q'adah* 499/July 1106, received an order from the "*sulṭān* of the time" to resume public teaching at Nishāpūr. Sulṭān Sanjar's order was delivered by his *wazīr* Fakhr al-Mulk, son of Niẓām al-Mulk.[197] Ghazālī, however, could not disobey this order because he now realized that his clinging to retirement in the hope of preserving himself from worldly contamination had been selfish in motive.[198] Therefore, he spent about three years in teaching at the Niẓāmiyah College at Nishāpūr, Sanjar's capital. In or about 503/1109, he again retired to Ṭūs, and lived a Ṣūfī life, while continuing to

---

195. Ibid.

 Ghazālī abandoned all the occupations in which he had been engaged including the office of *muddaris* (head) of the Niẓāmiya in Baghdad, and a year later he vowed never to take money from the *sulṭān*, to attend the audience of a *sulṭān* or to engage in Legal disputations (*manaẓarah*) in public, *Cambridge History of Islam*, p. 208.

196. *Naṣīḥat al-Mulūk*, p. 36.

197. Ibid., p. 36.

198. *Naṣīḥat al-Mulūk*.

impart private lessons and to write until his death at the age of fifty-three.[199] Apart from writing a number of works on Ṣūfism, logic, *kalām*, jurisprudence and philosophy, which we have not enumerated in detail, he seems to have spent many of his last days in compiling his book of counsel for kings entitled *Naṣīḥat al-Mulūk*, which is a commendable work on Islamic political theory.[200]

Besides having a bulk of traditional Islamic and old Persian counsel, *Naṣīḥat al-Mulūk* expresses a Ṣūfī view of life and politics. The book is divided into two parts. The main thesis of part one is regarding the spiritual life wherein Ghazālī holds that the ruler must sincerely believe in the true faith and fulfil its imperatives, he should govern justly, and sincerely resist the temptations to love worldly power and wealth and pleasure.[201] These themes include the fact that *saltanah* (rulership) is a gift bestowed, i.e. predestined by Allāh and that the ruler will be accountable for it to Allāh on the Day of Judgement.[202]

In part two, chapter first of the book on *Qualities Required in the Kings*, Ghazālī reiterates the importance given to examples and practices of the Sasānīd kings: "You must understand that the development or desolation of this universe depends upon the kings for if the king is just, the universe is prosperous and the subjects are secure, whereas when the king is tyrannical the universe becomes desolate as it was in the times of Dahak, Afrasiyab and others like them."[203]

199. Ibid.
200. Ibid.
201. *Naṣīḥat al-Mulūk*, p. 138.
202. Ibid., pp. 1-39.
203. *Naṣīḥat al-Mulūk*, pp. 46-47.

Another recurring theme in *Naṣīḥat al-Mulūk* is the need for security. "To establish security, the *sulṭān* must ruthlessly enforce discipline and inspire awe, for, insecurity is even worse than injustice."[204] Ghazālī points out that the complaints of bribery are prevalent in the administration of justice as a result of slackness and negligence by the *sulṭān*,[205] and the extortion of taxes by the revenue officials of the *sulṭān* is declared as the *sulṭān*'s personal responsibility.

Ghazālī enumerates the moral and intellectual qualities required in kings. One of these qualities is the ruler's determination to avoid drunkenness, which is a form of madness. "Happy and radiant-faced is the king who is vigilant against royal drunkenness."[206]

In general, the detailed maxims of the first chapter embody two basic principles of the need for royal justice and the need for royal vigilance. In the second and third chapters of *Naṣīḥat al-Mulūk*, Ghazālī describes the qualities required in *wuzarā'* and secretaries, who were the pillars of the civilian bureaucracy in Medieval Muslim State.[207]

Commenting upon the origin of the institution of *wuzāra*[208] Ghazālī holds that the need for a *wazīr* is attested by the Qur'ānic verses.

"And give me a minister from my family, Aaron, my brother; add to my strength through him."[209]

---

204. Ibid., p. 77
205. Ibid., p. 93.
206. *Naṣīḥat al-Mulūk*, p. 85.
207. Ibid., p. 85
208. *Naṣīḥat al-Mulūk*, p. 106.
209. *Al-Qur'ān*, XX:29-32.

Ghazālī further says, "You should understand that a king will never be successful without the help of a virtuous, worthy and competent minister, because no king can reign without a minister and any king who acts (solely) on his own judgement will surely fall.[210] Ghazālī has praised the role of Barmikid *wuzarā'* and the great Niẓām al-Mulk Ṭūsī. He asserts that it is the duty of *wuzarā'* and officials to work for the welfare of the subjects and that they must levy taxes according to the capacity of the subjects and in due seasons.[211]

The necessity of secretaries[212] for the state is similarly attested by Qur'ānic verses and Persian maxims.[213] In order to justify the inevitable nature of secretaries Ghazālī quotes two Qur'ānic verses, viz.:

(i) "Nūn, by the pen and what they inscribe."[214]

(ii) "And your Lord is the most generous who taught by the pen."[215]

The position and necessity of secretaries is extolled in the light of the historical fact that military upheavals seldom disturbed the position of the secretaries, who continued under Arab caliphs, Persian princes and Turkish *sulṭāns* alike, to perform the indispensable tasks of recording tax and revenue assessments and composing official correspondence.[216]

---

210. *Naṣīḥat al-Mulūk*, p. 106.
211. *Naṣīḥat al-Mulūk*, p. 112.
212. For details about secretaries, see Ibid., pp. 46-47.
213. Ibid., p. 113.
214. *Al-Qur'ān*, 48:01.
215. Ibid.; 96:3-4.
216. *Naṣīḥat al-Mulūk*, pp. 46-47.

Ghazālī, in his *Naṣīḥat al-Mulūk*, deals in detail with the "Magnanimity in Kings."[217] He defines magnanimity or high-mindedness as courage and self-respect derived from self-restraint and self-knowledge — a concept perhaps Greek in origin.[218] Ghazālī believes that courage and magnanimity[219] are innate in kings and noblemen and it is not readily acquired by others. In spite of insisting on the kings to be generous in financial matters, it seems that Ghazālī, at the same time, does not want the kings to do it at the cost of state treasury, for he praises the conscientious stewardship of Caliph 'Umar I and Umar II, who never spent money from the public treasury improperly.[220]

The last three chapters of the book *Naṣīḥat al-Mulūk* deal with "the aphorism of sages and saints," "intelligence and intelligent persons," and "describing women and their good and bad points" respectively.

This period (eleventh and twelfth centuries) witnessed not merely the re-imposition of Sunnism after a considerable time of Shī'a supremacy, but a reaffirmation of the caliph's position as head of the Islamic community[221] together with the incorporation of sultanate as a necessary element into the ideal of Islamic government.[222] This development gave birth to such a system of administration, whose stability depended, not on the separation of civil administration from the military,

217. Ibid., p. 49.

218. Ibid., p. 47.

219. Ibid., p. 49.

220. *Naṣīḥat al-Mulūk*, p. 47.

221. The position of caliph was rendered to a sheer non-entity during the period of Buyids.

222. *Cambridge History of Iran*, p. 207.

but on orthodoxy or "right religion" and personal loyalty of the sulṭān to the caliph and of subordinate officials to the *sulṭān*. The man who formulated this new relationship between the caliphate and the sultanate was Ghazālī.[223] He envisaged a new relationship between the caliph and the *sulṭān* and assumed co-operation between them.[224] On the one hand the caliph was to be designated by the *sulṭān*, who through his exercise of constituent authority, recognized the institutional authority of the caliph, and on the other hand the validity of the *sulṭān*'s government was established by his oath of allegiance to that caliph who authorized his rule.

In his *Naṣīḥat al-Mulūk* Ghazālī puts forward his conception of the sultanate as distinct from the caliphate, describing the *sulṭān* as the shadow of God upon earth.[225] Ghazālī seems to have had in mind not only the preservation of the religious life of the community, but also the maintenance of the power of the sultanate, which was necessary for the establishment of order.[226] He, further, wanted to emphasize that the power of the sultanate should be used with justice. He writes, "Known that Allāh has singled out two groups of men and given them preferences over others: first prophets, upon them be peace, and secondly kings. Prophets He sent to his servants to lead them to Him and kings to restrain from aggression against each other and in His wisdom He assigned them (kings) a high status."[227] Therefore, the obedience and love for the kings

---

223. Ibid.

224. Ibid., see also L. Binder, "Al Ghazālī's Theory of Islamic Government", *The Muslim World*, 1955, pp. 229-47.

225. *Naṣīḥat al-Mulūk*, p. 9.

226. *Cambridge History of Iran*, p. 208.

227. *Naṣīḥat al-Mulūk*, p. 39; cf. *Cambridge History of Iran*, ibid.

was incumbent upon men, and opposition and enmity towards them was unseemly, provided that the *sulṭān* acted with justice.[228]

The main thrust of Ghazālī in *Naṣīḥat al-Mulūk* is on political ethics based on the grounds of political expediency. His exposition of government is over-influenced by Islamic ethics. At the same time this theory of government seems influenced by the old Persian theory of state.[229]

In the light of the above discussion it becomes abundantly clear that the approach of Ṭūsī as a political thinker differs from that of the Ghazālī's. The former bases his exposition of the administration of state and the duties of the ruler on his long-drawn personal experience and the administrative legacy of the Sāsānian state, whereas Ghazālī's approach is more juristic and philosophic.

PATTERN OF ADMINISTRATION

In order to understand the nature of the state and pattern of administration during the period of our study it seems desirable to discuss in brief the political scenario of the world so that one can appreciate the exact position and conditions in which Shaikh 'Abdu'l Qādir (R.'A.) lived.

If we look at the political conditions in the West, we find that the eleventh century of the Christian era was one of great turmoils there. On the one hand both Spain and Portugal were ruled by Asiatic and African races and on the other, Europe was still a prey to schism and disunion. England had already

228. Ibid.; cf. "The Theory of Kingship in the Naṣīḥat al-Mulūk of Ghazālī", *The Islamic Quarterly*, 1954, pp. 47-55.

229. Cf. H.A.R. Gibb, "The Evolution of Government in early Islam", in *Studies on the Civilization of Islam*, London, 1962, pp. 34-35.

been weakened by the civil wars and France and Germany were on a perpetual war path with each other. The church had come to exercise the most direct influence over the politics of this continent and the Christian Europe was full of monasteries and nunneries, the inmates of which lived a life of luxury at the cost of the sweat and blood of common masses, which, of course, was the worst phase of religious hegemony and exploitation.

In the face of this state of affairs, the Muslims were acting as the champions of a political and social order. They had already disseminated the political and moral influence of the Prophet's (SAW) "world order," to the farthest possible lands of the earth. They had already established the political as well as the cultural superiority over a formidable part of the globe, which roughly extended to the Pyrenees in the West and Central India in the East.

Although during the period of our study there was not as much coherence among the Muslims, as had existed during the tenure of the first four caliphs, however, still if we take into consideration the fact that in all the countries which were under the control of the Muslims the same legal system and the constitution of government was in force, we are obliged to affirm that a real similarity existed between the various parts which composed the Muslim world.

It can't be denied that in the gamut of this vast empire the person and the office of the caliph at Baghdad had greatly been weakened in prestige and the caliph had become a puppet in the hands of the Turkish guards.[230] But even then, contrary to the general belief of the students of Islamic history, the power of the Muslim state was not decreasing at all and the

---

230. *Cambridge History of Iran*, pp. 205-6.

tremendous prestige it had was not underestimated by the rival contemporary political powers. The Ghaznavid *sulṭāns*, who had sought the recognition from the ruling caliph of Baghdad, were making inroads in the Indian subcontinent and had defeated the Eastern Roman empire in Asia Minor, while the falcons of the family of Umayyads were bravely knocking at the gates of France, Germany and Italy in the West.

But then the fact is that the downward trend during the successors of Hārūn al-Rashid and Māmūn al-Rashid had set in. The centre of gravity of the Islamic state was gradually shifted from Baghdad towards east where the Sāsānīds and Ghaznavids had established their independent kingdoms.[231]

As early as the reign of the Caliph Abul Qāsim Abdullah al-Mustakfi Billah (CE 944-46), Bani Buwaih (Buyids CE 932-1055) had taken possession of Isfahan and had invaded the rich plains of Iraq and risen to such power and prominence that the caliph became dependent on their military support. Their overwhelming rapport and prestige in Baghdad knew no bounds and checks. They were not only granted the high-sounding titles of *M'uizz-ud-Daulah* (Honour of the State) *'Imād ud-Daulah* (Pillar of the State) and *Rukn ud-Daullah* (Corner-stone of the State) but the caliph had also designated the oldest of them as *amir al-umara* and the *sulṭān*. The *sulṭān*'s name also began to appear on the coins of the realm along with that of the caliph himself. Ultimately, the power of Buyids began to wane owing to internecine feuds, and they failed to check the rising power of the Fāṭimīds (CE 909-1171) of Egypt, who had

231. J.J. Saunders, *A History of Medieval Islam*, London, 1965, pp. 143-47; Bashir ud-din. "Political Theory of Islam", *Islamic Culture*, October 1934, pp. 586 ff; Lane Poole, *Muhammadan Dynasties*, London, 1898, p. 149.

captured a number of provinces of the Baghdad caliphate including the Hijaz itself. In Spain the Umayyads were running their own caliphate.

In the east, Mahmūd of Ghazna, became famous by his daring exploits, earning the gratitude of Caliph al-Qādir (991-1031) who honoured him by granting the titles of *Yamīn ud-Daulah* (Right arm of the State) and *Amīn al-Millat* (Guardian of the Ummah/community).[232] Sulṭān Maḥmūd, the hero of "Thousand Romances," became the ruler of all the lands from the Oxus and Jaxartes to the Ganges and the city of Khurasan.[233] However, Sulṭān Maḥmūd's successors were not capable and his own son Mas'ūd was defeated by Turk leader of Khurasan, Saljūq by name.[234] After the latter's death, his people elected Tughril Beg as their leader who put to flight the Buyid forces at a number of places, thus taking possession of various provinces in charge of Jurjan and Khawārizm.

Like their predecessor Turk families, the Saljūqs soon became the power behind the throne of the 'Abbāsid Caliph who supported the Saljūqs against the Buyids and Fatimids. He also recognized them as the real defenders of the caliphate and *Dār ul-Islam*. In CE 1058, Caliph Qā'im in a magnificent ceremony at Baghdad put two crowns over the head of Tughril Beg which were the symbols of his legal authority over East and West (*Sulṭān al-Mashriq wa al-Magrib*).[235] In this way the

232. Hamid Allah Mustawfi, *Tarikh-I Guzīda,* abridged tr. E.G. Browne, London, 1910-13, p. 391.

233. Hamid Allah Mustawfi, op. cit., pp. 378-85; *Tarikh-i-Guzida*, pp. 394-95.

234. Rāwandi, p. 102; *Tārīkh-Gūzida*, p. 398.

235. Rāwandi, op. cit., pp. 98, 105-6; Ibnal-Athīr, op. cit., IX, p. 436; Hitti, op. cit., p. 474.

Amir ul-Muminīn (Commander of the Faithful) had delegated his sultanate to his Turkish lieutenant, the Saljūq *sulṭān*. It was now the *sulṭān*'s duty to defend the *Ummah,* to extirpate schism and heresy and to resume his war against the nations that rejected Allāh and His Prophet (SAW). Thus Saljūqs became the most powerful people of Western and Central Asia.

The Perso-Islamic traits and the true nature of the 'Abbāsid state can be understood by studying some of the prominent official positions and institutions of this state and their administrative ethics.

Shahna

Shahna was the *sulṭān*'s ambassador to the caliph and chief administrator of the city of caliph and head of *sulṭān*'s officials there.[236] Usually being a Turkish *amīr, shahna* as military governor, was mainly responsible for the restoration of law and order in the chief cities of his province and the caliph's residence at Baghdad.[237]

The word *shahna* is used in sources for this period under other shades of meaning as well.[238] Precisely, the *shahna* was the military governor of a province and the special representative of the *sulṭān*.

Court

At the apex of the administration was the *sulṭān*'s court (cabinet) which consisted of *umarā'* who were for the most

236. *Cambridge History of Iran*, vol. V, p. 213.

237. *Cambridge History of Iran*, p. 99.

238. There are a number of instances of the same person being referred to variously as *shahna, wālī* and *muqta*. The holder of a large provincial government was, however, seldom called a

→

part *mamlūks* or freedmen. The relationship between the *sulṭān* and the *umarā'* was not that of lord and vassal; however, the source of all grants of authority for them was the *sulṭān*.[239]

The chief official of the court, until the end of reign of Muhammad bin Malikshah, was the *Vakil-idar*, who appears to have been a kind of intermediary between the *sulṭān* and the *wazīr*. Sometimes he was the *wazīr*'s deputy[240] and in Muhammad bin Malik Shah's reign he was replaced by Amīr Ḥājib.

The Amīr Ḥājib, normally a Turkish *amīr*, was concerned with the maintenance of military discipline as well as court ceremonial.[241] Amīr-i Hirs (chief of the guard) and *jandar* (chief executioner) the two other officials at court, ranked after him.[242] He also regulated the audience of the *sulṭān* and transmitted the *sulṭān*'s commands to the *waẓīr*.

Akhūr sālār (master of the horse), who looked after the royal stables and the *khawān-sālār*, who was in-charge of the royal kitchens, were two other officials at the court.

→ *shahna*. See Lambton, A.K.S. "The Administration of Sanjar's Empire", *BSOAS*, vol. XX, p. 380.

The Amir 'Abbas is called *shahna* of Ray by Ibn al-Jawzi al-Muntazam, Hyderabad, AH 1357-59, X, p. 102, but *wali* of Ray by Awlia ullah Amuli, *Tarikh-I Ruyan*, ed. 'Abbas Khalili, Tehran, 1934-35, p. 89.

Similarly, Ibn al-Athir calls Qumaj as *muqta* of Balkh, whereas Rāwandi calls him *wali* al-Kamil, XI, p. 116 and Rāwandi, op. cit., p. 177.

239. *Cambridge History of Iran*, vol. V, p. 225.

240. Ibn al-Balkhi, *Fars Nāma*, ed. Lestrange (G.M.S), London, 1921, p. 91.

241. *Cambridge History of Iran*, vol. V, p. 226.

242. *Cambridge History of Iran*, vol. V, p. 226.

Judicial

On the judicial side the head of the department was Qāḍī ul-Quḍāh (the Chief Justice) under whom *qāḍīs* (the judges) worked in each province. The *sulṭān* exercised "administrative" justice in the *maẓālim* court, personally or through his agents.[243] The *qāḍī* in his court would administer justice in accordance with the *sharī'ah* and the legal rules of evidence and procedure, whereas the justice in *maẓālim* courts was administered on the basis of custom, equity and government regulations.[244]

The local courts seem to have three main types; the *qāḍīs* court, the *dīwān-i riyāsat* and *shahna*'s court. These were dealing with the *sharī'ah* affairs, cases relating to taxation and affairs concerning the public security respectively.

'Ulamā'

During eleventh and twelfth centuries the *'ulamā'* had their own organizations free from the control of the state. They played a significant role in the society and could call the rulers to account.[245] *'Ulamā'* of various theological outlooks including Mu'tazilites, Ashar'rites, Ḥanbalites, Shāfi'tes flourished during this period.[246] *'Ulamā'* were capable of prodding the caliph to act and carry out his primary constitutional function, namely the defence and maintenance of religion.[247]

---

243. *Cambridge History of Iran*, op. cit., p. 269.

244. Cf. J. Schacht, *An Introduction to Islamic Law*, Oxford, 1994, p. 49.

245. George Makdisi, *The Sunnī Revival in Islamic Civilization*, ed. D.S. Richards, Oxford, 1973, pp. 164-66.

246. Ibid.

247. Taju'd-Din Subki, *Tabaqāt al-Shāfi'iya*, vol. III, Cairo, 1905-6, p. 26. Also see Makdisi, op. cit., p. 164.

Apart from crucial socio-political role, the *'Ulamā'* were the custodians of *'ilm* that is of the religious patrimony of the Prophet (SAW), especially his *aḥādith* (Traditions), *fiqh* (Islamic Jurisprudence) and *uṣūl al-dīn* (theology). Their *ijmā* (consensus) represented the consensus of all the Muslims.

Although the executive power during this period was in the hands of the officials of "temporal government" they were nevertheless expected to consult and seek the approval of the *'ulamā'*, *i'imā'* and *muftīs* in the punishment of criminals.[248]

Muḥtasib

It was one of the prominent administrative positions. *Muḥtasib* was supposed to ensure the observance of public morals and performance of fundamental religious duties by the Muslims.[249] He was to oversee markets and to prevent dishonest dealings, as well as to supervise the guilds and corporations. He was empowered to inflict suitable punishments on offenders.[250] He was also charged with the supervision of public amenities.

The deed of investiture issued for Auhadud-din as *muḥtasib* of Mazandaran, from Sanjar's Court, commands him to ensure that people practise what is "good" and forbid what is "evil" and that commandments of *sharī'ah* are carried out properly. He was also entrusted with the responsibility of punishing corrupt officials, prevention of transaction of intoxicants and mixing of women in the gatherings of *'ulamā.'*[251]

---

248. Muntajab al-Din Juvaynī, *Atabat al-Katāba*, ed. 'Abbas Iqbal, Tehran, 1329/1950, p. 79.
249. *Cambridge History of Iran*, p. 278.
250. Ibid.
251. Juvaynī, op. cit., p. 827.

Ra'īs

Each town used to have a *ra'īs* (head) who resembled the modern mayor and acted on ceremonial occasions such as the coronation of the new *sulṭān*.[252] The deed of investiture for Abu'l Makārim Ahmad as *ra'īs* of Mazandarān, Gurgan, Dihistān, Astarābād, Bisṭām and Gulpayagan enjoins him to seek, in all dealings, the will of Allāh, to show solicitude for the good treatment of the people and to preserve them from unjust treatment.[253]

A commission for Naj ud-Dīn as *Ra'īs* of Sarkhs and its dependencies emphasizes the importance of the office of *ra'īs*, pointing out that this important office had always been in the charges of notables and eminent men of the State.[254]

The *ra'īs* was, in some measure, a link between the government and the people and his duties included financial affairs as well.[255] A careful study of *Atabat al-Katāba* also reveals that *ra'īs* exercised certain powers of supervision over religious affairs also.[256] On some occasions it seems that *ra'īs* had even wider powers than a *qāḍī*, so far as the supervision over religious affairs is concerned. The deed of investiture to Tajud-Din Abu'l Makārim as *ra'īs* of Mazandarān, instructs him to guide the *qāḍīs* and *hukkām* in the execution of their decrees and the restitution of rights.[257]

252. Rāwandī, op. cit., pp. 140-41.

253. Juvaynī, op. cit., p. 23.

254. Juvaynī, Ibid., p. 23.

255. Lambton, op. cit., p. 384.

256. Juvaynī, op. cit., p. 29.

257. Ibid., p. 24.

Armed Forces

As regards the armed forces of the Abbāsid state it appears that *'askar* formed the regular standing army and the *jund* the territorial reserve.[258] Although it is difficult to show exactly the numerical strength of the *'askar* and the *jund* yet the sources contain the number of the armed forces of the *sulṭāns* while in the battlefields.[259] Turks were an important element in the *'askar* while the *jund* were a heterogeneous mixture of Turks, Turkomans, 'Arabs and Kurds.[260] The *ahadīth* (regular volunteers), yet another force, were organized under *Ra'īs ul-Ahadāth*. The commander-in-chief of the army bore the title of *Amīr ul-Juyush* or more commonly *amīr* and sometimes called as *Ṣāḥib ul-Jaish* and *'Arid ul-Jaish. Qa'id ul-Quwwād* or colonel was under him and he was in turn the head of *qā'ids* or captains. Rabble or the Camp-followers were called *suqah* or *hawashi*.[261]

Duzdar[262] was the title given to the military governor of a fort and *Ṣāḥib ul-Shurtah* (Prefect of Police) to the head of the police in each town. The police was semi-military in organization for purely civil purposes. There was another police force under the *muḥtāsib* or *wālī ul-hisbah* (inquisitor).[263]

---

258. Ibn al-Qalanisi, *Dhail Tarikh Dimashq*, ed. M.F. Amedroz, Leiden, 1908, pp. 130, 132, 134.
259. Ibn al-Athir, op. cit., p. 201.
260. M.F. Sanaullah, *The Decline of the Saljūqid Empire*, Calcutta, 1938, p. 19.
261. Sannaullah, op. cit., p. 20.
262. Ibn al-Athir, op. cit., pp. 131, 179, 211.
263. Sannaullah, op. cit., p. 98.

2

Life of Shaikh Sayyid 'Abdu'l Qādir Jīlānī (R.'A.)

A Contemporaneous Appraisal

Abū Muḥammad 'Abdu'l Qādir,[1] son of Abū Ṣālih Jangī Dost, was a Hanbalite Theologian, a Ṣūfī and an influential Preacher of Islam. He was born in Jīlān[2] (470-471/1077-78),[3] migrated

---

1. Most of his biographers draw his genealogy as; Son of Abu Salih — son of 'Abdu'llah — son of Yaḥyā — son of Muḥammad — son of Dawud — son of Musa — son of 'Abdu'llah, the pure, — son of Musa — son of 'Abdu'llah — son of Hasan — son of al-Hasan (R.'A.) — son of Hadrat 'Ali (R.'A.) — son of Abū Talib.

   The Shaikh's pedigree on his mother's side is also traced back to Hadrat Ali (R.'A.) through Hadrat Husayn bin Ali (R.'A.). See Shatanaufi, *Bahjat al-Asrār*, p. 88.

2. Gīlān or Jīlān and also known as Vailām, is a north-western province of Iran, south of the Caspian Sea and north of the Elburz Chain. It is bounded in the east by Tabaristan or Mazandaran and its northern limit is marked by the juncture of the Kur and Araxes, its political boundary with Russia is marked by Astara stream. It is one of the most beautiful areas of Iran. — *Encyclopaedia of Islam*, vol. II, p. 170.

3. Asqalānī holds that this year was inferred from the statement of the Shaikh that he came to Baghdad when he was eighteen, in the year in which al-Tamīmī died. This Tamīmī was identified as Rizq Allāh Ibn Abd al-Wahhab, (ob. Jumada-i AH 488).

   For details see, Ibn Hajar al-Asqalānī, *Ghibtat al-Naẓīr fi Tarjamat al-Shaikh 'Abdu'l Qādir*. This work is precisely termed as *Gibṭah* in this book.

to Baghdad[4] while in his teen age, where he studied law with Qāḍī, Abū Sa'id al-Mukharrimī,[5] and studied Traditions under the guidance of a galaxy of scholars including Abū Bakr Ahmad Ibn al-Muẓaffar Ibn Sausan al-Tammār, Abū Ghālib al-Baqillānī,[6] Abu'l Qāsim Ibn Bayān al-Razzāz,[7] Abū Muḥammad Ja'far al-Sarrāj,[8] Abū Sa'id Ibn Hashīsh,[9] Abū Ṭālib Ibn Yūsuf[10] and others. Traditions were cited on his authority

4. It was perhaps not merely fortuitous that he arrived at Baghdad to acquire education almost at the same time when another reputed teacher, al-Ghazālī (d. CE 1111) was leaving the city in search of truth. (Ibn Kathīr, *al-Bidāyah wa an-Nihāya*, vol. XII, p. 149).

5. His name was Mubarak and we shall hear of his school later on. Mukharrim was a place in Baghdad where the palace of the Buyids was situated (see le Strange, *Baghdad*, Index).

6. From al-Shattanufi's (d. AH 713), *Bahjah al-Asrār wa Maadin al-Anwār*. (This work is precisely termed as *Bahjah* in this book.) We learn that this person's full name was Muḥammad Ibn al-Hasan Ibn Ahmad Ibn al-Hasan. Possibly he was a descendant of the famous Qadi Abū Bakr Muḥammad about whom a life is given by Ibn Khallikan in his *Wafāyāt al-A'yān*, vol. I, p. 609. For this person, dying in AH 403, left a son, al-Hasan, who might have been the great-grandfather of Abū Ghalib. He taught in the *Jami' al-Qasr*.

7. The *Bahjah* adds the names 'Ali Ibn Ahmad of Karkh. A brief notice of him is given in *Tāju'l-'Arūs*, thus: 'Ali Ibn Ahmad Ibn Muḥammad Ibn Dāwūd Ibn Mūsā Ibn Bayān heard Traditions from Abu'l Hasan Muḥammad Ibn Muḥammad al-Razzāz; he is distinguished from another Razzāz (AH 501-72), who must have been later than the Razzāz mentioned in the text.

8. The famous author of the *Masarial-'uss* Ibn Khallikān, op. cit., p. 139.

9. In *Bahjat al-Asrār*, this name is given as Muḥammad Ibn 'Abd al-Karim Ibn Khunaish.

10. His name was 'Abdu'l Qādir Ibn Muḥammad Ibn 'Abdu'l Qādir Ibn Muḥammad Ibn-Yusuf.

by Abū Sa'id al-Sam'anī,[11] 'Umar Ibn 'Ali al-Qurashī,[12] 'Abd al-Qādir's two sons, 'Abd al-Razzāq[13] and Mūsā,[14] the Hāfiz Abd al-Ghani,[15] the Shaikh al-Muwāffaq,[16] Yaḥyā Ibn Sa'idullah

11. The well-known author of the book on *Nisbahs* of whom Ibn Khallikan (op. cit., pp. 378-79) gives fairly a full account. His life lasted from AH 506 to 562. He heard more than 4000 Shaikhs, of whom he made a dictionary for his son's benefit.

12. Mentioned by Yāqūt (*Mu'jam al-Buldān*, vol. IV, p. 121), who calls him *Qāḍī*, and states that he composed a dictionary of his Shaikhs.

13. A brief account of him is given in the *Bahjah al-Asrar* (p. 114). He took the titles Taj al-dīn Siraj al-Iraqi, Jamal al-A'immah and Fakhr al-Huffāz.

14. Called Diya al-dīn Abū Nasr, he went to Egypt, and thence to Damascus, where he died.

15. His name was Abū Muḥammad Abd al-Ghani ibn Abd al-Wahid of Jerusalem. Many of his family were Qādirīs. He was called commander of the faithful in the Tradition. Yāqūt (geogr. ii, p. 113) gives the following account of him.

    Jamma'il village in the mountain of Nablus in the land of Palestine, is birthplace of Abd al-Ghani Ibn Abd al-Wahid Ibn Ali Ibn Surur Ibn Nafi Ibn Hasan Ibn Ja'far Abū Muḥammad al-Maqdisi. He took his *nisbah* from Jerusalem because Jamma'il is near it, and because Nablus and the territory appertaining thereto are all attached to Jerusalem, and there is only a day's journey between them. He was brought up in Damascus whence he went in pursuit of knowledge, and went to Baghdad, where he heard Ibn al-Nākur and others in the year AH 560; then he departed to Isfahan, and returned to Baghdad in the year AH 578, where he taught Tradition: thence he migrated to Syria, and then to Egypt, where he was successful and got together a following of Hanbalites. In Damascus he had been accused of openly avowing his belief in the bodily nature of the deity, and this accusation being signed by various juris consults, he was expelled from Damascus, and even in the Egypt, whither he went, he underwent some trouble from this suspicion. He wrote various excellent books on Tradition, such as *al-Kamal fi-Ma'rifat al-Rijāl*. He died in the year AH 600 in Egypt. Suyuti (*Hasan al-Muhadarah*, vol. I, p. 165) gives →

of Takrīt,[17] the Shaikh 'Ali Ibn Idrīs al-Ba'kūbī,[18] Ahmad Ibn Muti al-Bajisraā'i,[19] Abū Hurrairah Muḥmmad Ibn Laith Ibn al Wastānī,[20] Akmal Ibn Mas'ūd al-Hāshimī[21] and many others, of whom the last to die was Abū Talib Abū Latif Ibn Ahmad al-Qubbaitī,[22] whereas the last to repeat Traditions from him with licence was al-Rashid Ibn Ahmad Ibn Maslamah.[23]

'Abdu'l Qādir was the *imām* of his time, the *Quṭb*[24] of his age and the teacher of teachers of his epoch without question.

→ the name of another book of his, the *'Umdah;* he adds that he had the title Taqi al-dīn, and died at the age of 59. He was therefore, 20 years of age when he read with Jīlānī.

16. Muwaffaq al-dīn Abū Muḥammad Abdullah Ibn Ahmad Ibn Muḥammad Ibn Khudāmah of Jerusalem. He was also of Jamma'il, and Yāqūt (loc. cit.), gives an account of him. He was a voluminous author.

17. Abūl Faraj Ibn Abil Sa'adat Ibn al-Husayn Ibn Muḥammad al-Takriti is said to have been an author.

18. Abūl Hasan. A lengthy account of him is given in *Bahjah al-Asrār,* (pp. 227-30), most of it in superlatives. His *nisbah* refers to a place called Bakuba. This *nisbah* is regularly corrupted to Yakubi in Mss and printed books. He was also called Rauhan from Rauha, a village near Bakuba. He died in AH 619.

19. His Kunyah was Abūl-Abbas. Bajisra is near Baghdad.

20. His names are thus given in the *Bahjah* (p. 113): Muḥammad Ibn Abi'l Futuh al-Azaji al-Dinari. The Blind, known as Ibn al-Wastani. Dinari is a *nisbah* from the name of a Street in Baghdad.

21. The *Bahjah* (p. 94) adds Ibn 'Umar.

22. The author of *Taj-al-Arūs* mentions the man as a famous Traditionalist. In the *Bahjah* (p. 113) his *nisbah* is given as Ibn al-Saqati, and we are told that he lived first in Halwan, and then in Baghdad, and was a dealer in jewels Qubbaiti should mean dealer in a sweetmeat called *natif.*

23. Mentioned by Dhahabi in his life of Ibn Shāfi.

24. The word *Quṭb* is largely used by the Ṣūfīs and is the subject of considerable discussion. It would be interesting to know when →

Those who have seen 'Abdu'l Qādir have paid a glowing tribute to his moral excellence, large-heartedness, hospitality, modesty and generosity. He was always humble and unpretentious. Never evading the company of the poor, he even washed their clothes or performed similar other personal services for them, yet he never stood up in the honour of any person of the rank or the elīte.[25] If the Caliph ever paid a visit to him, the chroniclers of his time report that he deliberately went inside his house so that he might not have to stand up to welcome the king.[26] He used to come out of the house after the Caliph had seated himself. In fact, Jīlānī never paid back the courtesy call to any *wazīr* or the king.[27]

One of his contemporaries who had the opportunity of enjoying the company of Jīlānī remarks that he had not seen a man more polite, large-hearted and charitable than the Shaikh. Despite his erudition and eminence, he respected his elders, met the youngsters with a good grace, always saluted first, hailed the poor courteously with deference but never stood up to welcome the grandees or nobles, nor did he ever pay a visit to any minister or governor.[28]

The testimony of Moḥi-ud-dīn Abū 'Abdu'llāh Muḥammad Ibn Hamīd al-Baghdādī, a jurist-scholar of those times, runs as follows:

→ the Ṣūfīs first took to employing it. In the *Bahjuh* (p. 81), 'Abdu'l Qādir has an eloquent sermon on the subject, which is not very clear. Since Qushayri does not explain the word in his technicalities, it probably came into use about this time; and very likely Yusuf of Hamadan was the first person so called.

25. Abdul Wahhab Sha'rani, *Tabaqat al-Kubrā*, vol. I, p. 127.

26. Ibid., p. 128.

27. Ibid., p. 127.

28. Ibid.

> Always disposed to avoid things unseemly and indecorous, he only pressed for the desirable and befitting. He would boil with indignation if the Divine commandments were overstepped but remained listless to the wrongs and ill-treatments to his own person. He would never seek revenge save for the sake of Allāh, the Almighty, nor, send back a beggar without giving him something. If he had nothing to give he would part with the clothes he had been putting on.[29]

Another contemporary of 'Abdu'l Qādir, Ḥāfiẓ Abū-'Abdu'llāh Muḥammad ibn Yūsuf al-Barzālī reports:

> His prayers were readily granted. Being extremely tender-hearted, he would burst into tears (if anything sorrowful or touching was mentioned to him). More often he was to be found immersed in meditation and recollection of Allāh. He was soft-hearted, courteous, cheerful, generous and compassionate. Being the offspring of a noble family, he was also highly reputed for his profound knowledge and piety.[30]

Feeding the poor and spending freely to meet the needs of the destitute was a pleasure for Shaikh 'Abdu'l Qādir. Ibn al-Najjār narrates that 'Abdu'l Qādir often used to say, "If I were given treasures of the whole world, I would spend it all on feeding the poor." Sometimes he would say, "It seems that I have a hole in my hands. I cannot keep anything with me. If I had a thousand *dīnārs*, I would spend every single shell before the day break."[31]

He had given instructions to his servants that as many guests as possible should be invited for the dinner. At such occasions he always sat with the poor and lowly, chatted with

29. Ibn Yaḥyā al-Tādifī, *Qala'id al-Jawāhir*, p. 9.
30. Ibid.
31. Ibid., p. 10.

his students and enquired about the welfare of those who did not happen to be present there. His behaviour was so affectionate that everyone who met him felt that the Shaikh had the highest regard for him. He overlooked the faults of others and if anyone stated something on oath, he readily accepted his statement. He neither revealed the secrets of others nor stated anything before others that might put someone to shame.[32]

Ibn al-Sam'ānī's[33] description of Shaikh 'Abdu'l Qādir Jīlānī is as follows:

> Abū Muhammnd 'Abd al-Qādir was of Jīlān, and was the head and Shaikh of the Hanbalites in his time. He was a pious jurist, orthodox, frequently repeating the *Qur'ān*, constantly meditating, readily moved to tears. He got his training as a jurist from al-Mukharrimī, and was the companion of the Shaikh Ḥammād al-Dabbās. He dwelt at the Azaj Gate[34] in the School which they built for him. One day I went to bid farewell to one of my companions, and as we were going away one of those who were with me asked if I should not like to pay a visit to 'Abd al-Qādir and get his blessings. So, we went and I entered his school when it was morning. The Shaikh presently came out, and made a circle of his followers, and they recited the *Qur'ān*. When they had done it, I wanted to rise but he advised me to be seated and wait till the lesson was over. He proceeded to read out a lecture to his students, of which I did not understand a

32. Ibn Yaḥyā al-Tadifi, *Qala'id al-Jawahir*, p. 9.

33. He was called Abu'l Muzaffar 'Abd al-Rahim and lived AH 537-614. He is often quoted for Traditions. In his father's work on *nisbahs* 'Abdu'l Qādir is mentioned and a space left for a notice, which apparently was not filled up.

34. An inner gate in East Baghdad, shutting off the Ma'muniyyah Quarter, see Le Strange's, *Baghdad*, map (viii).

> word. What was still more curious was that the students presently rose and repeated his lecture, apparently understanding it, whereas we understood neither the terms nor the expressions.[35]

Abu'l-Farāj Ibn al-Jauzi (AH 508-97) sums up his views about the Shaikh in these words:

> Abū Sa'id al-Mukharrimī had built a fine school at the Azaj Gate. This came into the possession of Jīlānī, who preached there. He got a reputation for asceticism, and started a method and silence of his own.[36] The school presently became too small for the audience and he took the sitting at the wall of Baghdad with his back leaning against his cell. Great crowds used to be reverted at a single meeting. Then the school was repaired and enlarged, the common people making great efforts. There he remained preaching and teaching till he died.

Abū Bakar Ibn Tarkhān[37] (AH 600-90) states that Shaikh al-

35. This description, which would apply very well to Ibn 'Arabi's works, seems strange as applied to 'Abdu'l Qādirī's statements, which contain no difficulties.
36. The word *ṭarīqah* which is ordinarily used in this context, signifies a system in Ṣūfism. So in Harir's last *Maqāmah* Hasan al-Basri is said to have the best *tarīqah.* A brief summary of his *tarīqah* is given in the *Bahjah* itself (p. 84). The leading doctrine of the *Fath-i-Rabbāni* is doubtless that of *Fanā*. The Shaykh probably recommended a period of asceticism wherein the devotee could be weaned from the world, to which afterwards he should return; only, however, to take a minimum share therein. The period of asceticism in his own case is put 25 years (*Bahjah* p. 59). If the word rendered "silence" be anything more than a jingle with the other, it must signify a negative as well as positive system.
37. He is also called 'Izzal-dīn Ibrahim Ibn Muḥammad Ibn al-Suwaidi. He was a personal friend of Ibn Abi Usaibi'ah, who hạs an appreciative notice of him and his works.

Muwāffaq,[38] being asked about the Shaikh 'Abdu'l Qādir, gave the following reply:

We found him still living, but at the end of his life he lodged us in his school, and looked after us. He often sent his son Yaḥyā[39] (AH 550-600) to light the lamp, and would frequently send us food from his own lodging. He used to lead in the regular prayers, and I recited to him from memory out of the book of al-Khiraqī[40] in the morning. Whereas 'Abd al-Ghanī,[41] the *ḥāfiẓ* used to recite to him from the book called *al-Hidayah fi'l-Kitāb*.[42] We were the only persons studying with him during that time. We remained with him a month and nine days, when he died, and we prayed over him at night in his school. I never heard more tales of miracles told about any one than about him, nor did I ever see anyone more generally respected for his piety than he was. We only went through with him a few portions of his books.

Saif al-dīn Ibn Majd al-dīn[43] writes as follows: "I heard

---

38. See note 16.
39. According to the *Bahjah* (p. 115) he would have been 11 years of age at this time.
40. It refers to the *Mukhtasar* of Hanbalite law by Abu'l Qasim 'Umar al-Khiraqi, ob. AH 334.
41. See note 15.
42. A Hanbalite *Hidāyah* is mentioned by Ibn Khallikān as the work of Ibn al-Khattab Mahfuz al-Tubadi, which is probably to be corrected Abu'l -Khattab al-Kalwadhi (AH 432-515) a Hanbalite jurist, grammarian, and poet, of whom Yāqūt has a notice (op. cit., p. 302).
43. In the *Ghibtah* (p. 47) this story is ascribed to Sharaf al-dīn Ibn al-Majd 'Isa Ibn al-Muwaffaq, the son of the person mentioned in note 16.

Abū Abdullah Muḥammad Ibn Maḥmūd al-Maratibi[44] say, that he heard the late Shaikh Abū Bakr 'Imād al-dīn[45] commenting on Shaykh 'Abdu'l Qādir in these words:

> I had been reading about the metaphysics of religion, and certain doubts had been instilled into my mind, but I thought I had best to wait till I had attended a lecture by the Shaikh 'Abdu'l Qādir, since he was supposed to address himself to the inmost thoughts of his audience. So I went to his lecture room, and the first words I heard were "Our faith is the faith of our pious ancestors and Companions." I thought to myself that this remark was incidental. Then he went on, and turning to the part of the room in which I was, he repeated the observation. But I said to myself, "A preacher is always turning in one direction or another." Then he turned towards me a third time, and said: Abū Bakr! Abū Bakr! rise, for your father has come." Now he had been away; So I rose and hastened homeward, and found my father had, in fact, just arrived.

A similar story to this effect is told by jurist Abul-Qāsim Ibn Muḥammad Ibn Khālid[46] who says that they were informed by their Shaykh, Jamal al-Dīn Yaḥyā Ibn al-Sayrafī (AH 583-678)[47]

44. Rukn al-dīn al-Maratibi is mentioned in the *Bahjah* (p. 112) as one of those who claimed to be disciples of Jīlānī. The *Ghibtah* has al-Murai, clearly a corruption. From Dhahabi's *Ushtabih*, p. 471, we learn that this person's title was Taqi al-dīn, that he was head of the Hanbalites in Damascus, and a close friend of al-Muwāffaq.

45. Perhaps identical with the Shaikh Abū Bakr 'Atiq or Ma'tūq al-Bandaniji of the *Bahjah* (p. 110) and 'Imad al-dīn Ibn Kamāl al-Bandanji of Yāqūt (op. cit., vol. I, p. 745).

46. In the *Bahjah* (p. 136) a Majid Ibn Muḥammad ibn Khalid al-'Iraqi is mentioned whose Kunyah was Abū Muḥammad. Perhaps the person was a brother of Abū Qāsim.

47. He was also called Ibn al-Habashi (d. 748/1348), he was born in Harran, went to Baghdad in AH 607 where he heard, among others, 'Umar al-Suhrawardī, then to Damascus, and thence →

that he heard the grammarian Abu'l Baqā,[48] say:

> I attended a lecture of the Shaikh 'Abdu'l Qādir, and found the students reading in his presence with wrong intonation, and I said to myself," I wonder that the Shaikh does not censure them." The Shaikh thereupon said, "Here comes a man who has studied a few chapters of Law, and finds fault." I thought to myself, "Perhaps he means someone else and not me." Then he said, "It is you I mean." So, I repented inwardly of having criticized the Shaikh. . . .

Ibnu'l Sayrafī also quotes Shaikh Ibn Taimiyyah[49] (AH 661-728) to have said that he heard the Shaikh 'Izz al-dīn Ahmad al-Faruthi[50] (AH 614-73), quoting Shaikh Shihab al-dīn al-

---

→ returned to Harran. He taught at all these places and included Ibn Taymiyyah among his pupils, (*Tadhkiratu'l Huffaẓ, Da'iratu'l Ma'arif,* Hyderabad, AH 1355, p. 678).

48. 'Abdu'llah Ibn al-Husayn Ibn 'Abdu'llah al-'Ukabari al-Basri, the blind grammarian and commentator on *Mutanabbi.* Ibn Khallikan has a short notice of him. The story told in the *Bahjah* (p. 110), is somewhat different, Al-'Ukabari, passing by Jīlānī's lecture-room, said to himself, "I will enter and hear the talk of this foreigner." He entered; Jīlānī stopped his discourse and said, "O blind of eye and heart, what have you to do with this foreigner's talk?" Al 'Ukbari went up and demanded the *Khirka* which Jīlānī gave him. This story and that in the text are mutually exclusive.

49. The famous theologian, born in Harran and grew up in Damascus. He became a jurist of Hanbali School of Law. Taught first in Damascus then in Cairo. He was imprisoned a number of times in Syria and Egypt for his religious and political opinions.

50. His name was Abu'l-'Abbas Ahmad Ibn Ibrahim. He was preacher at the Muayyad *Masjid* (in Damascus), and wrote on Tradition, etc. (Appendix to Ibn. *Khallikan's* work). Faruth is a large village with a market on the Bank of the Tigris, between Wāsit and al-Madhar.

Suhrawardī's[51] (AH 539-632) comments as:

> I intended to apply myself to the study of metaphysics, but said to myself, I will first seek the advice of the Shaikh 'Abdu'l Qādir, so, I went to see him. Before I could utter a word he said, "Umar, it is no preparation for the grave"!, which he repeated twice. So I abandoned the subject.

Abū Abdullāh Muḥammad Ibn Mahm'd al-Marātibī[52] says that he asked the Shaikh al-Muwāffaq whether, when he was staying with Shaikh 'Abdu'l Qādir, he had seen any miracle wrought by him? He replied, "I fancy not. However, he used to lecture on Fridays, then we would leave him and go to hear *Aḥādith* from Ibn Sani[53] (d. AH 560). The books they studied under the guidance of latter were the *Musnad* and *Bukhārī.*" Shaikh Abūl-Husain al-Yuninī[54] states on the authority of Shaikh 'Izz al-dīn Ibn 'Abd al-Salām[55] (AH 577-660) that the

---

51. Abū Abdullah Umar Ibn Muḥammad. Ibn Khallikan has a notice of him. His visit to Jīlān is dated AH 560. In the *Bahjah* (p. 235), this story is told with the variation that Jīlānī passed his hand over 'Umar's breast, in consequence of which he entirely forgot the books on the subject that he had learned. Suhrawardī mentions Jīlānī occasionally in his *'Awārif-al Ma'ārif.*

52. See note 44.

53. We should probably read Ibn Shāfi'ī, who is cited twice in Yākūt's geographical dictionary. He is probably identical with Abu'l-Fadl Abmad Ibn Salih Ibn Shāfi'ī al-Jīlī (*Ghibtah,* p. 30; *Bahjah,* p. 89). And indeed, Dhahabi, in his life of this person, states that these two persons studied Tradition with him.

54. Qutb al-dīn Musa Ibn Muḥammad (ob. AH 726), author of an abridgement and continuation of Sibt Ibn al-Jauzi's *Mir'at al-Zamān.* He wrote a biography of 'Abdu'l Qādir called *Manāqib.* His *nisbah* comes from Yunin of Yunan, near Baalbek, and he had two brothers, Sharaf al-dīn 'Ali and Badr al-dīn Hasan, and a sister, Amat al-Rahim. See *Taj 'al-'Arus* for details.

55. 'Abd al-Aziz of Damscus. Yunini is mentioned among his disciples.

only miracles that had been transmitted by a continuous chain of narrators were those of the Shaikh 'Abdu'l Qādir.

Ibn al-Najjār, in his account of 'Abdu'l Qādir affirms as follows:

> He (Shaikh 'Abdu'l Qādir) came to Baghdad in the year AH 488 having then attained 18 years of age. He studied Law with Abū'l-Wafā Ibn-i-'Aqīl,[56] Abu'l-Khaṭṭāb,[57] Abū Sa'id al-Mubārak al-Mukharrimī, and Abū'l Husain Ibn al-Farrā,[58] till he had mastered Roots, Branches and Differences. He also heard Traditions from a good number of teachers. He read literature with Abū Zakariyya al-Tabrīzī (ob. AH 502). He devoted himself to preaching till he became an adept. Then he took himself to solitude,[59] asceticism, wandering, self-denial, sleeplessness, residences in wastes and deserts, and became the companion of the Shaikh Ḥammād al-Dabbās[60] (ob. AH 525), from whom he learnt the doctrine of the path. Then Allāh revealed him to mankind

---

56. His name was 'Ali (*Bahjah*, p. 106). Ibn Khallikān states that he died in AH 513, and enumerates various books of his, among them an encyclopaedia in many volumes.

57. Maḥfūẓ Ibn Ahmad al-Kalwadhani, ob. AH 510 or 515.

58. Abu'l Hasan Muḥammad son of the Qadi Muḥammad Ibn Ya'li who died in AH 438. The son is mentioned (with Kunyah Abūl-Husain, among the teachers of Ibn Hubairah. (Ibn Khallikān, tr. De slane, IV, p. 115). In the *Bahjah* (p. 107) the father of this person (ob. AH 438) is mentioned to have declared himself as the disciple of 'Abdu'l Qādir (b. AH 470) on the authority of Ibn al-Akhdar (b. AH 524) which, however, seems to have no bearing upon reality.

59. He professed to have wandered in the desert for twenty-five years, *Bahjah*, p. 85.

60. There is a brief notice of him in *Lawāqih al-Anwār* (vol. I, p. 180), where an attempt is made to show that he was the pupil, not the master: Sibt Ibn al-Jauzī gives some more details: he used to give all who were suffering from the fever almonds and dried grapes to →

and caused him to be favourably received. He formed his first congregation in the year AH 521, when Allāh revealed wisdom by his tongue; then in the year AH 528 he sat in his Shaikh's school[61] to lecture and answer legal questions. He formed the object of pious visits and vows, wrote on the Roots and Branches[62] and was a powerful preacher in the style of the people of the path. Traditions have been transmitted to us on his authority by his son 'Abd al-Razzāq, Ahmad Ibn al-Bandanijī,[63] Ibn al-Qubbaitī,[64] and others.

Abdullāh Ibn Abul Hassan al-Jubbā'i[65] narrates[66] that Jīlānī (R.'A.) apprised him:

→ eat, and this remedy was effective. He used at first to accept vows and distribute them; afterwards he refused. The *Bahjah* (p. 53) makes 'Abdu'l Qādir associate with him in AH 499 and 508 when Dabbās professed to have significant number of disciples (*Bahjah*, p. 20). Also see Sha'rani, *Ṭabaqāt*, vol. I, p. 134.

61. The Mukharrimī's school which was enlarged by public subscriptions.

62. His work *Ghunyah* is rather in the style of Ghazālī's *Iḥyā*. A work called *yawaqit al-Ḥikmah* mentioned by Ibn Khallikan was probably homiletic. Some other works include *Fath-i-Rubbānī*, *Futūh al-Ghaib* and *Jila'l-i-Khaṭīr*.

63. According to *Bahjah* (p. 110) all the jurists of Bandanjain, a district near Nahrawan, professed to be followers of 'Abdu'l Qādir. A story is told on his authority in the *Qalā'id* (p. 48) where he is associated with Jamal al-dīn Ibn al-Jauzi.

64. See note 22.

65. According to Yāqūt and Dhahabī, *Mushtabih* (p. 84), where we are told that he came from Jubbah, in the distt of Tarābulus and went to Isfahān. This person is called in the *Bahjah* (p. 109) with its usual superlatives "chief of the jurists." His written communication to Ibn al-Najjār form perhaps our chief source of information about 'Abdu'l Qādir. Besides those copied by Dhahabi, there is one given in the *Bahjah* (p. 102), according to which Bishr al-Kurazi recovered four camels in the desert by →

> My soul one day worried me for a lust, which I resisted, going down street after street till I could get to the desert. Whilst I was walking I saw a leaf of paper flung on the ground, which I found contained the words; "What have the strong to do with the lusts? Lusts were created for the weak, that they might fortify themselves thereby to obey Me." When I read this, the lust departed from my heart. He went on to say that he used to sustain himself by wild carobs and lettuce from the river bank.

Dhahabī claims that he read in the handwriting of Abū Bakr 'Abdu'llah Ibn Naṣr Hamzah al-Taymī[67] that he heard Shaikh 'Abdu'l Qādir Jīlānī say:

> During a famine that befell Baghdad I was in such straitened circumstances that I remained some days without food, trying to find refuses, and one day I went to the river-bank on the chance of finding a lettuce or other vegetable. Wherever I went I found that others had been there before me; so, I went towards the country, and could find no place where there was likely to be any refuse where I had not anticipated. Finally, weakness overcame me, and being unable to hold out any longer I entered a *masjid*,[68] and was just facing death, when a young Persian came in, who had with him some bread and roast meat. He sat down and began to eat. Each time he raised his hand to his mouth I nearly opened mine, so hungry was I and I blamed myself

---

→ involving 'Abdu'l Qādir's name. He saw a man in dazzling white raiment pointing out where they were.

66. The same story is told in *Ghibṭah* (p. 8).

67. Author of a work called *Anwār al-Nazir*, In the *Ghibtah* (p. 8) this story is told as part of the narrative given by Talhah Ibn Muzafar al-'Althi, ob AH 593.

68. According to the *Ghibṭah* the *Masjid* of Yāsīn, according to the *Qalā'id* of al-Tādifi, in the Suq al-Raihaniyyin.

> for my want of self control. Presently the lad turned round and saw me. He said, "In the name of Allāh" (handing me a morsel), but I refused, he conjured me, and anxious as I was to accept, I still resisted my inclination, and refused. Finally, he conjured me till I accepted, and ate, yet sparingly. Then he asked me what my business was and whence I came. I replied that I was a law student, and that I came from Jīlān. "I too" he replied, "am from Jīlān, and do you know a young man of Jīlān called 'Abdu'l Qādir," "that it is me" I said. He was alarmed thereat and the colour of his face changed. Then he said, "By Allāh, my brother, I came to Baghdad having still some journey money with me, and asked about you, but no one could give me any information, till all my journey money was exhausted, after which I remained for three days, in which I could not find the cost of my maintenance except from your money which was in my possession. On this fourth day I said to myself, "Three days have passed in which I have eaten nothing, and I am now permitted by law to eat dead flesh." So, I took some of your money which had been entrusted to me, and with it brought this bread and roast meat, so you may eat it with a conscience, since it is your own, and I here am your guest." "What do you mean?" I asked. He replied, "your mother sent with me eight *dīnār*s for you, and I assure you I have not cheated you till today." So I quitted and comforted him and gave him part of the money.

Abdullāh Ibn Abul Hassan al-Jubbā'i narrates, that Shaikh 'Abdu'l Qādir shared with him:

> I was in the desert repeating my law lesson in a terrible state of poverty, when some one, whose person I did not see, said to me, "Borrow enough to maintain you while you are studying law." I replied, "How am I to borrow, when I am

so poor,[69] and could never pay?" He answered, "Borrow and we undertake the payment." So, I went to a grocer and said to him, "would you deal with me on the condition that I am to pay you whenever Allāh eases my way, while if I die I am to be acquitted of payment?" The man burst into tears and said to me, "Sir, I am at your service." So I took his goods for a certain time, till I could endure it no longer. Then, a voice said to me, "Go to a certain place, take whatever you find on the seat, and give it to the grocer." So I went and found a large piece of gold on a bench, there. So I took it and gave it to the grocer.[70]

Jīlānī continued:

At one time I had a fit of insanity, and was taken to the madhouse; a series of ecstasies seized and till I almost died. Grave-clothes were brought, and I was placed in the lavatory, and then my fits passed over. I rose up and bethought me that I would leave Baghdad owing to the constant disturbances there. So, I went to the Halbah Gate,[71] when someone said to me, whither goest thou? He then gave me a push which knocked me down. "Go back," he said, "for you can do the people good." I said, "I wish to

---

69. In the *Ghibtah* (p. 33) Ibn al-Najjār is quoted for the statement that 'Abdu'l Qādir was the owner of land which was cultivated for him by disciples, while others undertook to grind his corn and bake his bread. At a later time he (like other saints) lived largely by vows, i.e. money vowed by persons who were desirous of obtaining something, and obtained it. In the *Bahjah* (p. 104) there is a case quoted in which a vow of this sort amounted to 30 *dīnārs*; ordinarily they were of far less value: 'Abdu'l Qādir kept open house on these receipts.

70. In the *Ghibṭah* a similar story is given on the authority of 'Abdu'llah al-Salamī with slight variations. Shattanuafi in *Bahjat al-Asrār* narrates a similar account.

71. "The present Bala-Tilsam" (Le Strange, *Baghdād,* p. 291).

> keep my religion sound." He said, "That is granted to you." All this time I did not see the speaker. Then I was seized with a fresh set of ecstasies and wished to find someone to remove them. As I passed by al-Zafariyyah,[72] a man, opening his door, said to me, "'Abdu'l Qādir, what did you seek yesterday?" Having forgotten, I was silent. The man got angry, and slammed the door violently in my face. When I went on I recollected what I had been asking Allāh and went back to look for the door, but could not recognize it. Now the man was Ḥammād al-Dabbās, whom I got to know afterwards, and who cleared up all my difficulties. If I ever absented myself from him in the pursuit of knowledge, when I returned he would say to me, "what has brought you to us? You are a jurist, and had better go to jurists"; and I had no answer.

Shaikh 'Abdu'l Qādir Jīlānī (R.'A.) rehearses some of his experiences in these words:

> One Friday we went with him (Ḥammād) to the place of prayer[73] on a very cold day. When we got to the bridge over the river, the Qāḍī[74] knocked me into the water. I said to myself, this is the Friday washing. In the name of Allāh, I had on me a woollen *jubbah*, there were manuscripts in my sleeve. So I raised my sleeve that the manuscripts might not be injured. The others then left me and went on. I squeezed out my *jubbah* and followed the party, but suffered severely from the cold. The Shaikh used to ill-treat me and beat me, and if ever I came to him hungry he would say, "Lots of bread and cake had come for us today; we have eaten all,

---

72. Took its name from the Garden of Zaffar, one of the chief servants of the Caliph.
73. The Rusāfah *masjid* (*Ghibtah*, p. 13; *Bahjah*, p. 53).
74. This title implies that in another form of the story Mukharrimī was the man who pushed Jīlānī into the water.

and left none for you, because we did not want your company." His pupils used to take the hint, and say to me, "you are a jurist; what do you want with us?" But when the Shaikh saw them annoy me, he took my part, and said to them, "You boys, what do you mean by teasing him, when there is not one among you to be compared with him? I am only teasing him in order to prove him. And now I find him to be an immovable mountain."

After a time there came a man from Hamadān, called Yūsuf al-Hamadānī[75] (AH 440-535), he used to be called the *Quṭb*. He took up his abode in a monastery. When I heard about him I went thither, not seeing him I asked about him and was told that he was in the cellar.[76] So I descended and when he saw me he rose up, made me sit down, and scrutinized my features, he then recounted to me all the experiences which I had undergone, and solved all my difficulties. Then he advised me to speak in public. "Sir," I replied, "I am a foreigner, without admixture, and speechless, how am I to speak before the orators of Baghdad?" He rejoined, "you have committed to memory

75. A life of him is given by Ibn Khallikān, after Ibn al-Najjār and Sam'āni. According to this, born in the village of Buza Najirid Hamadani, came to Baghdad, where he studied with Abū Ishāq al-Shirāzī and other eminent jurists, and travelled to Isfahān and Samarqand, where he acquired further knowledge and also devoted himself to piety and asceticism. Afterwards he returned to Baghdad in AH 515 where for a time he taught and preached in the Nizāmiyyah. After this he spent his life in Merv and Herat, and died at Bama' in on the Merv road. In the *Lawā Qih al-Anwār* we are told that his body was afterwards transferred to sanctuary at Merv. Some of his miracles are recorded in this work. Further details about him are given in *Haqā'iq al-Naqshabandhiyya* (Cairo, 1308, p. 109), where we learn the names of some of his books — *Khutbāt al-Hayāt, Manāzil al-Sa'irīn and Manāzil al-Sālikīn.*

76. It was a form of asceticism to dwell underground. In the *Bahjah* (p. 31), a certain Ibn Qa'id is said to have lived thus for 14 years.

> the law, its roots, the differences, the vocabulary, and the interpretation of the *Qur'ān*; surely you are qualified to speak. Mount the pulpit, therefore, and address the people. I see in you a cutting that will develop into a palm."

The Shaikh 'Abdu'l Qādir continues,

> "I used to receive orders[77] and prohibitions both in sleep and working hours, and the things to be said used to crown upon my heart and overwhelm me. If I did not utter them I should have choked and could not be silent. At first two or three men sat with me and listened, then people heard about me, and numbers crowded to hear, till about 70,000 (seventy thousand) used to gather at a single meeting." "I have examined," he said, "all acts, and can find none more meritorious than the bestowing of food. How I wish the whole world were in my possession so that I might feed the hungry therewith. My hand has a hole in it. It can retain nothing. If I were to receive two thousand *dīnārs*, not one would be left with me by nightfall."

If anyone brought him gold, he would ask him to put it under the prayercarpet.[78]

Jīlānī (R.'A.) continues:

> I should like to be in the desert and waste places as I was at first, neither seeing mankind nor being seen. Yet, I feel, Allāh desired to benefit mankind through me, and indeed more than five hundred persons[79] have by me been reverted to

77. Shattanaufi, *Bahjah,* op. cit., p. 49.

78. *Bahjah,* op. cit., p. 104. Where the passage goes on, "nor would he touch it with his hand. And when his servant came, he would say to him "take what is under the carpet, and give it to the baker and grocer."

79. *Bahjah,* op. cit., p. 96, where this citation from al-Jubbai is followed by example of such conversions. Similar stories are told of other saints, like that of Abū Sa'd.

> Islam, and more than 100,000 (hundred thousand) robbers[80] and bandits have been brought by me to repentance. And this is a great deal of good by the grace of Allāh.

The Shaikh adds:

> Burdens come down upon me so heavy that mountains would be crushed beneath them. When this happens I lie on my side on the ground and read the verse,[81] "Verily in difficulty there is ease," presently I raise my head, and troubles have all disappeared. When a child is born to me,[82] I take him in my arms and say, this is doomed to die, I remove it from my heart and if the child dies it leaves no impression on me."

Ibn Najjār recounts, 'Ab. Razzaq, son of 'Abdu'l Qādir remarked, "Forty-nine children[83] were born to my father, twenty-seven males and rest females."

Ibn Najjār comments that 'Abdu'llah Ibn al-Abi'l Ḥasan al-Jubba'i wrote to him:

---

80. The *'ayyārūn* are frequently mentioned in the histories of this time.

81. *Holy Qur'ān*, XCIV: 5-6.

82. *Bahjah*, op. cit., p. 87, where we learn that the Shaikh would continue his sermon after such news had been brought to him and he would go and bury his offspring only when he had finished his sermon.

83. Since the last citation implied that many of them died, Carra de vaux believes some of these to have been spiritual descendants. Rinn in his work *Marabouts Khouan* (Algiers, 1884, p. 178), however, gives the names of nine (09) sons of Jīlāni: 'Isā (died in Cairo, AH 573); Abdullah (b. AH 508, and died at Baghdad in AH 589); Ibrahim (d. at Wasit, AH 592); Abdal Wahhāb (d. at Baghdad, AH 593); Yahyā and Muḥammad (both died at Baghdad AH 600. Abd al-Razzāq (b. AH 528 d. at Baghdad AH 603); Mūsā (b. AH 539, d. at Damascus, AH 613); Abd-al-Aziz (AH 532-602).

→

> I used to hear the book *al-Hilyah*[84] read before Ibn Nāṣir[85] (AH 467-550) and my heart softened, till I said to myself, I should like to separate myself from mankind, and devote myself to the service of Allāh. I prayed behind the Shaikh 'Abdu'l Qādir, and when he had finished we sat down. He looked at me and said "If you want to retreat, then before you study Law, attend the courses of the Shaikhs and learn some literature, otherwise you will remain as you are, an unfledged chick."

Ibn al-Najjār states that he was informed by Abū Abdullah Muḥammad Ibn Sa'id[86] al-Dubaiṯhī (AH 558-637) that 'Abū Thana Ibn Abi'l Barakāt al-Nahrmalki communicated to him that he learnt it from one of his friends that no fly ever alighted

---

→ Also see for details Tadifi's *Qala'id*, op. cit., p. 54 and Shattanaufi's, *Bahjah*, op. cit., p. 114, Abd al-Gaffar, Abd al-Ghani, Abd al-Salam and Sālih who they further add, were grandsons. To the list of twelve we may further add from *Bahjah* the eldest son, Abd al-Rahmān AH 508-87 perhaps the most interesting figure is Abd al-Salām son of Abd al-Wahhāb (ob. AH 611) who (according to Ibn al-Athir) held several important posts, but was suspected of being a philosopher, he was imprisoned in consequence and his books burned at the *Bāb al-ammah*, but he was himself released presently by his father's intercession. Though the 49 children were not all by one mother, it is not clear that the saint (though he married late), had more than one wife at one time. Their births, therefore, may have been some twins. It is however, to be observed that with the Ṣūfīs, as interpreted by Sha'rani, polygyny was rather a merit than the reverse in a saint. The *Qala'id* gives full details of the family up to many generations.

84. Probably the *Hilayat al-Awliya* of Abū Nu'aim (ob. AH 430).

85. Abu'l Fadl Muḥammad Ibn Nasir al-Salami. A short account of him is given by Ibn Khallikān. (*Wafayat al-A'yan*, Eng. tr. T.B.M. de Slane, Paris, reprint. 1961, vol. I, p. 618.)

86. Ibn Khallikān gives an account of his life. He wrote in continuation of Sam'āni's supplement. Also see *Gibtah*, op. cit., p. 44.

on the garments of the Shaikh 'Abdu'l Qādir. I asserted that I know nothing of this. The following Friday we went in the morning to the Shaikh's meeting house. He turned to us and said, "What should a fly want with me, who have neither the big-paste of this world nor the honey of the other?"

He continues[87] and affirms that he was informed by Abu'l Baqā Abdullah Ibn al-Husain al-Hanbalī that he heard Yaḥyā Ibn al-Najah al-Adīb[88] say:

> I said to myself, I should like to count the number of times the Shaikh cuts off penitents' hair,[89] so I went to his meeting house, taking with me a thread, and each time he cut-off some hair I made a knot in the thread under my garment. And although I was quite in the back row, the Shaikh called out to me, "while I loosen, you tie!"

He goes on:

> I heard the Shaikh of the Ṣūfīs, 'Umar Ibn Muḥammad al-Suhrawardī[90] (ob. AH 563) say, "In my youth I studied Law, and it struck to my mind to read some treatise on metaphysical theology, yet I communicated my intention to no one. Now, it happened that I prayed with my uncle, the Shaikh Abu'l-Najib[91] (AH 524-611) with whom the Shaikh

---

87. *Bahjah,* op. cit., p. 94, *Ghibtuh,* op. cit., p. 44 where, however, for al-Ikrimi we should read al-Ukbari, this Abu'l-Baqa being the same as mentioned earlier

88. Not to be confused with the author of *Subul al-Khairāt,* a Spanish writer who died in AH 422.

89. Apparently this was a symbolic act, signifying that the person was let go free-(Ibn Khallikān, tr. de Slane, II, p. 382).

90. See Ibn Khallikan, tr. de Slane, II, p. 150.

91. His name was 'Abdu'llah Ibn Abi Nasr Mahmūd Ibn al-Mubarak al-Junaybidhi (*Bahjah,* op. cit., p. 110). Yaqūt, however (op. cit., p. 121), calls him 'Abd al-Aziz and states that he lived in Darbal- →

> 'Abdu'l Qādir happened to be on a friendly visit. My uncle asked him to invoke a blessing on me, and informed him that I was a law student. So, I rose up and kissed his hand. Taking my hand he said to me. 'Repent of your design! So will you prosper." Then he was silent and let go my hand. Still, I did not alter my design of studying metaphysical theology, till all my affairs went out of order, and my life was embittered and I knew that the reason was my disobedience to the Shaikh.

Ibn Najjār quotes Abū Muḥammad Ibn al-Akhḍar's statement that he used to visit the Shaikh 'Abdu'l Qādir in mid-winter, when it was bitterly cold. He found on him a single tunic, and a *Taqiyah*[92] on his head, while around him were people fanning him and all the time he was perspiring as though it were exceedingly hot.

→ Qayyar in the district Nahr al-Mu'alla in East Baghdad. Yaqut was his pupil and praises him highly. The story is told in the *Bahjah* (op. cit., p. 88).

92. Originally a skull-cap worn under the turban, according to Dozy, *Noms des vetements,* who was not then aware that it formed part of Ṣūfī livery. In the *Bahjah* (op. cit., p. 69) a certain Khalaf Ibn 'Ayyash al-Shari'i al-Shafi'ī, being sent to Baghdad to buy a copy of the *Musnad* of Ibn Hanbal, determines to visit 'Abdu'l Qādir and arranges in his mind a number of things that the saint should do, among them that "he should put on me the *Taqiyah* before I ask him." The saint reads his thoughts exactly and does all that had been in the Khalaf's mind. Similarly in *Bahjah,* op. cit., p. 43, it is narrated, "Then 'Abdu'l Qādir placed on my head a *Taqiyah* and when it touched my skull felt a coolness spread therefrom to my heart." In *Lawaqih al-Anwār* (I) p. 192, we read of the two *Khirqahs,* the garment and the *Taqiyyah,* and so in the *Bahjah,* op. cit., p. 133, the reverted brigand Abū Bakr al-Bataihi receives both from Abū Bakr the Caliph in a dream.

He further elaborates that he heard 'Abd al-Aziz Ibn 'Abd al-Malik al-Shaibānī say that Ḥāfiẓ 'Abd al-Ghani[93] communicated to him that he [Hāfiz] was informed by Abū Muḥammad Ibn al-Khashshāb (AH 492-567), the grammarian as:

> When I was a lad I studied grammar, and heard people describe the beauty of the language of the Shaikh 'Abdu'l Qādir. I wanted, in consequence, to hear him but could not find time. One day however, I at last went to his meeting house but when he spoke, I neither admired his language nor could I understand it. So I said to myself "This is a wasted day." Turning to the part of the room where I was seated he said, "What! you prefer grammar to sermons! You definitely make choice of the former? Follow me. . . ."

He elaborates that Shaikh Ahmad son of Zafar son of Ibn al-Hubayrah[94] (AH 497-560) communicated to him that he asked his grandfather to grant him leave to visit Shaikh 'Abdu'l Qādir. He not only granted him leave, but sent a sum of money with him to pay it to the Shaikh, and also advised him to greet him. He narrates his experience as, "I presented myself, and when the meeting was over, and he had come down from the pulpit I saluted him but recoiled from handing the money to him before that assembly. The Shaikh anticipated my thoughts and said, 'Hand over what you have got, never mind.'"

93. See note 15.

94. Yaḥyā Ibn Muḥammad Ibn Hubairah. Ibn Khallikān has a full biography. He was a Hanbalite. According to Ibn Khallikān he left two sons, 'Izz al-dīn Muḥammad and Sharaf al-dīn Muzaffar. The first of these is brought twice into Jīlānī's lecture-room, according to the author of the *Bahjah*.

The author of the *al-Muntaẓam fi al-Tārīkh*[95] says that the silence of the Shaikh 'Abdu'l Qādir was more lengthy than his discourse, and he spoke direct to the peoples' hearts, and he enjoyed great fame and perfect popularity. He never quitted his school except on Friday or when he went to his cell. The bulk of the people of Baghdad repented through him and many of the Jews and Christians were reverted by him to Islam. No one could see him except at prayer time. He would speak the truth boldly from the pulpit and reproach those who were put in authority over the people. When al-Muqtafī[96] (AH 530-556) appointed the wicked Ibn al-Murakkhīm as judge, the Shaikh pronounced from the pulpit,[97] "You have appointed over the Muslims the wickedest of the wicked: how will you answer presently before the Lord of the world?"

The Shaikh performed striking miracles, of which a number were related by many Shaikhs whom Dhahabī met. He says, "I was told by my maternal uncle Khass Bey,[98] and by Muzaffar al-Harbī,[99] a pious man as follows: "I used," he said, "to sleep

95. Sibt Ibn al-Jauzi (AH 583-654).

96. According to one of 'Abdu'l Qādir's servants Muḥammad Ibn al-Khidr al-Husain al-Mausili (*Bahjah,* op. cit., p. 86) he used to receive visits from Caliphs and viziers, and Jīlānī used to warn the Caliphs on their misdeeds. He, at one occasion rebuked al-Mustanji'd, (*Bahjah,* op. cit., pp. 61, 77).

97. Similar boldness was displayed by Ibn 'Abd al-Salam. He was in consequence deprived of the office of *Khātib*.

98. Ibn Balankri, *wazīr,* of the Sulṭān Mas'ud the Saljūq, who, on his death in AH 547 set his son Malikshah on the throne. Presently he deposed Malikshah and made his brother Muḥammad successor, with the object of deposing him also; he was, however, forestalled by Muḥammad and killed.

99. This person figures as 'Abdu'l Qādir's servant in the *Qalā'id al-Jawahar* of Ibn Yahyā al-Tādifī.

in the school of 'Abdu'l Qādir for the sake of his sermons. One night I went and climbed on the roof of the school, when the heat was very great, and I longed for fresh dates, till I said, "O Lord! Allāh! If I could only have five dates!" Now the Shaikh had a trap-door in the roof, which he opened, and he came out with five dates in his hand. And he called out, not that he knew me, "Muẓẓafar, find what you sought!" He adds that there were many more stories of the sort. He states also that Ibn Yūnus, vizier of the Caliph Nāṣir, assailed 'Abdu'l Qādir's family, dispersed them, and injured them in every possible way. He banished them to Wāsiṭ. Allāh in requital dispersed the power of Ibn Yūnus and dispatched him so that he died a most horrible death.

Shaikh 'Abdu'l Qādir (R.'A.) was matchless, far-famed, and a leader both in knowledge and conduct. The Shaikh Nur al-dīn al-Shaṭṭanaufi composed a lengthy work in three volumes on his life and works. On the authority of certain people he asserts that Shaikh took thirteen steps in air off his pulpit at a meeting;[100] and that once when the Shaykh was discussing and no one was moved he said, "you are not moved, and feel no pleasure. Ye lamps, manifest your delight!" whereupon the lamps moved about and the dishes danced. In general, however, his miracles are recorded by a sound chain, and he left no one after him like himself. The Shaikh died on 10 Rabi (ii), AH 561 being 90 years old. His funeral was attended by a countless multitude. A saying reported by al-Jubbā'i as uttered by the Shaikh 'Abdu'l-Qādir is, "Mankind screen you from your soul, and your soul screens you from Allāh."[101]

---

100. *Bahjah*, op. cit., p. 74.

101. Shaykh 'Abdu'l Qādir Jīlānī, *Al-Fath al-Rabbānī*, 43rd discourse.

WORKS

Works of Shaikh Sayyid 'Abdu'l Qādir Jīlānī (Raḥ.'A)

1. *Futūḥ al-Ghaib*[102] (Arabic)

It comprises eighty (80) discourses of the Shaikh (Raḥ.'A) dealing with multi-dimensional aspects of *taṣawwuf* ranging from esoteric interpretation of *īmān* (faith) to Ṣūfī *aḥwāl* (states),

---

102. The description of some of the manuscript copies available in different libraries of the subcontinent is given hereunder:

(a) Raza Library, Rampur

Acc. no.	*Script*	*Size, Folios and Lines per page*	*Condition & Age*	*Additional Particulars*
7948 M	'Arabic (Naskh)	S. 21.1 ×15.3 F. 157; L. 11	Good, worm eaten & water stained 1104/1693	The autograph and seal of Sulṭān Hasan Barilawi along with a seal of Nasru'llah dated 1223/ 1808 is borne on fol. 1a. Copied by Hafiz 'Abdu'l Halim. Beginning الحمد للهِ رب العالمين اولاً و آخراآه See Brock. 1/435, Sup. 1/778 & Patna 13/38.
5262 M	'Arabic (Naskh)	S. 22.5 × 13.1 F. 198 L. 9	Good, worm eaten 13th/19th century.	With blue and red Jidwal. The old seal of the library, in which is inscribed the following Bait, is borne on fol. 1a. چسنت ایں مہر برکتب خانہ والی رام پور فرزانہ

maqāmāt (stations) and spiritual worlds. It has been translated into many languages including English (one translation by M. Aftab-ud-Din Ahmad) and Urdu (one tr. published by Naz Publishing House, Delhi).

(b) Maulana Azad Library (Manuscript Section, Ḥabīb Gunj Collection), A.M.U., Aligarh

Acc. no.	*Script*	*Size, Folios and Lines per page*	*Condition & Age*	*Additional Particulars*
H.G. 21/ 69	'Arabic (Naskh)	S. 19 × 14 F. 135; L. 12	Good, Not dated	Copied by Abur-Razzaq Kashmiri. The words قال رضى الله عنه and ارضا are transcribed in gold. Bears seals; "فدوى محمد شاه بادشاه غازى" "فدوى شاه عالم بادشاه غازى" beginning الحمد لله رب العالمين اولاً وآخراً و باطناً عدد خلقه

(c) The details of some other manuscript copies are as under:

- *Tarjama Futūḥ al-Ghaib* (Ms), Salar Jang Museum, Hyderabad.
- *Khulāsah Futūḥ al-Ghaib* (Ms), Raza Library, Rampur, U.P.
- *Sharh-i Futūḥ al-Ghaib* (Ms), Kutub Khāna, Khanqāh-I Mujibiyya, Phaidi Sharif, Patna (Bihar).
- *Miftāh-i-Futūḥ al-Ghaib* (Ms), Asiatic Society of Bengal, Calcutta.
- *Miftāh-i-Futūḥ* (Ms) (*Sharh-i Futūḥ al-Ghaib*), Oriental Manuscript Library, (Asfiyya Library), Hyderabad.

Sharhu Kalimati'l Jīlānī fi'l-Futūḥ, by Ibn Taimiyyah (Ms), Raza Library, Rampur.

→

2. al-Ghunyah li-Ṭālibi Ṭariqi'l Ḥaqq:[103]

→ Arabic (*Nasta'liq*); S. 24.7 × 17.5 Good An annotation on
F. 24 slightly worm eaten *Futūḥ al-Ghaib*
L. 19

103. The details of some manuscript copies are as under:

Manuscript copies of the work available in Raza Library Rampur

Acc. no	*Script*	*Size, Folios and Lines per page*	*Condition & Age*	*Additional Particulars*
143 D	'Arabic (Naskh)	S. 26.3 × 18.2 F. 347; L. 16-8	Good, worm eaten 12th/18th century	Placed in new margins Beginning: الحمد لله الذى نحمده يفلغ كل كتاب آه See Brock. 1435, Sup. 1/778 & Patna 13/38
10283 D	'Arabic (Naskh)	S. 21.3 × 12.7 F. 343 (The last 4 folios missing)	Good, worm eaten 12th/18th century	Preceded by the table of contents of which the 1st fol. is missing. The paper has become brittle.
5128 M	'Arabic (Nasta 'liq)	S. 22 × 12.6 F. 512 L. 15-23	Good. worm eaten 12th/18th century	
8347 M	'Arabic (Nasta'liq)	S. 25 × 16.8 F. 312 L. 19	Good. Worm-eaten 13th/19th century	Written on reddish paper.

Also

- *Sharh-i Ghunnyat al-Talibin* (Ms); Hamdard.
- *Ghuniyāt al-Talibin* (Ms); tr. 'Abdu'l Haq Mkuhadith Dehlawi, Khuda Bakhsh Library.
- *Ghuniyāt al-Talibin* (Ms); tr. 'Abdu'l Hakim Sialkoti; Khuda Bakhsh (2), Pir Wa Madya, Asiatic, Raza and Tonk.

(*Ghunyāt aṭ-Ṭālibīn*) ('Arabic): It is an ethico-legal manual divided into thirty-nine chapters including fundamentals of Islam, Islamic manners, rituals, juristic issues, Praises of Prophet (SAW), different sections of Muslim Society, *mā'rifat* (gnosis), types of *ṣalāh* and qualities of Prophets. It has been translated into Persian and Urdu (one translation by Amanullah Khan, Arman Sirhadi).

3. *Fath-i Rubbānī*[104] (Arabic)

It comprises sixty-two sermons of the Shaikh (Raḥ.'A) delivered in the same number of *majālis* (religious gatherings). All the sermons are properly dated and in some cases the time forenoon or afternoon is also mentioned. Most of the sermons were delivered either in Madrasa Ma'murah or Khānqāh Sharif in Baghdad. *Tawḥid* (oneness of Allāh), physical and spiritual purification of one's self, purging of heart of all evil and dross, secrets of spiritual life, *mā'arifat* (gnosis), transitoriness of the world and the identification of *a'māl* (deeds) that lead to *qurbat* (nearness) to Allāh are some of the recurring themes of these sermons. This work has been translated into a number of languages including Persian and Urdu.

4. *Jila'l-i Khaṭīr*[105]

It is a collection of discourses of the Shaikh (Raḥ.'A) which

---

- *Daulat-i Qahirah* (Ms) (Persian tr. of *Ghuniyāt al-Talibin;* Pakistan.
- *Ghuniyāt al-Talibin* (tr. Persian and Tlkhis by Ibrahim Tatwi; (Ms) Pakistan.
- *Risāla Marji* (*Sharh-i Ghuniyāt al-Talibin*) by Fakhru'd-Din Awrangabadi; Ms (Pakistan).

104. Also, Fathi Rubbāni (Persian tr.) - Shaikh 'Abdu'l Qādir Jīlānī vide; (Catalogue (vol. V), (Ms) Markazi Tahqiqati Farsi, Iran wa Pakistan, Islamabad).

105. This work has also been edited by Shaikh Muḥammad al- →

deal with various aspects of spiritual life. Company of Shaikhs

→ Description of Some Manuscript copies of the work available in Raza Library Rampur

Acc. no.	*Script*	*Size, Folios and Lines per page*	*Condition & Age*	*Additional Particulars*
4025 M	'Arabic (Naskh)	S. 25.2 × 16 F. 136; L. 25 1169/1756	Good, worm eaten & water stained	Copied by Sayyid Taha al-Qadiri al-Hamawi al-Madani ash-Shafi'i Beginning: نسب السيراولياء الله. قال الشيخ الاعتراض على الحق موت الدين آه See Brock. 1/435, Sup. 1/778 Patna 13/39
470 M	'Arabic (Naskh)	S. 22.7 × 14.1 F. 472 L. 15	Good 12th/18th century	A nice copy with gold Jidwal and Damdani Mush. Beginning: الاعتراض على الحق عزوجل عند نزول الاقدار آه
26565 D	'Arabic (Naskh) L.16	S. 20.2 × 12.5 F. 8 (44a-51b)	Good 13th/19th century	A very small portion of the preceding work corresponding to foll. 228b-41a of the preceding copy. The autograph and seal of Jamalu-'d-Din Husain Qutbi are found at the end preceded by the Du'ai, 'Adilah & other prayers. Beginning: وقال رضي، الله عنه بعد كلام ماغلام خطوتان، وقد وصلت خطوة عن الدين آه

(preceptors), repentance, love, *tawwakul* (trust in Allāh), *ṣabr* (patience), *ikhlāṣ* (sincerity), *taqwā* (piety), deeds of heart, denunciation of the world, *nūr* (divine light), prohibition of injustice, contrition, and benefits of mercy are some of the recurring themes in these discourses of Jīlānī (Raḥ.'A).

5. *Al-Qaṣīdatu'l-Ghawthiya*[106]

It is a mystic poem composed by the Shaikh (Raḥ.'A). Certain Sūfic concepts like *mā'rifat* (gnosis), *wisāl* (mystical union), divine wine, *qurbat* (nearness to Allāh), spiritual *maqām* (stages)

→ Casnazani al-Husseini (Master of *Tarqiq 'Aliyyah* Qadiriyyah Casnazaniyyah) on the basis of three manuscript copies available to him, one at the Department of Manuscripts of the Iraqi Musuem, one at the Library of the Iraqi Ministry of Waqf and Religious Affairs and the third at the library of Shaikh 'Abd al-Qāḍir al-Gaylani in Baghdad (Iraq). This edited work has been translated into English by Professor Shetha al-Dargazelli and Louay Fatoohi (both the translators are *khalifa*s of the above-mentioned al-Husseni and are associated with Durham University).

106. Details of the Manuscripts of the work available in Raza Library, Rampur:

(a) Acc. No. 211 M, *Script:* 'Arabic (Nasta'liq); *Condition and age:* good, worm eaten 13th/19th century; *Additional particulars*: Composed in 546/1152. Copied by M. Azim b. Ghulam Muhammad, *Size folios and lines*: 27.7 ḻ 18.8; F. 95 (1a — 95b) L. 16.

Also see Brock 1/435, Sup. 1/778 and Asaf 1/364.

(b) Acc. no. 8347 M; *Script* 'Arabic (Naskh); *Size Folios and lines,* Same as above.

Condition and age: Good, 13th/19th century; *Additional particulars:* Written on the margins of fols. 1b-28a ends abruptly.

The details of some manuscript copies of the work are as under:

- *Sharh-i (Qasidah) Ghowthiyya* by Ghulam Mahyud-Din Ms. Jame'i.

→

and *aḥwāl* (states), find an esoteric interpretation and expression in this *qaṣidah*. It is also known as *Qaṣidah Khamriyya*.

6. *Kibriyat al-Aḥmar*[107] (Arabic)

It is a treatise in the praise of the status of Prophet Muḥammad

---

→ - *Sharh-i (Qasidah) Ghawthiyya* by Dawud bin Khalifa Fath 'Ali — Ms. Asfiyya.
- *Sharh-i (Qasidah) Ghawthiyya* by Muḥammad Fadil al-Din Patialiyya - Ms. Asfiya.
- -do- by Ibrahim bin Budh; Ms. Abul Khair.
- *Qasidiyya al-Khamriyya al-Ghawthiyya*; Ms. Phulwari.
- *Al-Qasidah al-Ghawthiyya*, tr. Shah Fadl al-Din, Ms. Phulwari.
- *Qasidah Ghawthiyya* (tr. Persian) by Muḥammad Ashiq.
- *Sharh-i Qasidah Khamriyya Ghawthiyya* (Arabic) eight Mss. Copies in Daru'l 'ulum, Peshawar, Pakistan, transcribed by different people.

107. This treatise has been published a number of times and translated into various languages including Persian and Urdu. A significant number of *sharh* (annotations) have been written on it. *Location of some manuscript copies is as under:*

(i) *Qasidah Kibriyat-i-Ahmar* (transcribed by Kamal al-Din Muḥammad) Ms. A.M.U.

Acc. no.	*Script*	*Size, Folios and Lines per page*	*Condition & Age*	*Additional Particulars*
H.G. 28/207 (2/35)	'Arabic (Naskh)	S. 15 × 11, 9 × 4 F. 6; L. 8	Good, not dated	Copied by Hafiz Muhammad Shaikh. Transcribed within blue and red ruled borders. Beginning: سقانی الحب کاسات الوصال فقلت الخمرتی نحوی تعال

→

(ṢAW). Certain *du'a* (prayers) also find an exposition in this

---

(ii) *Kibriyat-i-Ahmar* (transcribed by 'Abdu'llah) MS. Asfiyya and Buhar.

(iii) *Zary'e Sa'adat* (*Sharh-I Kibriyyat-I Ahmar*) (transcribed by Sa'id 'Asi); Ms. Pakistan.

(iv) Details of Manuscripts copies available in

Maulana Azad Library, AMU

Acc. no	*Script*	*Size, Folios and Lines per page*	*Con-dition & Age*	*Additional Particulars*
656 M	'Arabic (Naskh)	S. 29.3 × 16.4 F. 13 (1b-13a) L.11	Good, 12th/ 18th cen-tury	A very nice copy of a tract consisting of divine inspira-tions each beginning with a *lawh*, gold and coloured Jidwal and gold line under each line of the text. The first folio is in a later hand. Begin-ning: الحمد لله كاشف الغمه قال الغوث الاعظ المستوحش عن غير الله آه... See Brock sup. 1/778 under *Kalimat al Qudsiyyah.*
19353 D	-do-	S. 19 × 13.7 F. 8; L. 10-19	Good, water stained 1228/ 1813	
8626 M	'Arabic (Nasta-'liq)	S. 23.9 × 14 F. 6; L. 14	Good, worm eaten 13th/19th century	Copied by M A 'zim b. Ghulam Muhammad.

(v) *Kibriyat-i-Ahmar* (*Sharh*); transcribed by M. A'ezam Didamari. (MS. Pakistan).

treatise. It is regarded of great mystical value and many followers of the Shaikh (Raḥ.'A) recite it after *Ṣalāt-i-Fajr* (morning prayers).

7. *al-Mukhtūbātu'l Ghawthiyya*[108]

It is a treatise dealing with different dimensions of mystical life and divine inspirations.

8. *Risāla Ghawthiyya*[109] (Arabic)

It is another treatise that deals with some aspects of the contemplative life. A number of people have contributed to the *sharh* (annotation) on this treatise. It has been translated into Persian and Urdu.

---

108. Details of Manuscript copies available in Raza Library Rampur.

109. The details of some manuscript copies available in various libraries are as under:
    - *Risāla Ghawthiyya* (Ms, Persian) — Khuda Bakhsh (2 Nos).
    - *Risāla Ghawthiyya* (Ms, Persian) transcribed by Wali Muḥammad bin Muluk Shah Qādirī — Khuda Bakhsh, Raza.
    - *Risāla Ghawthiyya* (Ms, Persian) transcribed by Abdul Rahman Hasan bin 'Ali Mekki al-Husaini al-Jīlānī, Raza.
    - *Sharh-i Risāla Ghawthiyya* (Ms) transcribed by Wali Muḥammad bin Muluk Shah, Khuda Bakhsh (5 Nos.), Raza, Asifiyya, Asiatic (3 Nos.), Madras; also one copy with Persian text and Urdu tr. available in *Khānqāh-i-Munimi.*
    - *Sharh-i (Risāla) Ghawthiyya* (Ms) = transcribed by 'Abdu'llah bin Husain 'Ali al-Husaini al-Jīlānī, Phulwari.
    - *Al-Kalimat al 'Arabiyya Fi Sharh-I Risāla Ghawthiyya* — transcribed by Mulla Mu'azam Naqshbandī, Ms (Hamdard).
    - *Risāla Ghawthiyya* (Ms): Khuda Bakhsh (2) (AMU, Asfiyya, Raza, Jami, Nadwah).
    - *Risāla-Ghawth al-A'zam* (Ms): Khuda Bakhsh.
    - *Risāla-Ghawth al-Azam* (Ms) (Persian): Khuda Bakhsh.

9. *Maktūbāt*[110] (Persian)

From time to time the Shaikh (Raḥ.'A) has written a number of letters mostly addressed to his sons and disciples. Eighteen of these letters have been compiled in the form of a *risāla* (treatise). These letters are orginally written in Persian with frequent references to Qur'ānic verses and '*Aḥādīth*. Most of the *maktūbāt* deal with fundamental religious beliefs and their esoteric interpretation.

10. *Chahal Kāf*[111]

It comprises three verses of extreme mystical depth. The letter (ک) (kāf) occurs forty times in these verses. In these verses Shaikh (Raḥ.'A) addresses his inner self to entrust all the affairs

---

110. Details of some of the manuscript copies of this work are as under:
   (i) *Maktubat-i 'Abdu'l Qādir Jīlānī* (Persian (Ms no. 21/300 Habib Ganj collection, AMU). Also available in Asiatic.
   (ii) *Maktubat-i Ghawth-i A'ezam* (Ms no. 21/44) H.G. (AMU). Also available in Pir Wa Madya.
   (iii) *Chand Maktubat-i Sarmad Wa Ghawth-i Pak*, Chahar Dah Khanwadah; Ms no. 477. AMU, transcribed by 'Ali bin Hasam al-Din).
   (iv) *Makatib-i Shaikh 'Abdu'l Qādir Jīlānī* (transcribed by 'Ali Muttaqi; Ms Jamia Millia).
   (v) *Makatib-i Ghawth-I A'ezam* (Ms Phulwari).
   (vi) *Maktubat-i Ghawth al-Thaqalyn;* (Ms *'Abdu'l Salam;* transcribed by Abul Khair Muḥammad bin Ahmad Muradabad-i). *Al-Maktubat-I 'Abdu'l Qādir Jīlānī* (Ms Khuda Bakhsh).

111. The Ms copies of this treatise with *sharh* (annotation) are available in Pakistan, transcribed by
   (i) Muḥammad Hasan J'an Mujaddadi.
   (ii) Rafi'ud-Din.
   (iii) Shaikh 'Abdu'l Ḥaqq Mahadith Dihlawi.

→

to Allāh. He warns that one should not become a prey to the desires of the flesh.

11. *Tuḥfat al-Qādriyya*[112]

This treatise also deals with some aspects of mystical life.

12. *Risāla Ṣamadiyya*[113]

It deals with the praises of the attributes of Allāh and His unlimited favours to man. Besides, the treatise explains some aspects of the contemplative behaviour.

13. *Risāla Waṣl-i-Ḥaqq*[114]

It is a treatise in which the Shaikh (Raḥ.'A) explains some requirements that lead to the attainment of purity and perfection in the Ṣūfī way.

14. *Naw Dah Naw Nām*[115]

This treatise explains the mystical dimensions of ninety-nine

---

(iv) Khwaja 'Ali Muḥammad Ni'amatullah.

112. Ms copies of this treatise are available in a number of libraries including:

(i) Furqaniyya, Phulwari, Abu'lkhair, Khalil al-Rahman (transcribed by Shah Abul Ma'ali).

(ii) Deoband (transcribed by Shair Muḥammad Lahori).

(iii) Khuda Bakhsh and Asfiyya (transcribed by Karāmāt 'Ali Shah Lahori).

113. Ms copies available in Phulwari and Balkhiyya. Also, a Ms copy of its *sharh* (annotation) under the title *Risāla Fardiyya* (*Sharh-i Samadiyya*) transcribed by Ja'far Muḥammad bin Mubarak Qādirī is available in Balkhiyya.

114. Ms copies available in Pir Wa Madya and State Archives, Allahabad.

115. (i) Ms copy available in AMU.

→

attributes of Allāh. The significance and implications of these attributes are dealt with in detail.

15. *al-Ilhāmiyya*[116]

This treatise deals with divine inspiration, its causes, significance, requirements and implications in an elaborated way.

16. *al-Waṣiyah*[117]

This treatise comprises the instructions and the advice imparted by the Shaikh (Raḥ.'A) to his sons during the last days of his life. The Shaikh (Raḥ.'A) explains various dimensions of *tawḥīd* (oneness of Allāh), reminds of the life Hereafter, transitoriness of the world, impact of association with the pious people and reward for virtuous deeds.

17. *Kanz al-'Ibād Fi Sharḥ-al-Awrād*[118] (Arabic)

In this treatise the Shaikh (Raḥ.'A) explains the necessity of concentration and conformity of one's inner self with his physical devotion while performing various fundamental rituals. Some forms of *dhikr* (way of remembering Allāh) and *du'a* (prayers) are also explained in it.

18. *Bayān al-Asrār*[119]

This treatise deals with the exposition of some secrets of mystical life and their relevance for the perfection of inner self and personality of a Ṣūfī.

(ii) Ms copy under the title *Naw Dah Naw Nam Haḍrat-i-Ghawth al-A'ezam wa Sharh-I Qasidah Seryani*, available in Asfiyya.

116. Ms. copy available in Jami.

117. Ms. copy in Khuda Bakhsh.

118. Copy available in Darul'ulum Peshawar.

119. Ms. copy available in Darul'ulum Peshawar.

3

Origin and Development of Taṣawwuf

Origin

Iṣṭilahāt (terms) and *tāwilāt* (interpretations) at occasions have played a vital role in giving rise to different schools of thought and sects. But, if we forget about these new *iṣṭilahāt* and turn to the period of *aslāf* (the people of our glorious past), when people used very simple vocabulary, we may be able to derive a clear message from even very complex concepts and terms. *Taṣawwuf*, in fact, is one such new *iṣṭilahāt*. Scholars in our contemporary times wrangle about the origin and derivation of the term *taṣawwuf*. In fact, the word *taṣawwuf* did not find a place in the *Qur'ān*, *Sihāh-i-sitta* (compiled in AH 392) and *Qāmūs*, the standard Arabic dictionary, compiled in AH 817. According to the research of Imām Qushayrī[1] (d. 465/1072) the word Ṣūfī came into vogue a little before the expiry of the second century Hijra or CE 822.[2]

After prophet Muḥammad (SAW), *Ṣaḥāba* (companions) was the title adopted by the Muslims of that period. They needed no better title, for it was unanimously regarded to be the highest and the best one. Those who associated with the

---

1. See N.D. Ab. Rahman Jāmī, *Nafaḥāt al-Uns*, Urdu tr. Shams Barelvī, Delhi, 1994, p. 548 for the biography of Qushayrī.

2. Ibid., p. 74.

Ṣaḥāba were called in their own times *Tāba 'yīn* (followers). *Taba Tāba 'yīn* (followers of the followers) was the title conferred upon those who associated themselves with *Tāba 'yin* (followers).

Now, let us cast a glance at the various attempts of lexicographers on the derivation of the word Ṣūfī. One group considers it to come from *ṣaff* (a row) as these men, in their opinion, will stand in the first row on the Day of Judgement. But then it would be *ṣaffī* and not *ṣūfī*. Some contend that the word *ṣūfī* is derived from *ṣafā* (purity), but grammar would then yield *safavī* and not *ṣūfī*. Yet others hold this opinion that the qualities of Ṣūfīs resembled those of the *Aṣḥāb al-Suffā* (the people, of the Bench). But then it would be *ṣuffi* and not *ṣūfī*. There are scholars including Alfred Guillaume, Thomas Arnold, R.'A. Nicholson, and A.J. Arberry who contend that Ṣūfī is derived from the word *'ṣūf* (meaning wool). In their opinion, the pious people wearing woollen garments came to be described as Ṣūfīs. Abū Bakr al-Kalabādhi (d. 390/1000) and Ibn Khaldūn (d. 808/1406) also hold that the word *ṣūfī* is derived from *ṣūf* (wool). There is yet another derivation of the word *ṣūfī* from the Greek, *sophia* (wisdom). But in this case they would become sophists and not Ṣūfīs. Many others are of the opinion that Ṣūfīs are known in the *Qur'ān* by the terms: *muqarrabīn* (near ones to Allāh), *ṣābirīn* (patient men), *abrār* (virtuous men) and *zuhhād* (pious men). In fact, some of the Ṣūfīs were known as *muqarrabīn* for 600 years in the region of Turkistan and Mavarā-un-nahr. The author of *Ghiathul-Lughāt* states another theory that *suffa* was the name of a tribe of Arabs who in the time of ignorance separated from their people and engaged themselves in the service of *K'aba*. This Arab tribe *suffa* lived in Bani Muzar.

Unfortunately, misunderstanding has been created by

some scholars with regard to Ṣūfism being independent of *shari'at*, the Islamic doctrine and law. But the explanation of Ṣūfism presented by the prominent Ṣūfis as well as the evidence available in the biographies and sayings of the early Ṣūfis and saints completely rules out any question of Ṣūfism being independent of *shari'at*. In fact, the process of spiritual ascent in Ṣūfism is interwoven with and based upon *shari'at* that the possibility of separating the two cannot be conceived of. The dependence of *ṭarīqat* on *shari'at* is well illustrated in a Ṣūfī symbol in which Islam is compared to a walnut whose shell is *shari'at* which protects it from external forces, its kernel is *ṭarīqat* and the oil, which although invisible but present, corresponds to *ḥaqīqat* or the ultimate reality itself. It is not possible for the kernel to grow without a shell, nor is shell without a kernel of any value. They are complementary to each other. Thus, Ṣūfism becomes a mediator between *shari'at* and *ḥaqīqat*, precisely as it intends to push a man to the extreme of what he only accepts intellectually at the beginning. Ṣūfism can also be explained from the perspective of the three basic religious attitudes mentioned in the holy *Qur'ān*, viz. attitudes of Islam, *īmān* and *iḥsān*. In a *ḥadīth*, Prophet (SAW) describes these attitudes as components of *al-Dīn* (religion), while several other *Aḥādīth* in the Kitabūl *īmān* of *Ṣaḥīḥ al-Bukhāri* discuss Islam and *Īmān* as distinct attitudes varying in religious significance. *Iḥsān* is regarded as the highest stage of spiritual advancement. It was later termed as *Mushahadah* (direct seeing) by the Ṣufıs.

Abu Abdullah Sahl Ibn Abdullah al-Tastārī (d. AH 273), a famous Ṣūfī says:

اصول طريقتنا سبعة التمسك بالكتاب، والاقتداء بالسنة واكل
الحلال وكف لاذى و تجنب المعاصى والتوبه واداء الحقوق

Our way has seven principles; to hold fast by the Book (al-*Qur'ān*), to model ourselves upon the *Sunnah* (of Prophet

Muḥammad (SAW), to eat only what is lawful, to refrain from hurting people, to avoid borbidden things, *tawbah* (repentence/return to Allāh), and to fulfil obligations (*Haqūqullāh* and *Ḥaqūq ul'Ibād*).

Another Ṣūfī Ab'ul Husain Ahmad Ibn Abul Hawārī says,

من عمل عملا بلا اتباء سنة رسول الله صلى الله عليه وسلم فباطل عمله

whosoever acted not in conformity with *Sunnah*, his such act will prove futile.[3]

Ab'ul Qāsim Junaid Ibn Muḥammad (d. AH 297) says, "One who could not understand the *aḥkām* (instructions) of *Qur'ān* and *Aḥādith* and did not achieve their knowledge, he cannot be obeyed in (the field of) *taṣawwuf*, because our knowledge (of *taṣawwuf*) is outlined by the *Qur'ān* and *Sunnah* (of Prophet Muḥammad SAW) and these two (*Qur'ān* and *Sunnah*) are the source of *Ijma* and *Qiyas*."[4]

Abul Qasim Ibrahim (d. AH 367) says, "The basics of *taṣawwuf* are: observing the limits of *Qur'ān* and *Sunnah*, non-obedience of whims and *bid'at* (non-permissible innovations), respect for *mashā'ikh* (preceptors).[5]

Sayyid Shaikh 'Abdu'l Qādir Jīlānī (Raḥ.A) (d. AH 591) says:

اجعل الكتاب والسنة امامك وانظر فيهما بتامل و تدبر واعمل بهما ولا تغتر
بالقال والقيل والهوس

Keep *Qur'ān* and *Sunnah* in front of you (for guidance and obedience). Understand these with full vision and

3. Zakariyya Anṣārī, *Sharḥ-i Risāla Qushayrī*, vol. I, p. 126.
4. Ibid., vol. I, p. 143.
5. Ibid., vol. II, p. 15.

speculation, follow these and don't be misled by desires. . . .[6]

Abul Abbas Ahmad Ibn Muḥammad Ibn Sahl Ibn 'Aṭa (d. AH 309) while stressing upon the obedience to *Qur'ān* and *Sunnah* says, "One who follows the principles of *sharī'ah*, Allāh enlightens his heart and there is no better status than to obey the Prophet (SAW). . . ."[7]

Shaikh Shihābūddin Suhrawardī writes in his famous Ṣūfī compendium *'Awārif al-Ma'ārif*, "The use of word *ṣūfī* is not *m'arūf* (commonly used) and famous throughout the Islamic world, from east to the west, for the *ahl-i qurb* (near ones to Allāh). This title is used for those people who wear a special type of *libās* (dress). There are many *ahli-qurb* in the west, Turkestan Transoxiana, but they are not called Ṣūfīs simply on account of the fact that they don't wear the specific dress of Ṣūfīs. . . . So, by Ṣūfī we mean *muqarrabīn* (near ones to Allāh)."[8]

It means that up to seventh century Hijra the term *ṣūfī* was applied to those who wore a specific type of *libās* (dress). Later on, this restriction was diluted and all those who preached for a system of *murshid* (preceptor) and *murīd* (disciples) in a systematic, formal and consolidated way were called as Ṣūfīs. Shah Walī Allāh Dehlawī (d. 1175/1762) opines,

"علوم احسان ویقین کہ الیوم باسم تصوف
مشہور شدہ۔۔۔حقیقت تصوف کہ بعرف شرع
نام آں احسان است"

---

6. Shaikh 'Abdu'l'l Qādir Jīlānī, *Futūḥ al-Ghaib*, Eng.tr. Aftab-ud-din Ahmad, Delhi, rpt., 1990, Discourse no. 36.
7. Shaikhu'l Islam Zakariyya Anṣārī, *Sharḥ-I Risāla Qushayrī*, vol. I, p. 174.
8. Shaikh Shihābu'd-Din Suhrawardī, *'Awārif al-Ma'ārif* (Urdu tr. Shams Barelvi), Delhi, 1986, pp. 156-57.

> That *'ulūm* (sciences) of *iḥsān* (highest form of ethics) and *yaqīn* (belief) nowadays are being termed as *taṣawwuf*. . . . In reality *iḥsān* in common usage (in *shari'ah*), is called *taṣawwuf*.[9]

In reply to Jabriel's (A.S.) (the angel of first rank) enquiry about the interpretation of *iḥsān*, Prophet (SAW), in a big gathering of his *Ṣaḥāba* (companions), said,

ان تعبدا لله كانك تراه فان لم تكن تراه فانه يراك

> (*Iḥsān* means) to adore Allāh as though thou do see Him, for even if thou don't see Him. He nonetheless sees thee.[10]

Taṣawwuf may thus be defined as the spiritual progress of a devotee from the initial stage of Islam to the final stage of *Iḥsān*.

This *ḥadīth*, without any doubt, is the basis of *taṣawwuf*. In all the authentic books on *taṣawwuf* this *ḥadīth* has been quoted and commented upon. In fact, *taṣawwuf* has assumed the form of a science. It has also been interpreted as,

التصوف علم تعرف به احوال تزكيه النفوس و تصفية الاخلاق و

تعمير الظاهر و الباطن نسيل السعادة الابديه

> *Taṣawwuf* is a science which helps to know the states of purification of self, cleanliness of *ikhlāq* (manners) and construction of exoteric and esoteric aspects of life and its (chief) objective is the everlasting goodness (in this world and Hereafter).[11]

---

9. Dehlawi, Shah Wali Allāh, *Izālatul Khifā an Khilāfat al-Khulafā, maqsad* 2nd, p. 142.
10. Imām Muhyu'd-Din an-Nūwī, *Riyāḍ al-Ṣāliḥīn*, Urdu tr. M. Sadiq Khalil, Lahore, n.d., vol. I, *ḥadīth* no. 60.
11. Shaikhul Islam Zakariyya Ansari, *Sharh-i-Risālatul Qashayri*, vol. I, p. 69.

Ṣūfīs frequently quote the following two *Aḥādīth* of the Prophet (SAW):

العلماء ورثة الانبياء

> *'Ulamā'* are inheritors of Prophets.[12]

من عمل بما علم ورثة الله علم مالم يعلم

> When man acts on the basis of his knowledge (he possesses), (then) Allāh reveals/bestows to him the knowledge of such things which he does not know or which is unknown to him.

Ṣūfīs hold that this inherited (revealed) knowledge can also be termed as *fahm* (power of understanding) and *baṣīrah* (power of speculation) and it has also been termed as *ḥikma* (wisdom) in the *Qur'ān*;

يوتى الحكمة من يشاء و من يوت الحكمه فقد اوتى خيراً كثيراط وما

يزكر الا اولو الالباب [13]

Qur'ān specially points to *tazakiyya* (purification) as an important notion of religion and one of the four integral components of *nabūwat* (Prophethood). It reads as:

هوالذى بعث فى الامبين رسولا منهم يتلوعليهم اٰياته و يزكيهم و

يعلمهم الكتاب والحكمة و ان كانو من قبل لغى ضلال مبين [14]

In fact, Islamic *shari'at* comprises two complementary notions; one being *ẓāhirī* (exoteric) and another *bāṭinī* (esoteric) in nature. The esoteric component can be chiefly expressed in the form of *tazakiyya* and *iḥsān*. Thus, *taṣawwuf* specifically deals with this esoteric aspect of one's belief.

---

12. *An-Nūwī*, op. cit., vol. II, *ḥadīth* no. 496.
13. Holy *Qur'ān*, II:37.
14. Holy *Qur'ān*, Jum'a; 02.

DEVELOPMENT

Right from first century AH there were powerful ascetic tendencies within Islam. An exaggerated consciousness of sin and an overwhelming dread of divine retribution[15] appear as two chief factors in this early asceticism. In fact, the movement proceeded on orthodox lines, and with the passage of time asceticism passed into mysticism. Hasan of Basrah (d. 110/728) the most representative of the ascetic movement strove for spiritual righteousness and was not satisfied with only formal acts of devotion. He declared, "A grain of genuine piety is better than a thousandfold weight of fasting and prayer."[16] Again, "Cleanse ye these hearts (by meditation and remembrance of Allāh), for they are quick to rust, and restrain ye these souls, for they desire eagerly, and if ye restrain them not they will drag you to an evil end." "Still these ascetics were forerunners of Ṣūfism. The term *ṣūfī*, according to Qushayrī came into common use before the end of the second century AH or CE 815. It is possible that this epithet refers to the woollen garment adopted by Muslim ascetics in order to distinguish themselves from those who effected a more luxurious fashion of dress. The term *ṣūfī* was first applied to Abū Hāshim of Kūfā (d. AH 150), about whom Jāmī says, "Before him there were men eminent for *zuhd* (asceticism) and *taqwā* (piety) and well-doing in the path of *tawwakul* (trust) and in the path of love, but he was the first that was called *ṣūfī*."[17]

The first *khānqāh* (convent), according to Jamī, for Ṣūfīs was founded at Ramla in Palestine. The Ṣūfism of the ascetic

15. Jāmī, op. cit., p. 34.
16. Abdu'l Qāsim Qushayrī, *Risāla*, Cairo, 1959, p. 63.
17. Qushayrī, Ibid., p. 63.

and quietistic type, such as we find in the sayings of Ibrahim bin Adham (d. AH 161), Dāwūd al-Tai (d. AH 165), Fudayl bin 'Iyāḍ (d. AH 187) and Shaqīq of Bulkh (d. AH 194) was by and large the native product of Islam. Although the Ṣūfism of the Ṣūfīs mentioned above carried asceticism and quietism to extreme lengths still we find that their mysticism was very moderate. The raptures of later Ṣūfism were unknown to them as were its daring speculations.[18] They loved Allāh, but feared Him more and the end of their love was total surrender to His will.

With the dawn of third century AH Ṣūfism assumes an entirely new character. It is significant that the earliest definition of Ṣūfism occurs in the sayings of M'arūf al-Karkhī (d. AH 200), whose parents were of Persian nationality.[19] M'arūf, it is said, was a *mawla* (client) of 'Ali bin Mūsa al-Riḍā (d. 203/818) and accepted Islam at his hands.[20] The former associated with Dāwūd al-Ta'i (d. AH 165), but we learn from *Fihrist*[21] that his master in Ṣūfism was a certain Farqad al-Sanji[22] who derived from Hasan of Baṣrah (d. 110/728), who derived from

18. There is one conspicuous exception, namely, Rabi'a al-Adawiyya (d. AH 135 or 180 or 185, according to different authorities). In her sayings the doctrine of mystical love appears almost fully developed.
19. Ma'rūf belonged to the district of Wāsiṭ.
20. Ma'rūf lived in Baghdad in Karkh quarter, whence he is generally called Ma'rūf al-Karkhī, during the reign of Harun al-Rashid, and his tomb, which still exists in that city, has always been an object of profound veneration.
21. Ibn Nadim, *Fihrist*, ed. G. Flugel, Leipzig, 1871-72, p. 183.
22. The vocalization of this word is uncertain. It may refer to any one of several places named Sanj, Sinj or Sunj.

Mālik bin Anas (d. 179/795). M'arūf is described in *Tadhkiratu'l Awliyā* as a man filled with longing of Allāh.[23]

In the sayings of M'arūf we discern for the first time unmistakable traces of those new ideas which remain to this day the essential and most characteristic elements in Ṣūfism. Here are some examples:

> Love is not to be learnt from men; it is one of Allāh's gifts and comes by His grace.[24]
>
> The saints of Allāh are known by three signs: their thought is of Allāh, their dwelling is with Allāh, and their business is in (reciting the name of) Allāh.[25] If the *'ārif* (gnostic) has no bliss, he himself is in every bliss.[26]

One day M'arūf said to his pupil, Sari al-Saqati, "When you desire anything of Allāh فاقسم عليه بى (Swear Him by me)."

When we pursue the sayings of Ibrahim b. Adham and

---

23. His pupil, the celebrated Sarī al-Saqatī, relates as follows: "I dreamed that I saw M'arūf al-Karkhī beneath the throne of Allāh, and Allāh was saying to His angels, 'Who is this?' They answered, 'Thou knowest best, O Lord!' Then Allāh said, 'This is Mārūf al-Karkhī who was intoxicated with love of Me, and will not recover his senses except by meeting Me face to face'." (Qushayrī, Ibid., p. 11).

24. Aṭṭār, Farid-ud-Dīn 'Aṭṭār, *Tadhkirat al-Awliyya*, ed. R.'A. Nicholson, London, 1905-07, vol. I, p. 272. (This work will be abbreviated as *T.A.* henceforth in this book.)

25. *T.A.*, Ibid., I, p. 271.

26. *T.A.*, Ibid., I, p. 272. Compare with this Ibrahim bin Adham's definition, "This is the sign of the gnostic, that his thoughts are mostly engaged in meditation, and his words are mostly praise and glorification of Allāh, and his deeds are mostly devotional, and his eye is mostly fixed on the subtleties of Divine action and power" (cf. *T.A.*, Ibid., I, p. 93).

the group of Ṣūfīs mentioned above in connection with him, we perceive that these utterances of M'arūf al-Karkhi belong to a different order of ideas. Their *taṣawwuf* had a practical end, the attainment of salvation, but his was primarily a theosophy. It consisted as we see from his definition, الاخذ بلحقائق (the apprehension of Divine realities).

Many of the sayings of Abū Sulayman al-Darānī[27] (d. AH 215) are purely mystical in spirit and expression like;

> It may be that while the *'ārif* (gnostic) sleeps on his bed, Allāh will reveal to him the mystery and will make luminous that which He never will reveal to one standing in the prayer.[28] When the *'ārif* 's (gnostic's) spiritual eye is opened his bodily eye is shut. They see nothing but Him.[29]
>
> None refrains from the lusts of this world save him in whose heart there is light that keeps him always busied with the next world.[30]
>
> When the heart weeps because it has lost, the spirit laughs because it has found.[31]
>
> Gnosis is nearer to silence than to speech.[32]
>
> If gnosis were to take visible form, all that looked thereon would die at the sight of its beauty and loveliness and goodness and grace, and every brightness would become dark beside the splendour thereof.[33]

---

27. He was a native of Wāsiṭ, emigrated to Syria and settled in the village Darayat, west of Damascus.
28. *T.A.*, op. cit., I, p. 234.
29. *T.A.*, op. cit., I, p. 234.
30. *T.A.*, op. cit., I, p. 232.
31. Jami, *Nafahatul Uns*, op. cit., p. 44.
32. *T.A.*, op. cit., vol. I, p. 235.
33. Ibid.

The following passage many be quoted in full, in as much as it is one of the earliest specimens of the erotic symbolism which afterwards became very prominent in the religious language of the Ṣūfīs:

> Ahmad b. Abil Hawari[34] said: "One day I came to Abū Sulayman al-Darāni and found him weeping." I asked, "What makes you weep?" He answered: "O Ahmad, why should I not weep? for, when night falls, and eyes are closed in slumber, and every lover is alone with his beloved, and the people of love keep vigil," and tears stream over their cheeks and bedew their oratories, then Allāh Almighty looks from on high and cries aloud: 'O Gabriel, dear in my sight are they who take pleasure in My word and find peace in praising My name. Verily, I am regarding them in their loneliness, I hear their lamentation and I see their weeping. Wherefore, O Gabriel, dost thou not cry aloud amongst them? What is this weeping? Did ye ever see a beloved that chastised his lovers? Or how would it beseem Me to punish folk who, when night covers them, manifest fond affection towards Me تملّقو الى ? By myself I swear that when they shall come alone to resurrection I will surely unveil to them My glorious face, in order that they may behold Me and I may behold them."[35]

Passing over to Bishrul-Hāfi (the barefooted), who died in AH 227 and who described the gnostics (*'ārifīn*) as the peculiar favourites of Allāh,[36] we came to the period of Dhu-Nūn al-Miṣrī (d. AH 245)[37] the man who, more than any other, deserves

34. *T.A.*, Ibid., I, p. 286.

35. Qushayrī, op. cit., pp. 5, 18.

36. *T.A.* op. cit., pp. 112-13.

37. He was called Dhul Nūn (He of the fish) on account of a miracle which is related in *TA*, op. cit., I, pp. 116, 18.

to be entitled the founder of theosophical Ṣūfism. His right to this honour is acknowledged by oriental biographers and historians. Jāmī says, "He is the head of this sect; they all descend from him, and are related to him. There were shaykhs before him but he was the first who explained the Ṣūfī symbolism (اشارات با عبارت آورده) and spoke concerning this (path)."[38] According to Abul-Maḥāsin, "Dhul Nūn, was the first who spoke in Egypt concerning the system of States (الاحوال) and 'stages of saints' (مقامات اهل الولاية)." These assertions, though not literally exact, are amply borne out, on the whole, by the sayings of Dhul Nūn which are preserved in the *Tadhkiratu'l Awliya* and in other works. It may be remarked, however, that the definitions of *'ārif* (gnostic) and *m'arifat* (gnosis) alone occupy about two pages in Arbery's edition of *Tadhkiratu'l Awliya*.[39] Dhul Nūn distinguishes three kinds of knowledge, of which one is common to all Muslim, another is that of philosophers and divines, while the third sort, viz. the knowledge of the attributes of unity is peculiar to the saints "who see Allāh with their hearts."[40] When Dhul Nūn was asked how he knew Allāh, he replied, "I know Him by Himself";[41] yet he confessed that the highest knowledge is bewilderment[42]

اعرف الناس بالله تعالىٰ اشدهم تحيّرا فيه

Similary he thought that true praise of Allāh involves absorption of the worshipper in the object of worship.[43] He is reported to have said; "One that veils himself from mankind

38. Jāmī, op. cit., p. 36.
39. *T.A.*, op. cit., I, pp. 126-28.
40. *T.A.*, op. cit., p. 127.
41. (عرفت ربى بربى) Qushayrī, op, cit., p. 167.
42. Ibid., p. 166.
43. غيبة الذاكر عن الذكر (Ibid., p. 120.)

by means of Allāh[44] his deity is a Being that can be described only by negatives: whatever you imagine, Allāh is the opposite of that."[45] The idea that Ṣūfism is an esoteric aspect of religion finds frequent expression. Thus, توبة العوام is a different thing from توبة الخواص [46] and divine love is regarded as a mystery which must not be spoken about, lest it comes to the ears of the profane.[47] Dhul Nūn mentions, "the cup of love" handed to the lover of Allāh.[48] He is the author of the first definition of *wajd* and *samā'*[49] and *tawḥīd*.[50] It was unquestionably Dhul Nūn al-Miṣrī "who above all others gave to Ṣūfī doctrine a permanent shape."[51] Let us now see whether the facts recorded by his biographers afford any clue as to the origin of this doctrine. According to Ibn Khallikān[52] and Jāmī[53] the name of Dhul Nūn was Abul-Fayḍ Thawban b. Ibrahim or al-Fayḍ b. Ibrahim. His father, a native of Nubia or of Ikhmim in upper Egypt, was a slave enfranchised and adopted by the tribe of Quraysh. Dhul Nūn probably passed some time in the Hijaz, for it is said that he was a pupil of Imām Mālik b. Anas (d. AH 179) and learnt the *Muwaṭṭā* from his dictation. His master in Ṣūfism according to Ibn Khallikān was Shuqrān al-'Ābid or a

---

44. Qushayrī, op. cit., p. 60.
45. كل ما تصورفى رهمك فالله بخلاف ذالك (Ibid., pp. 5, 10).
46. Ibid., p. 10.
47. Ibid., p. 172.
48. *T.A.*, op. cit., I, p. 120.
49. Ibid., p. 129 and Qushayrī, op. cit., p. 180.
50. Qushayrī, op. cit., p. 5.
51. Mawlana Rūmi, *Mathnavi-i-Ma'navi*, tr. and abridged by E.H. Whinfield (2nd edn.), p. xvii, of the introduction.
52. Ibn-i Khallikān, *Wafāyāt al-A'yān Wa Anba' az-Zamān*, Eng. tr. De Slane, Paris, rpt. 1961, vol. I, p. 129.
53. Jāmī, op. cit., p. 35.

Maghribite named Isrāfīl. Ibn Khallikān tells us that Dhul Nūn was the "nonpareil of his age" for learning, devotion, communion with the divinity (*ḥal*), and acquaintance with literature (*adab*); also that he was a philosopher and spoke Arabic with elegance. He was a *Malāmatī*, i.e. he concealed his piety under a pretended contempt for the law, and most of the Egyptians regarded him as *zindīq* (free thinker), but after his death he was canonised[54] for several anecdotes. *Tadhkiratu'l Awliya* represents Dhul Nūn as turning pebbles and the like into precious stones, and in the *Fihrist*[55] his name occurs among "the philosophers who discoursed on alchemy," while a few pages further on we find him mentioned as the author of two alchemical works.[56] His true character appears distinctly in the account given by Qiftī in his *Akhbāral-Ḥukamā*: "Dhul Nūn possessed the art of alchemy, and belongs to the same class as Jabir b. Ḥayyān. He devoted himself to the science of esoterics (*ilmul-bāṭin*) and became proficient in many branches of philosophy. He used to frequent the ruined temple (*barba*) in the town of Ikhmim, wherein there one of the ancient Houses of Wisdom بيوت الحكمة containing marvellous figures and strange images and that enriches the believer's faith and the infidel's transgression. And it is said that knowledge of the mysteries therein was revealed to him by the way of saintship (بطريق الولاية); and he wrought miracles."[57]

Mas'ūdī, who died exactly a century after Dhul Nūn and is the first authority to mention him, derived his information from the inhabitants of Ikhmīm on the occasion of a visit which

54. *T.A.*, op. cit., I, p. 114.

55. Ibn Nadīm, op. cit., p. 353.

56. Ibid., p. 358.

57. Jamāl al-Dīn Abu'l Hasan al-Qiftī, Tārīkh al-Ḥukamā, ed. Jlippert Leipzig, 1903, p. 185.

he made to that place. He relates the local tradition as follows: "Abul-Fayd Dhul Nūn al-Miṣrī al-Ikhmīmī, the ascetic was a philosopher who trod a particular path (طريق) and pursued a course of his own in religion. He was one of those who elucidate the history of these temple ruins (*barabi*). He roamed among them and examined a great quantity of figures and inscriptions."[58] Mas'ūdi gives translations of some of the latter, which Dhul Nūn claimed to have deciphered and read.

It is now clear that Dhul Nūn was an alchemist and magician, but we must remember that at this time magic and alchemy had long been associated with theurgy and theosophy.

It would be easy to show that the old theurgic ideas exercised a poweful influence on Ṣūfism. J'afar al-Ṣādiq (d. AH 148), whose life is given in *Tadhkiratu'l Awliya* is said to have written a treatise on alchemy, augury and omens. His pupil Jabir b. Ḥayyān, the celebrated alchemist known to Europeans by the name Gebbar, was called "Jābir the Sūfi" and like Dhul Nūn he studied the science of esoterics علم الباطن which according to Qiftī, is identical with Ṣūfism.[59] More important evidence is offered by the biographers of the Ṣūfī saints. It is related that Ibrahim b. Adham, while travelling in the desert, met a man who taught him the greatest name of Allāh (اسم الله الاعظم), and as soon as he pronounced it he saw the Ḥaḍrat Khiḍr.[60] Dhul Nūn is represented as knowing the greatest name. One of his pupils, Yūsuf b. al-Husayn (d. AH 304) desired to learn it, but

58. Abu'l Hasan 'Alī bin Husain Mas'ūdī, *Murūjul-Dhahab*, ed. Barbier de Meynard, vol. II, p. 401.

59. Qiftī, op. cit., p. 160. This combination of natural science and religion is exemplified in the history of medieval mysticism in Europe.

60. Qushayrī, op. cit., p. 9.

failed to pass a simple preliminary test[61] which Dhul Nūn imposed on him.[62]

An ascetic, philospher, and theurgist, living in the ninth century among the Christian Copts, himself of Coptic or Nubian parentage — such was Dhul Nūn al-Miṣrī from whom, as his extant sayings bear witness, and as Jāmī, moreover, expressly states, the theosophy is mainly derived.

The principal Ṣūfī Shaykhs who died between AH 250 and 300 include, Sarī al-Saqatī (d. AH 253), Yaḥyā b. Mu'ādh al-Raḍī (d. 258), Abū Yazīd (Bāyazīd) al-Bisṭāmī (d. AH 261), Abu Hafs al-Haddād (d. circa. AH 260), Hamdun al-Qaṣṣar (d. AH 271), Abū Said al-Kharrāz (d. AH 277 or 286), Abū Hamza al-Baghdadi (d. AH 289), Sahl b. 'Abdu'llah al-Tustāri (d. AH 273 or 321 or 203 or 293), Abul Husayn al-Nūrī (d. AH 295), Junayd Baghdādī (d. AH 297), Amr b. Uthmān al-Makkī (d. AH 291, 297 or 301), Abū Uthmān al-Hiri (d. AH 298), and Mimshād al-Dinawari (d. AH 299).

The development of Ṣūfism down to the end of third century AH took place in two ways:

(1) Existing doctrine was amplified, elaborated, and systematized.

(2) New doctrines and practices were introduced.

(1) Ṣūfism which was at first a form of religion adopted by individuals, and only communicated to a comparatively small circle of *asḥāb* (companions), gradually became an organized system, a school for saints, with rules of discipline and devotion which the *murīd* (novice) learned from his *pīr*,

61. Ibn al-Athīr, al-Kāmil Fi'l Tārīkh, ed. C.J. Tornbargh, Leiden, 1851-76, vol. VII, p. 79.

62. *T.A.*, op. cit., vol. I, p. 316.

ustād (spiritual director), to whose guidance he submitted himself absolutely. Already in the third century it was increasingly evident that the typical *Ṣūfī* adept of the future would no longer be a solitary ascetic shunning the sight of men, but a great Shaykh and divinely inspired teacher, who appears on ceremonial occasions attended by numerous trains of admiring disciples. This notion is expressed by Bāyazīd in one of his sayings "If a man has no teacher (*ustād*), his *imām* is *saṭān*."[63] Divine favour and authority were claimed by the Ṣūfī theosophists from the very beginning, "Swear to Allāh by me," said *M'arūf al-karkhi* and Dhul Nūn declared that the true disciple should be more obedient to his master than to Allāh.[64]

In the sayings of the Shaykhs of this period the tendency to codify and systemize is apparent everywhere. The path of the novice was marked out into a series of stages[65] and different "paths" were distinguished. Yaḥya b. Mu'ādh al Raḍī (d. AH 258) said: "when you see that a man inculcates good works, know that his path is piety; and when you see that he points to the divine signs (*āyāt*), know that his path is that of the *abdāl*;"[66] and when you see that he points to the bounties of the Allāh, know that his path is that of the lovers; and when you see that he is attached to the praise of Allāh (*dhikr*) know that his path is that of the gnostics.[67] Hamdūn al-Qassar (d. AH 271) founded in Nishāpūr the sect of the *Malāmatīs* or

63. Qushayrī, op. cit., p. 213.

64. *T.A.*, op. cit., I, p. 131.

65. Ibid., I, p. 261.

66. The *abdāl* (substitutes) form a particular class in the mysterious *Ṣūfī* hierarchy at the head of which stands the *quṭb*. According to Ibn Khaldūn, they were derived from, and correspond to, the *Nuqabā* of the Shi'ites.

67. *T.A.*, op. cit., I, p. 305.

Qassaris who proved their sincerity and devotion to Allāh by cloaking it under an unaffected libertinism.[68]

Sarī al-Saqaṭī (d. AH 253) is said to have been the first who spoke in Baghdad concerning divine realities (*haqā'-iq*) and unification (*tawḥīd*).[69] The first to lecture on Ṣūfism in public بر منبر was Yaḥyā b. Mu'ādh al-Raḍī (d. AH 258)[70] and his example was followed in Baghdad by Abū Hamza al-Baghdadī (d. AH 289). According to Jāmī[71] the theory of Ṣūfism was formulated and explained in writing by Junayd (d. AH 297) who taught it only in private houses and in subterranean chambers (سردابها), whereas Shiblī (d. AH 334) made it the subject of public discourses. From this, we may conclude that the orthodox group, whom the accession of Mutawakkil (d. AH 232) re-established in power, treated the Ṣūfī mysticism with less intolerence than they displayed towards the liberal opinions of Mutazilites. Dhul Nūn, however, was denounced as a *zindīq* and was summoned to the presence of Mutawakkil, but a pious exhortation which he addressed to the caliph secured his honourable dismissal.[72] Junayd himself was more than once accused of being a free thinker, and mention is made of an inquisition directed against the Ṣūfī (*mihnati Sūfiyan*) in Baghdad in consequence of which Abū Said al-Kharrāz (d. AH 286) fled to Egypt.[73]

68. See Jāmī, op. cit., p. 8, *T.A.*, op. cit., I, pp. 7, 23, 319, 333. Other Ṣūfī sects are the Ṭayfūriyan, the Kharaiziyan and the Nūriyan, who followed Bāyazīd, Abū Said al-Kharrāz, and Abu-Husayn al-Nūrī respectively.

69. *T.A.*, op. cit., I, p. 274.

70. *T.A.*, op. cit., I, p. 299.

71. Jāmī, op. cit., p. 36.

72. Ibn Khallikān, op. cit., vol. II, p. 291.

73. Jāmī, op. cit., p. 81.

The Ṣūfīs of the third and fourth centuries worked out a complete theory and practice of mystical path, but they were not philosophers, and they took little interest in metaphysical problems, so that the philosophical terminology which later Ṣūfism borrowed, through Farābī' Ibn Senā (Avicena) and Ghazālī, from the Neo-platonists, does not concern us here. Traces of the symbolic language of the *ṣūfīs* appear very early.[74] It is told of Da'ud al-T'āī (d. AH 165) that a *dervish* saw him smiling and asked, "whence this cheerfulness, O Abū Sulayman?" Da'ud answered: "At dawn they gave me a wine which is called the wine of intimacy (*sharāb-i-uns*); today I have made festival, and have abandoned myself rejoicing."[75] Love symbolism occurs in the sayings ascribed to Rabi'ah (d. AH 135, 180, or 185) in a passage already quoted from Abū Salaiyma al -Darani (d. AH 215) and thence forwarded with increasing frequence. Hatim b. al-Asmm (d. AH 237) speaks of the four deaths of the Ṣūfīs: white death — hunger, black death — endurance of injuries, red death — sincere self-mortification, and green death — wearing a garment to which patches are always being added.[76] But the peculiar poetic imagery, which was afterwards developed by the famous Ṣūfī of Khurasan, Abu Sa'id b. Abil Khayr (d. AH 440), is first found full-blown in the sayings of Bāyazīd of Bisṭām (d. AH 261). Yaḥyā b. Mu'ādh al-Raḍī wrote to Bāyazīd: "I am intoxicated through having drunk deeply of the cup of His love," and

---

74. Ibn 'Ata (d. AH 309) was asked why the Ṣūfīs used strange and unusual expressions. He replied, "For as much as this practice (i.e. Ṣūfism) is honoured by us, we were unwilling that any one except Ṣūfīs should be acquianted with it, and we did not wish to employ ordinary language. Therefore, we used a particular language." (*T.A.*)

75. *T.A.* op. cit., I, pp. 2, 222.

76. Qushayrī, op. cit., p. 18.

Bāyazīd replied: "Another has drunk the seas of heaven and earth, and is not yet satisfied, but his tongue comes first and says, "Is there no more."[77] Here are some striking examples of the same kind:

> I went forth to the fields. Love had rained, and the earth was wet. My foot was sinking into love, even as a man's foot sinks in clay.[78]
>
> One day he was speaking of the truth, and was sucking his lips and saying: "I am the wine-drinker and the wine and the cup-bearer."[79]
>
> Dost thou hear how there comes a voice from the brooks of running water? But when they reach the sea they are quiet, and the sea is neither augmented by their incoming nor diminished by their outgoing.[80]
>
> Desire is the capital of lover's kingdom. In that capital there is a set of throne of the torment of parting, and there is drawn a sword of the terrror of separation, and there is laid on the hand of hope a branch of narcissus of union; and every moment a thousand heads fall by that sword. And seven thousand years (said he) have passed, and that narcissus is still fresh and blooming; never has the hand of any hope attained thereto[81]

(2) As has been said, the germ, at any rate, of nearly all the characteristic Ṣūfī doctrines may be traced back to Dhul Nūn al-Miṣrī and his immediate predecessors. The idea of ecstasy and self-annihilation was no doubt familiar to these early

77. Qushayrī, op. cit., p. 171.
78. *T.A.*, I, p. 155.
79. Ibid., p. 159.
80. Ibid., p. 163.
81. Ibid., p. 166.

theosophists, but the doctrine, which became of vital importance in the subsequent history of Ṣūfism, is nowhere clearly stated by them. It was a Persian, the celebrated Bāyazīd of Bisṭām, that first used the word *fanā* denoting self-annihilation and he probably is regarded as the earliest propounder of this doctrine.[82] Abū Yazīd Tayfūr b. Īsā b. Adam b. Surushan[83] was born at Biṣṭām, a town in the province of Qumis situated near the south-eastern corner of the Caspian Sea. His grandfather was Zoroastrian, and his master in Ṣūfism a Kurd.[84] Bāyazīd at first held the opinions of the *aṣḥābūl-roy* "but a saintship was revealed to him in which no positive religion (*madhhab*) appeared."[85] If we can assume the genuiness of the saying attributed to Bayazid by Faridud Din Attar in the *Tadhkiratu'l Awliya*, he was not only an antinomian pantheist of the most extravagant type — a precursor of Husayn b. Manṣūr al-Ḥallāj — but also a singularly imaginative and profound thinker, not unworthy to be compared with men like Aṭṭā'r and Rūmī. It is hard to say what the proportion of the utterances collected by his biographies is a fact and how much is fiction. Abdullah al-Ansāri of Herāt (d. AH 481) asserts that many falsehoods have been fathered on Bāyazīd, for instance his alleged saying. "I went into Heaven and pitched my tent opposite the throne of Allāh."[86] Out of this grew the

---

82. According to Jāmī Abū Sa'id al-Kharrāz (d. AH 286) was the first one who spoke concerning the theory of *fanā u baqā*, i.e. death to self and life in Allāh. See Jāmī, op. cit., p. 81.

83. He must not be confused with Abu Yazid Ṭayfūr b. Isa b. Adam who is known as al-Bisṭāmi al-asghar.

84. The text of the Jāmī, op. cit., p. 62, has گردی but کردی is the correct reading.

85. Jāmī, op. cit., p. 63.

86. Ibid.

story of his ascension (*mi'rāj*) which is told at great length by Aṭṭār.[87] Ibn Khallikān describes him as an ascetic, pure and simple, but the account of him given by Qushayrī, Attār and Jāmī is confirmed by what we know of his race and Magian ancestry. Bāyazīd became the legendary hero of Persian Ṣūfism just because he was in reality a thorough Persian and true representative of the religious aspirations of his countrymen. He it was who brought into Ṣūfism the extreme pantheistic ideas which even in Sasanian times were widely prevalent in Persia. This pantheistic (Perso-Indian) element is as distinctively oriental as the older theosophical tendency is distinctively Greek.

Let us now examine some of the most characteristic sayings ascribed to Bāyazīd, which illustrate (a) the doctrine of *fanā*, (b) his uncompromising pantheism, and (c) the poetical and imaginative colour of his thought.

(a) Creatures are subjected to "states" (*aḥwāl*), but the gnostic has no "state" because his vestiges are effaced and his essence is annihilated by the essence of another and his traces are lost in another's traces.[88]

> I went from God to God, until they cried from me in me, "Thou I!" that is I attained the stage of annihilation in God.[89]

(b) Verily, I am God, there is no God except me, so worship me.[90] Glory to me! how great is my majesty.[91]

---

87. *T.A.*, op. cit., I, pp. 172-76.
88. Qushayrī; op. cit., p. 166.
89. *T.A.*, op. cit., I, p. 160.
90. Ibid., p. 137.
91. Ibid., p. 140.

> I came forth from Bayazid-ness as a snake from its skin. Then I looked. I saw that lover, beloved and love are one, for in the world of unification all can be one.[92] He was asked, "what is the "arsh?" He said, "I am it." "What is the tablet and the pen?" "I am they."[93]

With the exception of Bāyazīd and Abū Sai'd al Kharrāz, the Ṣūfīs of the third century keep the doctrine of *fanā* in the background and seldom use the language of unguarded pantheism. . . . Now let us recapitulate the main points which we have endeavoured to bring out:

1. Ṣūfism, in the sense of "mysticism" and "quietism" was a natural development of the ascetic tendencies which manifested themselves within Islam during the Ummayad period (41/661–132/750).
2. This asceticism on the whole may be called purely a product of Islam, and the Ṣūfism which grew out of it is also essentially Islamic.
3. Towards the end of second century AH a new current of ideas began to flow into Ṣūfism. These ideas, which seem to be non-Islamic and theosophical in character, are discernible in the sayings of M'arūf al-Karkhī (d. AH 200).
4. During the first half of the third century AH the new ideas were greatly developed and became the dominating elements in Ṣūfism.
5. The man who above all others gave to the Ṣūfī doctrine its permanent shape was Dhul Nūn al-Miṣri (d. AH 245).
6. The historical environment in which this doctrine arose points clearly to Greek influence.

---

92. *T.A.* op. cit., , p. 160.

93. Ibid., p. 171.

7. As the theosophical element in Ṣūfism seems to be Greek, so the apparently extreme pantheistic ideas, which were first introduced by Abū Yazīd (Bāyazīd) al-Bisṭāmī (d. AH 261) are Persian or Indian.
8. During the later part of the third century AH Ṣūfism became an organized system with teachers, pupils, and rules of discipleship, and continual efforts were made to refine it and accomodate within the framework of Islamic *Shari'at*.

The Organization of Ṣūfī Silsilās (Orders)

The circle of pupils and adepts around a master was the first stage of Ṣūfī organization. In Khurāsān the location of such a group was a centre called *khānqāh*. It was simply a dwelling taken over to house a Shaikh and his dervishes. Even though it occupied a building in which rooms were set aside for *jama'āt* or *samā'at-khāna* (assembly) and for *muṣalla* (prayer), still this centre was a circle and frequently the whole centre went on tour for a year or longer. In the eleventh century many such centres are recorded in the life of Abū Sa'īd ibn Abi'il Khair (CE 967–1049),[94] among them Khānqāh-i Abū 'Ali at-Ta'rūsī (d. 364/974) founded in Nishāpūr, which survived until 548/1154 when it was destroyed. Another in the same city was Khānqāh-i Sarawi founded by Abū Ali ad-Daqqāq (d. CE 1016), who was the master of both Abū Sa'id and al-Qushayrī. The tombs of these early masters (or the site tradition) were preserved and during the stage two of *ṭarīqa* development, their mausoleums were restored or erected, and then there

94. Muḥammad ibn al-Munawwar, *Asrār at-Tawḥīd fī Maqāmāti ash-Shaikh Abi's sa'id* written *c.* CE 1200. This account of Abū Sa'id is the basis of R.'A. Nicholson's study of him in *Studies in Islamic Mysticism*, Cambridge, 1921, pp. 1-76.

took place the opposite process — the presence of the tomb leading to the association of a *k͟hānqāh* with it.

A minimum of rules had to regulate their lives in common at these stage-one associations. An early record of such rules, that of the just-mentioned Abū Sa'id for members of his *k͟hānqāh* at Mayhana in Khurāsān is translated by R.'A. Nicholson. We reproduce these rules here:[95]

(i) Let them keep their garments clean and themselves always pure.

(ii) Let them not sit in the *masjid* or in any holy place for the sake of gossiping.

(iii) In the first instance let them perform their prayers in common.

(iv) Let them pray much at night.

(v) At dawn let them ask for forgiveness of God and call unto Him.

(vi) In the morning let them read as much of the Qur'ān as they can, and let them not talk until the sun has risen.

(vii) Between evening prayers and bedtime prayers let them occupy themselves with repeating some litany (*wirdi u d͟hikri*).

(viii) Let them welcome the poor and needy and all who join their company, and let them bear patiently the trouble of (waiting upon) them.

(ix) Let them not eat anything save in participation with one another.

95. The various Ṣūfī manuals of the period deal in a general way with the manners of Ṣūfīs in association, see for example as-Sarrāj, *Luma*, p. 174; al-Hujwiri, *Kas͟hf*, pp. 341-45 (reception to be accorded to a visiting *dervish* and the rules he must observe), pp. 345-47 (rules to be observed when travelling).

(x) Let them not absent themselves without receiving permission from one another.

> Furthermore, let them spend their hours of leisure in one of the three things: either in the study of theology or in some devotional exercise (*wirdi*) or in bringing comfort to someone. Whosoever loves this community and helps them as much as he can, is a sharer in their merit and future recompense.[96]

Ribāṭs,[97] some of the frontier posts in Arab controlled regions, had become centres of devotees. But these are not to be equated with the Iranian *k͟hānqāh*s as the master–pupil relationship did not figure in them.

In stage two of the organizational development, however, the centre of the guiding master was designated by the term *ribāṭ*, such as that of the S͟haikh Najīb and S͟haikh S͟hihāb ud din Suhrawardī, on the banks of the Tigris, whilst the Iranian term *k͟hānqāh* was adopted in Iraq, Syria and Egypt. Both *ribāṭ* and *k͟hānqāh* type institutions were specially designed for Ṣūfī groupings and to serve their aims. However, in construction the two institutions were different in that the *ribāṭ* was centred upon a master, whilst in the *k͟hānqāh* the congregational outlook dominated and the officially appointed head was an administrator rather than a shepherd of souls. *Ribāṭ* at the same time was a non-committal term since there were also others, as in Makkah, which were little more than endowed hostels for Ṣūfī travellers and pilgrims.

---

96. Muḥammad Ibnu'l Munawwar, *Asrāru'l Tawḥīd fi Maqāmāt-i-Shaykh Abi Sa'id*, p. 416. Eng. tr. R.'A. Nicholson, *Studies in Islamic Mysticism*, p. 46.

97. *Ribāṭ* were founded in frontier regions as Muslim cells in a non-Muslim environment. They were watch-stations and frontier-posts, whose guards were often effective preachers of Islam. →

In the development of organized Ṣūfism, *zāwiyāhs*, the small modest establishments, were more important than most of the *k͟hānqāhs* and *ribāṭs*. Here, the institution was a man. They centred around one Shaikh; at first impermanent, especially since such men were frequently migrants themselves. Self- perpetuating *ṭariqās* came into being through these men. *Zāwiyāhs* were not endowed like *ribāṭs* and *k͟hānqāhs*, though in time when they became family residences they tended to accumulate *awqāf*.

Normally a *k͟hānqāh* consisted of a *ṣaḥn* (central courtyard) having *riwāqs* (cloisters) along two sides, within which were

---

→ Two early *ribāṭs* in northern Africa were those of Monastir (Tunisia) founded in 180/796 and Sus founded in 206/821. Al-Ya'qubi in his *al-Buldān*, composed in CE 891, writes "At every state there is a strong point, each close to the other, garrisoned by pious men and *murabitun*." The teaching centre established by Wajjaj ibn Zalwi al-Lamti, where 'Abdu'llah ibn Yāsīn (d. 1059), instigator of Murabī movement, recieved his training, was known as Dar al-Murabitin (*Rawḍ al-Qirtas*, ed. Tornbergh, 1839, p. 46). Al-Maqdisi in his *Ahsan at-Taqasim* (completed AH 375) mentions the *ribāṭs* found in the various Islamic countries. Many of those in Khurasan were associated with the tombs of Ṣaḥāba who had fallen in battle. Some were well endowed with *awqāf*. *Ribāṭ an-Nūr* near Buk͟hāra was associated with an annual *mawsim*. At the same time a place where an ascetic withdrew to wage the spiritual *jihād* was also known as a *ribāṭ* and in time the latter became the dominant usage. The frontier *ribāṭs* changed their character from centres of defence and proselytism to centres of *Ṣūfī* devotion and teaching. Al-Umari, in the middle of the fourteenth century, refers to "the pious men who are called *murabits* (*masalik*, tr. Gaudefroy-Demombynes, 1927, p. 204). On Maghribi *ribāts* see G. Marcais, "Note sur les *Ribāṭs* en Barberie, Mel. R. Basset, II (1925); J. Oliver Asin, "Origen arabe de rebato," Boletin de la Real Acacdemia Espanola, Madrid, 1928; and 'Ali Ibn Abdar-Rahman ibn Hudhail, L'Ornement des ames, tr. Mercier, Paris, 1939, pp. 115-21, and cf. pp. 71-74; *Encyclopaedia of Islam*, vol. III, pp. 1150-53.

situated *khalwas* or *tibāq* (the cells) of the Ṣūfīs. Common devotional exercises of the Ṣūfīs took place in the main hall. The Shaikh reclined upon the sheepskin, lying in front of the *mihrāb*, during ceremonies and receptions. The religious phrases such as *shahādah* and the name of the founder were engraved over the niche. Frequently there was a separate *masjid*, whilst kitchens and other offices and sometimes a bathhouse, were attached. Both migrant and resident Ṣūfīs were provided with food and lodging and the latter even with clothing and other prerequisites.

Many descriptions of *khānqāhs* are found in local topographies, but they provide little information about methods of administration, functions, and ceremonies. More can be gleaned from this description by Ibn Baṭṭūta of *khānqāh* in Cairo in CE 1326.

"Each *khānqāh* has a shaikh and superintendent (*hāris*) who organizes their affairs admirably. . . . These men are celibate, there being separate *khānqāhs* for the married.[98] Their duties include attendence at the five ritual prayers, passing the night in the *khānqāh*, and attendance at their *dhikr* gatherings held in its hall (*qubbā*). It is also customary for each one to occupy his own special prayer-mat. When they pray the Daybreak Prayer they recite *Sūrat al-Fath* (48), *Sūrat al-Muluk* (67), and *Sūrat al-'Amma* (78); then sections of the *Qur'ān* are brought in and

98. Many *khānqāhs* were not built specially for the purpose but existing houses were bequeathed by their owners as pious foundations. Thus Amir 'Ala ad-din Taibogha of Aleppo constituted his house a *waqf* or Arabized Ṣūfīs (*as-Ṣūfiyyatu'l-must'arabi*) in 631/1234; Abū Dharr Sibt ibn al-'Ajamī (d. 1479), *Kunūz adh-dhahab fi tārīkh Halab*, quoted by M. Raghib at -Tabbakh, *I'lām*, Aleppo, 1923, IV, p. 435. Although adapted and added to in the course of time there were very considerable architectural differences, but functionally they followed the same lines.

distributed among the *faqīrs*, who recite the whole *Qur'ān* and perform a *dhikr*. Following this the *Qur'ān*-reciters chant in the eastern fashion. They do the same after the *'Aṣr* Prayer.

Khānqāhs had their rules regarding the admission of Ṣūfī into their companionship, whether for a shorter or longer length of time. They were not strictly guidance-centres[99] but associations of people prepared to live a common life under discipline." Ibn Baṭṭūta continues:

"When a new arrival makes his appearance he has to take up his stand at the gateway of *khānqāh*, girded around the middle, with the prayer-mat slung over his back, his staff in his right hand and his ablution-jug in his left. The gatekeeper informs the steward who goes out and ascertains from what country he (new arrival) has come, what *khānqāhs* he has resided in during his journey (or training), and who was his initiator. If he is satisfied of the truth of his replies, he brings him into the *khānqāh*, arranges a suitable place for him to spread out his prayer-mat, and shows him the washroom. He then restores himself to a state of ritual cleanliness, goes to his mat, ungirds himself, and prays two *raka'at*. After this he clasps the hand of the shaikh and of those who are present, and takes his seat among them.

Tombs became a normal feature of these various types of establishments, but whilst the *ribāṭs* and *zāwiyāhs* housed the

99. Many *khānqāhs* gave courses in the Islamic sciences. Maqrīzī says (*khitat*, 1326 edn., IV, p. 283) that Khānqāh-i-Shaikhū (founded by Amir Saif ad-din Shaikhu in Cairo in 756/1355) offered courses in all four schools of *fiqh*, *ḥadīth*, and the seven readings of the *Qur'ān*. This particular *khānqāh* seems to have been more like a *madrasah*. From his description the Jamatiyya (founded in the same city in 730/1330) was a combined Hanafi *madrasah* and *khānqāh* (*khitat*, IV, pp. 237-40, 279), but this was unusual, and normally the Ṣūfī aspect was the dominant one.

remains of the founder and his successors, the *k͟hānqāhs* had only the tomb of the founder. A few possessed relics: *Ribāṭ al-āthār* situated outside Cairo had a piece of iron and wood said to have belonged to the Prophet (SAW)."[100]

The decline of the *k͟hānqāh*-type of Ṣūfī centre is associated with the *ṭā'if* stage, manifested institutionally in the form of tomb–*zāwiyāhs*. In non-'Arab Asia they continued to be called *k͟hānqāhs*, but the focal point, the justification for their existence, was the tomb. These tomb–*k͟hānqāhs*, especially in Central Asia, varied from the elaborate mausoleums built by Mongol and Turkish rulers to moderate structures where *īs͟hān*, the local term of Shaikh, lived with his family and followers. Hospitality to travellers as well as wandering Ṣūfīs were regular features with these *k͟hānqāhs*. These institutions were independent expressions of divine blessing upon mankind through a man whose holiness was perpetuated through his tomb and his successors.

Zāwiyāhs and tomb-*k͟hānqāhs* which, from their inception, were associated with a Shaikh, survived as long as their founder's *baraka* continued to manifest itself. If the *baraka* kept on functioning, whether in association with a living or dead *walī*, pilgrims and offerings flowed in. Their importance in the social life of Islamic countries can be gauged from traveller's narratives such as those of Ibn Jubair and Ibn Baṭṭūta. The latter, in Asia, finds hospitality everywhere. With groups of *fuqarā'* who are generally associated with a tomb as at the convent ascribed to Abū Ishāq al-Kazerūnī (d. CE 1034) at Kazarun, west of Shīrāz under the aegis of whose name and *baraka* a powerful insurance corporation came into being.[101]

100. Maqrizi, *khitat*, edn., IV, AH 1326, p. 295.

101. For details of their insurance system see Ibn Batuta, *Rihla*, Paris edn. (ii) pp. 64, 88-92, (iii) pp. 244-48; (iv) pp. 89, 103, 271.

Throughout the Arab world we find Shaikh, the head of *ṭā'ifa* is the spiritual heir of the founder, whose qualities and powers become inherent in him upon his succession. He is called *Shaikh as-Sajjādah* (master of the prayer-mat or skin) (Persian *Sajjādah-nishīn*), since he inherits that of the founder as symbol of his authority.

Under the Shaikh are a number of *khullafā'* or *muqadamms* appointed by him directly to take charge of districts or town sections. Each is given *ijāzah* (licence) stating what he is authorized to undertake. Heads of small local orders will retain the power of initiation in their own hands, but when an order expands *khullafā'* are authorized to confer it. Immediately under the Shaikh, especially in Egypt and Syria, there was *nā'ib* or deputy.

In the East the term *zāwiyā* is given to more humble places of prayer and *dervish* cells. Corresponding terms for the convent and the tomb-centred institution of the West are *k̲h̲ānqāh* in Central Asia and India, and *tekke*[102] or *dargāh*[103] in the Ottoman Turkish sphere. Whilst *k̲h̲ānqāh* in Egypt and Syria were unspecialized institutions, those in India from their inception and in Central Asia from the fourteenth century were the equivalent of the Arab world's *zāwiyāh*s, in that they tended to be specialized to a particular Shaikh and his line. The difference between the terms used in India is well explained by K.A. Niẓāmī.

> Though broadly used in the sense of hospices these terms differ in their connotation. The *k̲h̲ānqāh* was a spacious building which provided separate accommodation for each

102. *Tekke, tekye* or *tekiye*, a derivative from Arabic *ittika*, was perhaps first employed in the sense of "refectory."

103. *Dargāh* (Persian's court) used in India for a shrine or tomb.

> visitor and inmate. The *jamā'at khānah* was a large room where all the disciples slept, prayed and studied on the floor. The Chistī saints built *Jamā'at khānahs*; the Suhrawardīs constructed *k͟hānqāhs*. Common people, unable to appreciate the distinction used the word *k͟hānqāh* even for the Chistī *jamā'at khānahs*, and now the term is used for all places of spiritual activity without distinction. The *zāwiyahs* were smaller places where mystics lived and prayed, but unlike inmates of *k͟hānqāhs* and *jamā'at khānahs*, did not aim at establishing any vital contact with the world outside. In the seventeenth and eighteenth centuries another type of *khānqāhs*, the *daerhas*, came into existence. The primary aim of these *daerhas* was to provide place for men of one affiliation to devote their time to religious meditation. They were smaller than the *zāwiyahs*.[104]

The *qubbā* (domed tomb) of the founder is the focal point of the organization, a centre of veneration to which *ziyārat* (visitations) are made. *Ādāb az-ziyāra* (the ritual of approach to a tomb) has its place in the order manuals. The simplest form is to stand in front of the tomb and recite the *fātiḥa*. There are many procedures for intercession to God through the saint. Muḥammad al-Khatlānī gives an account of some of these in the preface to his book on the notables of Fez, *Salwat al-Nafas*, for example: "Among the peculiar properties of the *ṣaḥıḥ* of al-Buk͟hāri, so some say, is that he who opens it or a section of it before the tomb of a saint and reads whatever single *ḥadīth* his eyes fall upon, commending himself to God through the mediumship of the masters of his chain right back to the

104. K.A. Nizāmi, *Some Aspects of Religion and Politics in India During the Thirteenth Century*, 2nd edn., Delhi, 1974, p. 175. On the organization of K͟hānqāh, see the article "Some Aspects of K͟hānqāh" by the same author, *Life in Medieval India*, Studia Islamica, VIII (1957), pp. 51-69.

prophet at the same time expressing his need may, if God wills, find his wish fulfilled."[105]

An essential distinction between Eastern and Western *silsilās* (orders) is shown by comparing the stress laid by each upon training, apprenticeship in the discipline of mystical path, and in the ceremony of investiture. In the East the orders were stricter and more rigid in discipline and organization, and had many more *dervish-type* disciples than in the West.

Ṣūfī dress was an important outward sign of the *Ṣūfī* way of life. Like other material symbols it came to have an inner significance, and investiture with such a garment soon became a sign of initiation. The use of wool went out of fashion during the eleventh century CE in favour of the patched garment called *muraqqa'a or khirqa*. 'Ali al-Hujwīrī (d. 465/1072) writes that the Ṣūfī *shaykhs* observe the following rules:

> When a novice joins them, with the purpose of renouncing the world, they subject him to spiritual discipline for the space of three years. If he fullfils the requirements of this discipline, well and good; otherwise, they declare that he cannot be admitted to the (*ṭarīqa*) path. The first year is devoted to the service of the people, the second year to the service of God, and the third year to watching over his own heart. . . . The adept, then, who has attained the perfection of saintship takes the right course when he invests the novice with the *murāqqa'a* after a period of three years during which he has educated him in the necessary discipline. In respect of the qualifications which it demands, the *murāqqa'a* is comparable to a winding-sheet (*kafan*); the wearer must resign all his hopes of the pleasures of life, and purge his

105. M.B. Ja'far al-Khatlāni, *Salwat al-Nafas*, 1316/1898, I, pp. 65-66.

> heart of all sensual delights and devote his life entirely to the service of God.[106]

Evidence for donning of a *khirqa*, the double attribution this conveys, and the importance of credentials is shown in the following account of *dervish* life by Muḥammad ibn al-Munawwar, writing between CE 1180 and 1203.

> The *pīr*, by laying his hand on the disciple's head and clothing him in the *khirqa*, indicates to all and sundry that he knows and has verified the fitness of that person for companionship with the *Ṣūfīs*. . . . It is for this reason that the *Ṣūfīs*, when a dervish whom they do not know comes into the convent or desires to associate with a party of dervishes, enquire of him: Who was thy "*Pīr* of companionship? (*Pīr-i-ṣuḥbat*), and from whose hand didst thou receive the *khirqa*?" The Ṣūfīs hold these two *nasab* in very high regard: indeed, there is no *nasab* in the (*ṭarīqat*) path except these two. If anyone should fail to establish these two relationships to a *pīr* who is exemplary (*muqtadā*), they drive him forth and do not admit him to their society.[107]

In fact, three essential elements make up initiation or companionship to use the older term: *talqīn adh-dhikr, akhdh al-'ahd and libās'al-khirqa.*[108]

Talqīn, verbal noun of *laqqana*, has the meaning "to prompt, inculcate, teach by repetition," but in respect of Ṣūfī initiation it means "to give (secret) instruction." Mystery was associated

---

106. 'Alī al-Hujwīrī, *Kashf al-Maḥjūb*, tr. R.'A. Nicholson, London, 1959, pp. 54-55.
107. Muḥammad ibn al-Munawwar, *Asrār at-Tawḥīd fī Maqāmāt ash-Shaikh Abi Sa'īd*; ed. V.A. Zhukovski, St. Petersburg, 1899, p. 55.
108. Sanūsī, *Salsabīl*, p. 3.

with the giving (*laqqana*) of the Seven words[109] associated with the seven stages of the mystic Path.

Akhdh al-'ahd means literally "taking the compact" and involves a *bai'at*, homage, oath, or covenant of allegiance. It is used in such phrases as: *'ahd al-yād*, swearing obedience to the shaikh with the handclasp (*musāfaha*), which may be extended to *akhdh al-yād wa 'l-iqtidā'* (taking shaikh as exemplary). *'Ahd* (or *akhdh*) *al-khirqa* is the compact involved in investiture with the habit. The justification for investing with the habit is the Qur'ānic verse (VII, verse 26), *Libās at-taqwā dhālika khair*, a phrase frequently introduced into the ceremony. The particular type of *khirqa* may be indicated: *akhdh khirqat al-arāda*, means "assuming the habit of the novitiate." This was frequent in the East, but not in the West, where the *khirqa* did not become common.[110] In the Arab world too it tended to become a formal act, like "capping" in a European university, for the habit disappeared and only the headgear remained. Thus, the ceremony tended to become divested of its esoteric significance. The *khirqa* as a dual-*frock* consisted of *khirqat aṭ-tabaruk* corresponding to *silsilāt al-baraka* (chain of heads of the *ṭā'if* from the shaikh to the *ṭarīqah*-founder), and *khirqat al-*

109. These seven words are: *La ilāha illa 'llāh* (no god but, Allāh), *yā Allāh* (O Allāh), *yā Hwa* (O He), *yā Haqq* (O Truth), *yā Hayy* (O living), *yā Qayyūm* (O Eternal) and *yā Qahhār* (O Subduer).

110. The *khirqa* was apparently used by early Western Ṣūfīs, many of whom had been trained in the East, but later became merely a sign of *faqīr*-dom. The patched garment was more generally called *murāqqa'a*, but it represented only one aspect of the tradition and was not equivalent to the graduating *khirqa*. In the nineteenth century the *murāqqa'a* was worn especially by Darqāwīs and Haddawīs (whose special term was *handasa* or *derbala*), and by *Khalwatīs* and by the followers of Muḥammad Ahmad, the *mahdi* of Nilotic Sudan, a heritage from his repudiated *Ṣūfī* past.

wird, chain of heads of the *ṭarīqah* from the founder to the Prophet.[111] These two in association comprised, in stricter orders, *khirqat as-ṣuḥba* (the vestment of companionship), which term with earlier masters had the significance of "discipleship."[112] There were many other different types of *khirqa*: *khirqat al-khidma* (service), or *at-ta'līm* (teaching), or *at-tarbiya* (guidance). Obviously Ibn Baṭṭūta's investment with the *khirqa* of the Suhrawardiyya would mean nothing to genuine initiates. The founder of the order writes about the purpose of the *khirqa*.

---

111. This is to be distinguished from the wearing of two *khirqās*, indicating at one period investiture by two Shaikhs (as in as-Sirr'āj, *Lumā;* pp. 191, 194, and in Ibn Khallikān, ed. de Slane (1842), I, 256, 4, and tr. de Slane, I, p. 502, n. 5); and also from its double aspect in respect of clothing, since investment included the headgear as well as the frock. Shaikh Abū Bakr ibn Hawiz al-Hawazani al-Batā'ihi, a former highway robber, when repenting out in the desert, was invested with the *khirqa* consisting of a *thawb* (gown) and *taqiya* (headgear) by Abū Bakr as-Siddīq in a dream finding them on him when he woke up; see al-Wāsṭī, *Tiryāq al-muhibbīn*, Cairo, AH 1305, pp. 6, 42-3; and cf. Sha'rani, *Lawāqih*, II, p. 125. The headgear was important in eastern orders in that it served as a distinguishing mark. Ibn Baṭṭūta refers to these distinctive aspects of dress as when he writes of the tattered gown and felt hat (*libasuhu muraqqa'a wa qalansuwa libd*) of a devotee at Hali in 'Asir al-Yaman (*Rihla*, Cairo edn., 1928, I, p. 155).

112. *Ṣuḥba* is another of those terms whose actual significance needs to be ascertained, unless specified as in the following quotation from al-Wāstī (writing *c.* 1320); "Izz ad-din Ahmad al-Farūthi said, 'I associated with Shihāb ad-din 'Umar as-Suhrawardī *ṣuḥbat at-tabarruk* and attended his courses.' One day he suggested investing me with their *khirqa*, but when it was conveyed to him that my *khirqa* was Ahmadiyya he said, 'please excuse me, my boy, all of us are embraced within the *khirqa* of Ahmad ar-Rifa'i'" (*Tiryāq*, p. 62).

> Investment with the *khirqa* establishes a bond between the shaikh and the aspirant and makes the aspirant subject himself to the discipline (*taḥkīm*) of the Shaikh; this *taḥkīm* being permissible in law.[113]. . . This *khirqa* is the symbol of the oath of investiture (*mubaya'a*). It is the first step towards *ṣuḥba*, the ultimate goal (of the aspirant) being *ṣuḥba*, the basis of all the aspirant's expectations. It is related that Abū Yazīd (al-Bisṭāmī) said, "He who has no master then Saṭān is his master.

Shaikh Shihab al-dīn al-Suhrawardī distinguishes between two types of *khirqa* — that with which the novice was invested and that given to a *mutashābbih* (imitator) in these words:

> Know that the *khirqa* is of two types — that of the novitiate (*irāda*) and that of the benediction (*tabarruk*). The primal one which the masters intend for aspirants is that of the novitiate, whilst that of benediction is similar to the other, except that the first is for the genuine *murīd*, whilst that of benediction is for the *mutashābbih*; in other words, he who imitates the Ṣūfīs. The essence of the *khirqa* is that the genuine candidate who enters into discipleship (*ṣuḥba*) with the Shaikh, surrendering himself and becoming like a small child with his father, is reared up by the shaikh in his God-given wisdom.[114]

Ibn Baṭṭūta shows the way in which *khirqa* investiture had degenerated in his time. He writes: "I met in this city (Hurmūz) the holy peregrinating Shaikh, Abu'l-Hassan al-Aqsarāni, a Rūmi (Greek) in origin, who entertained me and returned my visit, when he garbed me with a garment (*thawb* = *khirqa*) and

---

113. Shihab ad-din as-Suhrawardī, *'Awārif al-Ma'ārif*, Egypt, 1289/1872-73, Eng. tr. H. Wilberforce Clarke, 1981, rpt. New York, 1970, p. 69.

114. Suhrawardī, Ibid., p. 73.

gave me the girdle of companionship[115] — this acts as a support when squatting (to carry out religious exercises). Most of the Persian dervishes gird themselves with it."[116]

There are three types of *ijāzah* (licence).

The first is that given to a *dervish* or adept giving his qualifications and permitting him to practise in the name of his master; the second is given to a *khalīfah* or *muqaddam* authorizing him to confer the *wird*, that is, admit others into the *ṭarīqah*; whilst the third type simply affirms that the holder has followed a particular course of Ṣūfī instruction. A clear distinction is made between one's true guide — *shaikh at-tarbiya* (upbringing), or *shaikh as-ṣuḥba* (discipleship)[117] — and the various *shuyūkh at-tā'līm* (instructors) whose courses one has followed. The fact that Ṣūfīs claimed several initiations and possessed a number of *ijāzā*s were only concerned with announcing that the recipient has followed a course, perhaps absorption of a Ṣūfī book, and being given a licence to teach it or to recite a word of power, such as ash-Shadhili's *Hizb a-Bahr,* with power. In India even choirmen (*qawwāl*s) were given a singing licence (*ijāzāt-nāma-samā'*).

An *ijāzah* at its simplest takes a recognized form: "This is to certify that Muḥammad, son of (full genealogy), who took the *ṭarīqa* from the Khalīfa Mustafa (then follows the *silsilā* of *khullafā'* back to the founder) has found his adept Ṭāhā, son of (full genealogy), worthy to be admitted to the Order. He is, accordingly, given authority to act according to the rules of

115. Ibn Baṭṭūta uses the Persian *kamar-i-ṣuḥbat.*

116. Ibn Baṭṭūta, *Rihla,* Cairo edn., 1928, p. 173.

117. He is generally, though not necessarily, the initiator into the *silsilā* covering both *ijāzah irāda,* that of the *murīd,* and *ijāza 't-tabarruk,* the permission which links with the Shaikh's *baraka.*

the order (then follows a statement of the things he is permitted to carry out) since its secrets have been revealed to him."[118] The *khalīfah* affixes his seal to the document,[119] and it is frequently worn rolled in a tubular case (a full *ijāzah* might well be two yards long) on the flank.[120] A complete *ijāzah* often contained the *wird* and recommendations such as, for example, the *waṣiyya* or testament said to have been given by 'Abd al-Qādirī al-Jīlānī to his son 'Abd ar-Razzāq.[121] The Nilotic Sudan Hagiographer, Wad Daif Allāh (d. CE 1809), reproduces part of an *ijāzah* given by Ibn Jābir to a disciple in CE 1574:

> Praise be to God, the Lord of the Universe, and peace be upon the Apostle. Verily, the brother of Faqih Ibrahim, the pious, learned and humble one, the son of Umm-i-Rab'a, I believe to be worthy of mastership and leadership. I, therefore, appoint him a *quṭb* in rank, an interpreter to his own age and time, a tutor to aspirants, an example to those who guide, a refuge for the poor and destitute, a revivifier of the sun of knowledge after its setting.
>
> I authorize him to pass on and teach to the people all that he has truly received and heard from me. I also authorize him

---

118. Thus Abū 'Amir al-'Azafī was given an *ijāzah* by al-Badisī to teach his *Maqsad*; tr. G.S Colin in *Archiv. Maroc*, XXVI (1926), p. 163.

119. Other attestations may be given and must be given if the recipient is the Shaikh's own son.

120. Richard Burton gives a translation (Appendix III of his *Pilgrimage*) of an *ijāzah*, which he says, gave him authority, as *Darwish* 'Abdallah, to act as a *murshid* in the *Qādirī* order, but in fact it simply says that he has been given instruction in the Saying of Unity with authority to recite it 165 times after each *fariḍa* (obligatory ritual prayer) and on any other occasion according to his ability. This *ijāzah* was four feet five inches long and about six and a half inches broad.

121. See Jīlānī, *al-Fuyūḍāt ar-Rabbāniyya*, pp. 35-38.

> to propagate and broadcast the knowledge we have referred to. Let anyone to whom such knowledge is communicated be exceedingly careful lest he be spiritually destroyed.[122]

In the past *ijāzā*s frequently dealt with the question of *rukhsā*s (sing. *rukhsa*), an aspect of Ṣūfī life we have hardly referred to. These are "dispensations" or "indulgences." They include such everyday necessities as the holding of private and public assemblies (*hadras*) at which they hold concerts (*samā'at*), and indulge in jesting (*mizah*), dancing (*raqs*), and the rending (*tamzīq*) and divesting of garments. They embrace "contemplation of youth" (*nazar ila'l-murd*), soliciting of alms (normally reprehensible), and taking up arms in a holy cause. They may cover the use of the *rosary*, neglect of *masjid* attendance, and non-observance of ritual *ṣalāh* during a period of *'uzlat* (retirement).

122. *Ṭabaqāt* of Wad Daif Allāh, ed. Sidaiq (1930), p. 33, ed. Mandil (1930), pp. 31-32.

4

Ṣūfī Thought of Shaikh 'Abdu'l Qādir Jīlānī (Raḥ.'A)

Shaikh 'Abdu'l Qādir Jīlānī (Raḥ.'A) infused breath of new life, zeal and self-confidence into countless persons through his power of speech and the spiritual power of his heart. He was, in truth, a blessing for the world of Islam for he renovated and revived the true content of the faith and tapped the sources of moral and spiritual strength for a religious renaissance.[1] Sheikh 'Amr al-Kaisāni reports that there was hardly a sermon delivered by 'Abdu'l Qādir after which a number of Jews and Christians did not embrace Islam, marauders and robbers did not repent for their sins, and heretics and apostates did not renounce their mistaken beliefs.[2]

Al-Jubba'i relates that 'Abdu'l Qādir once told him that he wished to lead the life of a recluse in the wilderness but God had willed that people should derive benefit from him. And, it was a blessing granted unto him that more than 5000 Jews and Christians embraced Islam and about a 100000 sinners and criminals repented for their misdeeds on account of him.[3]

Gifted with divine grace and enlightenment, 'Abdu'l Qādir

---

1. Muḥammad Ibn yaḥyā al-Tādifī, *Qalā'id al-Jawāhir* (composed about AH 980), Cairo, AH 1303, p. 8.
2. Ibid.
3. Ibid.

was ever conscious of the purification of spirit and rectitude of morals, yet he did not lose sight of the importance of teaching and disseminating the correct doctrines of the faith. Being a follower of the Hanbalite school of Sunnī theology, he endeavoured, like his mentor, to root out innovations and deviations from the orthodox faith and practice.

The discourses of 'Abdu'l Qādir had a magnetic effect which is still discernible in them. 'Abdu'l Qādir is at his best in *Futūḥ al-Ghaib, al-Fath-i al-Rubbānī* and *Jila'l-i Khaṭīr*. In describing the love and unity of the Divine Being he appears to be inspired by higher sources. The reader can still find the spirit of sincerity and enthusiasm running through these sermons.

Following in the footsteps of the Prophet (SAW), his successors and the enlightened saints of the earlier period, 'Abdu'l Qādir touched on the current problems of his days, analysed the reasons for the miseries and maladies of the people and provided answers to their doubts and deficiencies. Along with this, the tremendous sincerity and earnest zeal for the welfare of the people fired his haranguing with a frenzy of enthusiasm and magnetic effect capable of pulling the strings of the heart.

The Shaikh used to take daily a class each of the Qur'ānic exegesis, Traditions and Jurisprudence. The classes were held in the morning and evening, while 'Abdu'l Qādir listened to the recitation of the *Qur'ān* after the midday prayers and thereafter dictated *fatwā*s on religious or legal questions referred to him. In formulating his answers 'Abdu'l Qādir generally followed the Shafe'ite and Hanbalite schools of Jurisprudence. His juristic opinions were highly praised by the jurist-scholars of Iraq, for these provided a striking example of the acuteness of his intellect.[4]

---

4. 'Abdu'l Wahab Sha'rānī, *Ṭabaqāt al-Kubrā*, Egypt, AH 1305, vol. I, p. 126.

Once the question referred to him was that a man had taken an oath that he would perform a religious observance in a manner that nobody else in the whole world would be able to share the privilege with him but, if he failed to fulfil his undertaking, this would mean an irrevocable separation between him and his wife. The scholars were astounded by the strange oath taken by the man and could not suggest an observance which could be performed by him alone in the whole world. 'Abdu'l Qādir, however, replied that the man should be allowed to circumambulate K'aba alone seven times to perform the lesser *ḥajj*. Everyone agreed that this was the only authorized religious observance which he could perform alone at a time when no body else would be engaged in the same 'Ibādah.[5]

Profound knowledge of the religious lore and meticulous observance of the Traditions of the holy Prophet, aided by the grace of Allāh, had unveiled the mysteries of celestial world to 'Abdu'l Qādir, who had reached the stage where discrimination between truth and untruth, divine intuition and Demoniac imposition is born in a man. He had acquired the certitude of knowledge that the *sharī'ah* of the Last Prophet (SAW) was perfect and that any claim made contrary to the divine edict was simply a saṭānic suggestion. 'Abdu'l Qādir himself relates an incident that he once came across. He says:

> "Once I saw a dazzling light which filled the entire sky." Then a human frame appeared therein and said. "O 'Abdu'l Qādir, I am Lord, thy God. I have made every prohibited thing lawful unto thee." I replied, "Get away from me, O Devil." As soon as I uttered these words, the lustre in the sky turned into darkness and the human frame began to

5. 'Abdu'l Wahab Sha'rānī, *Ṭabaqāt al-Kubrā*, Egypt, AH 1305, vol. I, p. 126.

> fizzle out into smoke. Then I heard someone saying, " 'Abdu'l Qādir, I had misled seventy mystics with this device, but God saved thee on account of thy knowledge and piety." To this I rejoined, "No, It was simply a grace of Allāh." After 'Abdu'l Qādir had related the incident someone asked, "How did you know that it was the Satan." "Since he told me," replied 'Abdu'l Qādir, "that he had made the prohibited thing lawful for me."[6]

He used to tell his disciples that if any action transgresses the commandments of Allāh, then it is surely an imposition by the Satan. In such cases one should return to the tenets of the *sharī'ah,* inculcate an unflinching faith, and firmly reject the temptations of self-indulgence; for, whatever is not permitted by the *sharī'ah* is decidedly misleading.[7] Here, we refer now to some of the recurring themes of his thought.

Tawḥīd (Oneness of Allāh)

The Shaikh (Raḥ.'A) asks for the declaration of the Unity of Allāh and holds that whoever perishes for His (Allāh's) sake receives his compensation from Him. He asserts, "And proclaims the unity of Allāh and do not associate anything with Him and make yourself the target of the sorrows of providence which will strike you not to kill but to injure and whoever perishes for the sake of Allāh receives his compensation from Him."[8]

He affirms that one should seek assistance from Allāh alone because the whole humanity can neither harm nor benefit any person in contrary to the will of Allāh. He maintains:

---

6. Sha'rāni, *Tabaqāt al-Kubrā,* vol. I, p. 127.
7. Idem.
8. Shaikh 'Abdu'l Qādir Jīlānī, *Futūḥ al-Ghaib,* Eng. tr. M. Aftab-ud Dīn Ahmad, Delhi: Kitab Bhawan, 1990, Discourse no. 38.

> So when you ask, ask from Allāh, and when you seek assistance, seek it from Him. The pen dried after writing down all that is to happen, and if the servants of Allāh strive to benefit you with anything which Allāh has not decreed for you, they will not be able to do it, and if all the servants of Allāh strive to harm you with anything which Allāh has not decreed for you they will not be able to do so.[9]

Jīlānī (Raḥ.'A) holds that Allāh is alone in His knowledge of good and evil of things. He says, ". . . He (Allāh) transfers you from one state to another and to one that is the opposite of it, because you do not know wherein lies good — in poverty or affluence, in calamity or in ease. He has kept the knowledge of things hidden from you and He is alone in His knowledge of good and evil of things. . . ."[10]

Allāh, according to 'Abdu'l Qādir (Raḥ.'A), is unparallel in His might and power. He says, "Allāh alone is the giver of strength and the helper, because there is no might and power excepting in Allāh, the High, the Great."[11] He advises one to be with Allāh in such a way as if no other creation exists. He opines, "Be with Allāh, the Mighty, the Glorious, as if no creation exists. And be with the creation as if there is no self in you."[12]

When Jīlānī (Raḥ.'A) was suffering from the illness of which he died, his son Shaikh 'Abdu'l Wahhāb requested him, "Give me a parting admonition which I should act upon after you have left this world." The Shaikh advised him: "It is incumbent upon you to fear Allāh and not fear anyone excepting Him, and not to hope from anyone excepting Him

---

9. Jīlānī, *Futūḥ al-Ghaib*, op. cit., Discourse no. 42.
10. Ibid., no. 69.
11. Ibid., no. 76.
12. Ibid., no. 77.

and entrust all your needs to Him. And do not rely on anyone except Him and ask everything from Him and do not place confidence on anyone besides Him. Stand by His unity, stand by His Unity, all are agreed on this."[13]

At the last moment of his life the Shaikh (Raḥ.'A) praised Allāh and His attributes in these words, "I seek the help of Allāh . . . there is no object of worship excepting Allāh, glory be to Him and be He exalted, the everlasting, who does not fear annihilation; glory be to Him who has established His superiority through His power and overpowered His servants by means of death. There is no object of worship excepting Allāh and Muḥammad (SAW) is the Prophet of Allāh."[14]

In one of his sermons the Shaikh (Raḥ.'A) explains the significance of obedience to Allāh in these words: "Make obedience to Allāh the primary thing under which every other thing should come and make it the guiding factor and make whatever is besides this as of secondary and subordinate consideration."[15]

Commenting upon *tawḥīd* (oneness of Allāh) and seeker's behaviour, the Shaikh (Raḥ.'A) says, "Obey (Allāh and His Messenger) and do not create innovations (in religion); support (religion) and do not oppose it. Be obedient (to Allāh and His Messenger) and do not be disobedient (to them); Be sincere and not polytheist; believe in oneness of Allāh and do not escape from His door (in search of others); Ask from Him and none else; seek His assistance and no one else's; trust Him and none else."[16]

---

13. Jīlānī, *Futūḥ al-Ghaib*, op. cit., Discourse no. 79.
14. Ibid., no. 80.
15. Ibid., no. 59.
16. Shaikh 'Abdu'l Qādir Jīlānī, *Fatḥ-i Rubbānī*, Discourse no. 47.

Jīlānī (Raḥ.'A) holds that one should believe so much in the oneness of Allāh that not even a stray of the world should find any abode in his heart. He maintains, "Believe so much in the oneness of Allāh that not even a stray of this world be there in your heart. *Tawḥīd* abolishes everything (other than Allāh)."[17]

On the same theme the Shaikh (Raḥ.'A) comments, "How come do you claim Islam, *īmān* (belief) and *īqān* (faith) when you actually trust upon your energy, potential and your *asbāb* (worldly means)."[18] He adds, ". . . Ask for all things from one (Allāh) who is the Creator of all things, spend all your resources in His search."[19]

The Unity of the Divine Being

The forces of worldliness had become so strong during 'Abdu'l Qādir's time that the entire social and economic life of the community appeared to be woven into the context of political situation then prevailing; people had developed a tendency of depending upon the kings and nobles for realization of their worldly ends and had begun to treat them as ultimate dispensers of benefits and harms. In order to counteract this mistaken tendency of the people, the Shaikh comments in one of his sermons:

"This entire creation is like a man who has been imprisoned and chained by a king whose dominions are vast and countenance awesome. The prisoner has been hanged from a pine tree beneath which flows a river, wide and deep. The king is seated on an elevated chair, having arrows and bows, javelins and spears by his side. He hits the captive with

---

17. Jīlānī, *Fatḥ-i Rubbānī*, Discourse no. 62.
18. Ibid.
19. Ibid.

whatever weapon he desires. Now, would it be prudent for anyone witnessing the scene to divert his attention from the king and expect harm or favour from the captive instead of the king? Would not such a man be deemed a fool or even mad? O God, I seek thy refuge from blindness after having given eyes, from being cast off after getting near Thee, from regression after being promoted to Thy favour, from being misled after obtaining Thy guidance and from apostasy after having granted faith."[20]

In another sermon he asks to instil the love of Allāh to the exclusion of everything else.

"Keep your eyes fixed on Him who is looking at you; keep yourself before One who keeps Himself before you; love Him who loves you; hark unto Him who calls you; seek help from Him who can save you, take you out of the darkness of ignorance, cleanse you of the impurity of your soul, and redeem you from the baser self and misleading temptations, despair and timidity. Your earthly desires are like your foolish friends who keep you off the righteous path and deprive you of the things, pleasing and desirable. How long would you remain slaves of your desires, temptations, greed, pride, in short, in this transitory world? How long would you remain forgetful of the Hereafter and of your Creator, the Fashioner of everything, the First and the Last, the Manifest and the Hidden; everything is couched within His grasp from which emanates the love within your heart, the peace and solace, blessings and favours?"[21]

'Abdu'l Qādir throws light on the same topic in his yet another discourse in these words:

20. Jīlānī, *Futūḥ al-Ghaib*, op. cit., Discourse no. 17.

21. Ibid.

"The entire creation is helpless. Nothing can do good or harm to you. It is only Allāh who lets a thing be done by you, or, in other words, the will of Allāh finds expression through you or somebody else. Allāh has already destined whatever is to happen to you; whether it be beneficial or harmful; and the destiny cannot be changed. Those who are faithful and virtuous, they set an example unto other creations. There are a few among these who have so purified their heart that their interior and exterior selves have become one; even if they have riches, their desires never seethe with the worldly attachment. Verily, only those are courageous, valiant and powerful who have purified their hearts and attained this state of enlightenment. Unto these alone belongs the kingdom of Heaven and Earth for they have cleansed their heart of everything save Allāh; they are like a soldier who guards the door of his heart, with the sabre of *tawḥīd* (Unity) and the *sharī'ah* in his hand, to bar the entry of all creations to a place reserved for the Creator. Since they have attuned their hearts to the ultimate source of power, the *sharī'ah* beautifies their exterior while *tawḥīd* and the wisdom of God's knowledge decorate their interior."[22]

While warning against the worship of false objects the Shaikh (R.'A.) explains:

"You put your trust in your own self, in others, in your wealth, in your rites and customs, in your trade and business, or in your rulers; but, in whatever object you place your reliance, it becomes, to say the truth, your object of worship. If you fear someone, or expect harm, or favour from him or else deem him as an intercessor with Allāh, then he is the object of worship for you."[23]

---

22. Jīlānī, *Fath-i Rubbāni*, Discourse no. 13.

23. Ibid., no. 20.

On another occasion, 'Abdu'l Qādir vividly describes the jealousy and pride of Allāh and His abhorrence of all associates, as also the wisdom lying behind the loss of the things adored and loved by man.

"You often complain, as you would ever do, that you have to suffer the loss of whatever you set your affections on. The object of your fancy, if it is a human being, either separates or dies. If it is wealth that you care for, you incur losses or are deprived of it. Then, should I tell you, that Allāh is in love with you, and He is jealous too! He has created you for Himself but you want to be enraptured by others! Have you not heard what Allāh has said: *He holds them dear who love Him*, and also, *I created the jinn and humankind only that they might worship Me.*[24] And, are you not aware of what the Prophet once said: *When Allāh loves anyone; He places him in trouble but if he puts up with it with endurance and forbearance, Allāh then sets him apart for Himself.* Requested to elucidate what he meant by "setting apart of a man," the Prophet replied: *God deprives him of his possession and progeny*. This is so because it is natural for a man to love his offsprings and possessions and thus his love which should have been for Allāh alone is divided between the Creator and the created, between the Eternal and the finite."

The Shaikh continues: "God is, however, extremely Proud and Mighty and therefore, He destroys whatever threatens to become an associate in the love for Him. It is only then that the heart of the man whom He loves gets attuned to Him. And, then, this man can claim to enjoy the distinction of what has been described thus by Allāh: *He holds them dear who love Him*. It is the stage when the heart of the man is cleansed of all idols and associates (of God) such as the offsprings, riches,

---

24. Holy *Qur'ān*, *Adh-Dhāriyāt*, 56.

pleasures and desires. It has now no yearnings, no longings left, wordly or otherwise, not even those relating to piety and miraculous powers, stations and states, nearness and remoteness; the heart becomes a bottomless vessel in which nothing can be kept. Allāh Almighty being extremely Proud and Jealous makes the heart of His beloved incapable of nourishing any other desire; He shrouds the heart of His devotee with His awe and a gasp of admiration, and guards it with His Glory and Might so that nothing can get inside this heart; nor can the possessions and riches, family and progeny, friends and relations, piety and miraculous powers do any harm to it. None of these finds a place in the heart of such a man nor, then, Allāh remains, jealous of them. Whatever is granted thereafter to this man is a gift or reward from his Allāh so that he may be of help to those who are around him or visit him."[25]

Enforcing the lawful and forbidding the unlawful

(امر باالمعروف و نهی عن المنکر), Enforcement of lawful and forbidding of the unlawful is frequently stressed by Shaikh 'Abdu'l Qādir Jīlānī (Raḥ.'A) in his sermons. He says that holding the commandment of Allāh, abstension from forbidden things is indispensable for a believer in all the circumstances. He speaks; "Three things are indispensable for a believer in all conditions of life: he should keep the commandments of Allāh; he should abstain from the forbidden things, and should be pleased with the decree of providence."[26]

Shaikh says, "Abstinence from unlawful things is incumbent on you or else the rope of destruction is coiled round you."[27] He quotes a *ḥadīth* of Prophet (SAW) in support

25. Jīlānī, *Futūḥ al-Ghaib*, op. cit., Discourse no. 32.

26. Ibid., no. 1.

27. Ibid., no. 35.

of it, in which he has expressed that the foundation of religion is abstinence from unlawful things and its destruction is in greed, and that whoever goes round a protected pasture land is only too likely to fall himself into it as a cattle pasturing freely by the side of a cornfield is only too likely to stretch his mouth towards it. It is unlikely that the cornfield should remain safe from him.

Jīlānī (Raḥ.'A) also quotes sayings of Haḍrat 'Umar Ibn Khaṭṭāb and Haḍrat Abū Bakr in support of it. The former is reported to have said, "We used to abstain from nine-tenth of lawful things in the fear lest we should fall in the zone of unlawful things," and the latter is reported to have said, We used to avoid seventy doors of permissible things for fear of getting involved in sin."

Jīlānī (Raḥ.'A) adds that, "these personages did so just to be away from any proximity to unlawful things; and in doing so they acted on the saying of the Prophet (SAW), Beware! verily every king has a protected pastureland and the pastureland of Allāh is His forbidden things."[28]

In the beginning of *bāb* (chapter) 8 of his Ghuniya in order to express the significance of امر بالمعروف و نہی عن المنکر, the Shaikh quotes a few verses of the holy *Qur'ān*.[29] He opines that there are three groups to prohibit unlawful. The ruler . . . the *'ulamā'* . . . and the common people. He quotes a *ḥadīth*[30] of the Prophet (SAW) to substantiate his view.

---

28. Jīlānī, *Futūḥ al-Ghaib*, op. cit., Discourse no. 35.
29. یا مرون باالمعروف والناهون عن المنکر والحافظون لحدو الله.

كنتم خير امة اخرجت للناس تامرون باالمعروف و تنهون عن المنكر و تومنون بالله.

والمومنون والمومنات بعضهم اولياء بعض يامرون باالمعروف و ينهون عن المنكر
30. Abū Sa'id Khudri (Raḍ.'A) narrates that the Prophet (SAW) said, "If you witness violation of *sharī'ah*, you should check/stop it →

The Shaikh (Raḥ.'A) prescribes five conditions for the fulfilment of this duty:

1. The prohibitor should himself be fully equipped with the knowledge of prohibited actions in accordance with the *sharī'ah*.
2. To win the pleasure of Allāh and strengthen the Islam should be his sole aim in fulfilment of this task. . . .
3. He should adopt a generous and polite approach and not impolite and stern one in this task of prohibition of unlawful actions. He should advise the accused in an affectionate manner. The Shaikh warns of the designs of devil if one fails to adopt an Islamic approach. He quotes these verses of the holy *Qur'ān* to explain it.

   انما يدعو حزبه ليكونوا من اصحٰب السعير 31

   ". . . He (Satan) invites his adherents, that they may become companions of the Blazing Fire."

   Allāh addresses his Messenger in these words:

   فبما رحمةٍ من الله لنت لهم ولو كنت فظاً غليظ القلب لا تفضوا من حولك 32

   "It is the part of the Mercy of God that thou dost deal gently with them. . . ."
4. One who shares this responsibility should be *ṣābir* (patient), affectionate, dignified, courageous and polite and should be having full control and command over

---

→ with your hand (i.e. using your power/strength); if you are not capable enough then you stop it with your tongue (i.e. speak against it); if you have not this capacity too, then keep hatred (against the evil) in your heart; (but) it is the weakest (stage) of Īmān (faith)."

31. Holy *Qur'ān* XXXV: 6.

32. Ibid., III: 159.

his own whims. . . .

5. His way of life should be in conformity with his mission of امر باالمعروف و نهى عن المنكر so that others (the accursed ones) do not make it an excuse and he does not become blameworthy in front of Allāh, who says:

أتامرون الناس بالبر و تنسون انفسكم و انتم تتلون الكتٰب افلا تعقلون [33]

"Do ye enjoin the right conduct on the people, and forget (to paractise it) yourselves, and yet ye study the scripture? Will ye not understand?"

The Shaikh (Raḥ.'A) holds this view that it is better to impart advice, with regard to enforcement of lawful and prohibition of unlawful, in isolation because in such state it appeals to one deeply. 'Abdu'l Qādir Jīlānī (Raḥ.'A) affirms that in no case one should shun this responsibility as, in that case, it amounts to displeasure of Allāh.

It has been stated in the holy *Qur'ān*;

لولا ينههم الربانيون والاحبار عن قولهم الاثم واكلهم
السحت لبئس ماكانوا يصنعون [34]

"Why do not the Rabbis and the doctors of law forbid them from their (habit of) uttering sinful words and eating things forbidden? evil indee are their works."

Love of Humanity

The love of humanity, in general, and the affection for the *ummah*, in particular, was symptomatic of 'Abdu'l Qādir's sublimated soul and indicative of his close affinity to the successors of the Prophet. In one of his sermons he delineated the object and the mental states of different types of persons

33. Holy Qur'ān, II: 44.

34. Ibid., V: 66.

visiting a market. Coming to the last category, he perhaps describes his own feelings in these words:

"And there is the fifth man whose heart is filled, when he enters a market, with the awe and reverence of the Almighty to seek His blessings for those present in the market. He becomes oblivious of everything else save his benediction for the people; he remains immersed, from the time of his entry into the market till he comes out of it, in the solemn invocation of divine blessings and in repenting for the sins of those who happen to be there, and thus he hardly gets any time to see what they are selling or buying. His heart bleeds and eyes shed tears over the ingratitude of man while his tongue remains busy in thanking Allāh over what He has bestowed unto his bondsmen."[35]

About Shirk (Polytheism)

According to Jīlānī (Raḥ.'A) keeping expectations for gifts and favours with people tends to associate them with Allāh. He says "Thus, so long as you remain with people you hope for their gifts and favours and ask from them with expectations at their doors, you are associating Allāh's creation with Him."[36] In the same discourse he states that relying on one's earning while being forgetful about the favours of Allāh is a form of polytheism. He preaches, ". . . And you begin living on your earning and then rely on earning and become contented with it and forget the favour of your Lord (Allāh), you are again behaving like a polytheist and this polytheism is subtler than the previous one."[37]

35. Jīlānī, *Futūḥ al-Ghaib*, Discourse no. 72.

36. Ibid., no. 16.

37. Ibid.

Man, according to the Shaikh (Raḥ.'A) is the most unjust and greatest offender in the sense of ascribing partner to Allāh. He explains, "While you are the most unjust one and greatest offender because moved by your animal passion you have taken the initiative in your own self and the creation of Allāh and thereby indirectly you have ascribed a partner to Him."[38] He quotes a Qur'ānic verse in this context: "Verily Allāh will not forgive that any partner be ascribed to Him and will forgive what is besides that to whomsoever He pleases."[39] Jīlānī (Raḥ.'A) continues, "Keep away from associating anything with Allāh with utmost effort and do not go near this sin and shun it in all your movements and restful conditions during the night as well as during the day both in moments of solitude and when you are in company."[40]

In his another discourse 'Abdu'l Qādir Jīlānī (Raḥ.'A) asks for proclamation of the Unity of Allāh and not associating anything with Him. He holds, "And proclaim the Unity of Allāh and do not associate anything with Him and make yourself the target of the arrows of providence which will strike you not to kill but to injure and whoever perishes for the sake of Allāh receives his compensation from Him."[41]

According to the Shaikh (Raḥ.'A) the polytheistic tendencies amount to unbelief and take a man away from Allāh. He says, "How can comfort be claimed in face of the existence of diseases, both internal and external, and how can the faith in the unity of Allāh be claimed in face of polytheistic

---

38. Jīlānī, *Futūḥ al-Ghaib*, Discourse no. 22.
39. Holy Qur'ān, IV: 16.
40. Jīlānī, *Futūḥ al-Ghaib*, Discourse no. 22.
41. Ibid., no. 38.

tendencies which amount to unbelief and which take a man away from nearness to Allāh. . . ."[42]

Polytheism, according to the Shaikh, does not consist only in idol-worship but also following the desire of the flesh, and associating anything with Allāh is also polytheism. He says, "Polytheism consists not merely in idol-worship. It is also polytheism to follow the desire of the flesh and to adopt anything of this world and of the Hereafter in association with Allāh."[43]

When one, according to Jīlānī (Raḥ.'A), takes anything other than Allāh into account for bringing him profit or loss, he is performing an act of polytheism. He affirms, "You are slave of yourself, your world, your whims. You are slave of creatures for you regard them as partners unto Allāh because in any form of profit or loss you take them into account."[44]

The eyes of one's heart, according to Jīlānī (Raḥ.'A), remain closed till he regards people as partners unto Allāh. He says, ". . . Until you beg to people and regard them partners unto Allāh the eyes of your heart will remain closed."[45]

In one of his discourses the Shaikh (Raḥ.'A) strongly condmens the creation of innovations (*bid'at*) and ascribing anyone as partner to Allāh. He says, ". . . do not create innovations and do not transgress . . . and do not ascribe any partner to Him (Allāh)."[46]

---

42. Jīlānī, *Futūḥ al-Ghaib*, Discourse no. 73.
43. Ibid., no. 7.
44. Jīlānī, *Fatḥ-i-Rubbāni*, Discourse no. 17.
45. Ibid., no. 29.
46. Jīlānī, *Futūḥ al-Ghaib*; Discourse no. 2.

Ṣūfī, Taṣawwuf and Spiritual Struggle

The Shaikh (Raḥ.'A) holds that the Ṣūfī is such a person whose *bāṭin* (interior) and *ẓāhir* (exterior) have become pure and serene through following the *Qur'ān* and *Sunnah* (way) of the Prophet Muḥammad (SAW). In such case the Prophet becomes an ambassador between him and his (Ṣūfī's) Lord (Allāh). He elaborates:

"Woe unto you! You claim to be a Ṣūfi, yet you are disturbed! The Ṣūfī is one whose *bāṭin* (inward) and *ẓāhir* (outward) have become pure and serene through following the Book of Allāh and the *Sunnah* of the Messenger of Allāh. As this pure serenity increases, he will further emerge from the sea of his existence and give up his will, choice and volition."[47]

Again he comments: When someone's heart becomes pure and serene, the Prophet will become an ambassador between him and his Lord, as was Gabriel. The foundation of good is following the Prophet (SAW) in both his word and his deed."[48]

On the blessings of pure food, clothes and heart Jīlānī (R.'A.) asserts: "Purify your heart by taking the foods which are lawful. You will achieve *m'arifat* (gnosis) of Allāh. Purify your food, clothes and heart, you will become *safi*. *Taṣawwuf* is derived from *ṣaffa*. One who wears *ṣūf* (wool) and is true at his *taṣawwuf*, his heart remains purged of all except Allāh."[49]

According to Jīlānī (Raḥ.'A) Ṣūfī is one who is purified by Allāh. Commenting on purification the Shaikh says, "one who

---

47. Jīlānī, *Jila'al Khaṭīr*, Eng. tr. Setha al-Dargazellī and Louoy Fatoohī, Delhi, 1998, p. 146.

48. Ibid.

49. Jīlānī, *Fatḥ-i-Rubbānī*, p. 150.

purifies his heart of all calamities of *nafs* (self), remains aloof from vices, performs pious deeds, fulfils the rights of Allāh, whose heart feels anxiety in the love of people, remains attentive to Allāh by adopting solitude and feels satisfaction in his being attentive to Allāh, is the desired purified one."[50]

Commenting on the status of Ṣūfī, the Shaikh maintains; "Allāh purifies Ṣūfī by the spring of His wisdom and deeds, then he (Ṣūfī) attains the place of peace . . . deceives his *saṭān* (devil) and *nafs* (self), relinquishes his whims and desires, remains absorbed in the worship of Allāh, involves his *nafs* in self-mortification, spares himself for none but Allāh . . ."[51]

'Abdu'l Qādir Jīlānī (Raḥ.'A) puts forward eight qualities of *Ṣūfī*s in the following way:

(1) Generosity like that of Ḥaḍrat Ibrahim ('A.S.)

(2) Cheerful submission like that of Ḥaḍrat Isma'il ('A.S.)

(3) Patience like that of Ḥaḍrat Ya'qūb ('A.S.)

(4) Prayer like that of Ḥaḍrat Zakariyya ('A.S.)

(5) Poverty like that of Ḥaḍrat Yaḥyā ('A.S.)

(6) Wearing of woollen clothes like that of Ḥaḍrat Mūsa ('A.S.)

(7) Travelling about like that of Haḍrat 'Īsā ('A.S.)

(8) A life of poverty with resignation and content like that of Prophet Muḥammad (Ṣ'AW).[52]

Commenting upon the way for the achievement of *taṣawwuf*, Jīlānī (Raḥ.'A) asserts, "*Taṣawwuf* is obtained not

---

50. Jīlānī, *Ghuniyat ul Ṭālibīn*, Urdu. tr. Amānullāh Armān Sirhadī, Delhi, 1987, p. 629.

51. Ibid., pp. 629-30.

52. Jīlānī, *Futūḥ al-Ghaib*, Discourse no. 75.

through discussion and talk but through hunger and giving up even those things which are liked and approved of (in ordinery circumstances)."[53]

The Shaikh (Raḥ.'A) pronounces ten characteristics for those who are engaged in spiritual struggle and in self-introspection and are determined to attain the spiritual goal to which they must stick. While describing these charcteristics he says. ". . . The servant should not *swear* by Him whether truthfully or falsely, intentionally or by mistake. . . . He should avoid *untruth* seriously or out of joke. . . . He should be aware that when he *promises* anything to anyone he should not break his promise or he should not make any promise at all. . . . He should refrain from *cursing* anything in the creation nor should he cause any harm to anything. . . . He should refrain from praying for any *harm* to anyone among people, even if he has been treated unjustly. . . . He should not affirm his evidence on *polytheism, unbelief* and *hypocrisy* of one of those who follow the same *qibla* (direction of prayer). . . . He should refrain from looking at anything of a *sinful* nature both outwardly and inwardly and should restrain his organs of the body from it. . . . One should avoid putting any *burden* on anyone whether it be small or big. He should be free from all *expectations* from men, nor should he feel tempted in his heart by what is with them. . . . The tenth characteristic is *humility,* because it is with this trait that the station of the servant is raised high and his position made lofty and his honour and eminence made perfect in the sight of Allāh."[54]

Aḥwāl (States) and Maqāmāt (Stations)

Commenting upon different states and stations of the Sūfic

53. Jīlānī, *Futūḥ al-Ghaib,* Discourse no. 75.

54. Jīlānī, *Ghuniyat ul-Ṭālibīn,* pp. 670-72.

path, Jīlānī (Raḥ.'A), enumerates states of *ṣāliḥ* (piety), *wilāyat* (sainthood), *abdāl, ghawth* and *ṣiddīq* as the prominent ones. He preaches; "Follow the Law (of *sharī'ah*) in all that may happen to you if you are in a state of *ṣāliḥ* (piety) which is the first step and follow the commandment in the state of *wilāyat* and in the state of dying out of the existence of desire and do not go beyond this, and this is the second step. And be pleased with the action of Allāh and be reconciled to it and vanish into the state of *abdāl, ghawth* and *ṣiddīq*. These are the final stages."[55]

'Abdu'l Qādir Jīlānī (Raḥ.'A) holds that the spirit of man can be either in the state of happiness or in the state of trouble. He elaborates his statement in these words:

"The spirit of man can be in two conditions and there is no third one: the state of happiness and the state of trouble, so when it is in trouble there is anxiety and complaint and displeasure and criticism and finding fault with Allāh, the Mighty, the Exalted, lacking in patience and cheerful submission and reconcilement; sin of associating the creation and worldly means with the Creator and finally unbelief. Then when it is in comfort, it is a victim of greed and insolence and predominance of low desire and enjoyments. . . . Thus, when it is in trouble it does not desire anything except its removal and forgets all pleasure and desires and delightful things and does not ask anything out of these."[56]

The Shaikh holds that when this sufferer is blessed with an easy and comfortable life, he returns to arrogance and greediness and disobedience to his Lord and plunges in his sinful occupation. He forgets the misfortune he had lately been into and the calamity to which he had been a victim.

---

55. Jīlānī, *Futūḥ al-Ghaib*, Discourse no. 18.

56. Ibid., no. 40.

The Shaikh subscribes to this view that a man can either be close to Allāh or away from Him. He comments, "The state of your affairs can be either the one or the other of the following two:

(i) Either you are not in the nearness of Allāh, the Mighty, the Glorious, or

(ii) You are close to Him,"[57]

'Abdu'l Qādir (Raḥ.'A) enumerates four states in attaining the enjoyments and allotments. He says;

". . . There are four states in attaining the enjoyments and allotments. The first state is that of the urges of nature and this is an unlawful one. The second state is of the law and this is permissible and lawful. And the third state is that of inner commandment and this is the state of *wilāyat* and discarding of desires. And the fourth state is that of Divine favour, and this is the state of disappearance of purpose and attainment of *badaliyyat* and of being the (divine) objective, standing by the decree of destiny, which is the act of Allāh, and this is the state of knowledge and of being possessed of the quality of righteousness, and no one can be called righteous unless he has really attained this position."[58]

In his another discourse, the Shaikh regards the different states of spiritual experience as states of restraint. He observes; "All the different states of spiritual experience are states of restraint because the *walī* (pious saint) is commanded to look after them. And whatever is ordered to be looked after brings restraint."[59] Jīlānī (Raḥ.'A) also holds this opinion that a devotee

57. Jīlānī, *Futūḥ al-Ghaib*, Discourse no. 50.

58. Ibid., no. 55.

59. Ibid., no. 57.

is always either in the state of calamity or in that of blessing. He says, "Your condition must be either of the following two. It will be either a state of calamity or of blessing, so if it be a state of calamity you should ask therein for patience. . . . And if it be a state of blessing you should ask in it thankfulnes on account of it."[60]

At another place the Shaikh opines that when a believer persists in a spiritual struggle, Allāh gives him what He has guaranteed him. He explains, "So when a believer persists in a spiritual struggle like this, up to the point of the coming of death and meets his Lord with a drawn sword besmeared with the blood of his *nafs* (self) and his desires, He gives him what He has guaranteed him of the paradise in His words.[61] And as for him who fears to stand before his Lord and forbids the soul from low desires then surely the garden is his abode."[62]

Worldliness and its Fate

The execessive accumulation of worldly objects, according to Jīlānī (Raḥ.'A) will take the form of poisonous animals in *ākhirah*. He regards all the wordly objects as idols and warns against one's forgetfulness about the Almighty Allāh and worshipping of various forms of idols. According to him, it is advisable to worship the Creator of idols so that idols will humble themselves to the believer. He elaborates:

"Woe Unto you! You are busy in accumulating one gold coin on the top of another, and your accumulation is endless. These will be scorpions and snakes that will bite you (in *ākhirah*)."[63]

---

60. Jīlānī, *Futūḥ al-Ghaib*, Discourse no. 59.
61. Ibid., no. 67.
62. Holy *Qur'ān*, LXXIX: 41.
63. Jīlānī, *Jila'ali Khaṭīr*, p. 157.

"This world is your idol, the Hereafter is your idol . . . lustful desires and pleasures are your idols . . . praise, commendation and people's acceptance of you are your idols. (Remember) everything other than Allāh is an idol!".[64]

He contines: "You have made your only concern to work hard and secure your alloted shares in this world and protect them. You have forgotten death and what lies beyond it. You have forgotten Allāh, changed Him, replaced Him and left Him behind your backs."[65]

"Every heart that is filled with things of this world, lustful desires and pleasures is a shell that is only suitable for the Fire. If you find inside your heart anything from this world, you should know that you will be punished."[66]

"If you glorify the tyrants of this world, its Pharaohs, its kings and its rich, yet forget Allāh and do not glorify Him, the verdict on you will be the verdict passed on the worshippers of idols . . . worship the Creator of the idols and then the idols will humble themselves to you."[67]

The Shaikh (Raḥ.'A) explains the transitoriness of the world in different ways and asks to be in it with renouncing hearts. While comparing believers with hypocrites he says that hypocrites are slaves of the creatures and objects of the world while the believers are always with their Lord. His perception of the world is that it seeks anyone who runs away from her. He maintains:

"You earn, instead of religion, wordly status and you

64. Jīlānī, *Jila'ali Khaṭīr*, p. 158.
65. Ibid., p. 159.
66. Ibid., p. 163.
67. Ibid., p. 164.

amass rents, gold coins, clothes, houses, maidservants, horses and servants. All these things will soon be separated from you. Turn back to your Lord."[68]

"Be in this world with renouncing hearts. Do not settle in it. . . . This abode is the prison of the believer in comparison with the abode of the Hereafter."[69]

"The hypocrites are slaves of creatures . . . slaves of the might, strength, and earnings and slaves of the rich, kings and *sulṭāns* . . . the believers are always with their Lord."[70]

"O Seekers of this world, as long as you are seeking her, you will remain in tiredness! She seeks anyone who runs away from her."[71]

"O people, pay heed to my words and renounce this world for your desire and your love of it screen you from the Hereafter and from nearness of your Lord and blind your hearts."[72]

The Shaikh holds that sorrows, griefs, fear and apprehension in the heart of a person are the consequences of worldliness. He says "But so long as there remains in his heart any attraction for this world, sorrows and griefs and fear and apprehensions will have a standing abode in his heart and abasement will be a necessary concomitant for him as also the state of being veiled from Allāh, the Mighty, the Glorious, and from His nearness, by a veil thick in several folds."[73]

---

68. Jīlānī, *Jila'ali Khaṭīr*, p. 165.
69. Ibid., pp. 165-66.
70. Ibid., p. 167.
71. Ibid., p. 168
72. Ibid., p. 169.
73. Jīlānī, *Futūḥ al-Ghaib*, Discourse no. 54.

In his another discourse Jīlānī (Raḥ.'A) says that Allāh does not lessen the (worldly) wealth even if one turns indifferent towards it provided he is obedient to Allāh. He says, "And if you engage yourself with obedience to Him (Allāh) and become indifferent towards the wealth, Allāh will make a free gift of it to you and will not lessen it even by an atom."[74]

The Shaikh regards the worldly life as a cultivation ground of the life Hereafter. Good deeds, according to him, consist in observing the patience and reconcilement in the midst of trial. He affirms; "the worldly life is a cultivation ground of the life Hereafter and the good deeds of the Prophets and *awliyā* (pious people) after the performance of commandments and prohibitions consist in patience and pleasure and reconcilement in the midst of trial."[75]

Worldliness, according to Jīlānī (Raḥ.'A), spoils a seeker's heart the way the acid spoils honey. He warns, "Do not be a seeker of the world and do not be angry for not getting some share of it, because it will spoil your heart the way an acid spoils the honey."[76]

The world, according to the Shaikh (Raḥ.'A) remains in a bow position in front of the true believers. He advises a seeker to kill the ill desires of his *nafs* (self) with the sword of *tawḥīd*. He maintains "You are running after the world to get some share of it and the world is running after the true believers so as to give some share to them. It remains in a bow position in front of them. Kill (the ill desires of) your *nafs* (self) with the sword of *tawḥīd*. Carry cloth of *tawfīq* (generosity), arrow of *mujāhadah* (self mortification), shield of *taqwā* (piety), and

---

74. Jīlānī, *Futūḥ al-Ghaib*, Discourse no. 12.

75. Ibid., no. 71.

76. Jīlānī, *Fatḥ-i-Rubbāni*, Discourse no. 56.

sword of belief to fight against it."[77]

Jīlānī (Raḥ.'A) neither asks to give up the worldly pleasures in total nor does he preach monasticism. He emphasizes in his sermons that worldly things should be made use of by a man to the extent of need but he should never allow himself to become subservient to his desires and temptations. Explaining the purport of the *ḥadīth* (Tradition) which runs, "verily, the world has been created for you, and you have been created for the Hereafter," Jīlānī (R.'A.) affirms;

"Do not try to obtain your share of the worldly gifts in a way that you have to keep standing before it like a beggar. You ought to be like a sovereign who keeps himself seated while the gifts are presented before him. This world acclaims those who stand and wait at the door of God Almighty but it demeans those who wait upon it. Thereafter, get your share of the worldly benefits without demeaning yourself or compromising your dignity, and this is what Allāh expects of preachers (true believers)."[78]

In another sermon he says: "It is perfectly lawful to lay hands on the world and its gifts, to possess it or even to accumulate it for a commendable purpose, but it is forbidden to set your heart upon it. You may allow it to stand at the door of your heart but it is prohibited to allow it to get inside the door, for it shall not bring any honour to you."[79]

Jīlānī (Raḥ.'A) regards decorations, vanities and snares of the world as a fatal poison which is soft exteriorly and whose inside is injurious. He adds that the poison of the world keeps

77. Jīlānī, *Fatḥ-i-Rubbāni*, Discourse no. 62.

78. JIbid., no. 21.

79. Ibid., no. 51.

people indifferent towards its evils and treacheries and breaches of promises. He says, "Its (world's) fatal poison of which the outside is soft to touch and the inside injurious . . . and keeps them indifferent towards its evils and treacheries and breaches of promises."[80]

He advises a true believer to turn away his sight from world's tinsels and close his nose against the foul smell of its sensualities and gross enjoyments. He gives its logic/wisdom in these words, "So that you may remain safe from its trials."[81] In this connection he quotes the following verse from the Holy *Qur'ān*, "And do not cast your look of greed on what we have given to certain classes of men to enjoy the splendour of this world's life, that we may thereby try them and the sustenance given by your Lord is better and more abiding."[82]

Love of Allāh

Shaikh 'Abdu'l Qādir Jīlānī (Raḥ.'A) holds that the heart of a believer should be filled with the love of Allāh alone and one should purify his heart of all the things other than Allāh. This enables a person to see gold and clay as equal. As an effect of it one loses his own will. The Shaikh shows his surprise to see a believer who claims that he loves Allāh but does not obey Him. He affirms:

". . . You do not have two hearts, but it is a single heart; once filled with something, there will be no room for another. Allāh has said: 'Allāh has not made for any man two hearts within his body.'[83] A heart that loves the Creator and a heart

80. Jīlānī, *Futūḥ al-Ghaib*, Discourse no. 5.
81. Ibid.
82. Holy Qur'ān, XX: 131.
83. Ibid. (XXXIII: 4) ماجعل الله لرجل من قلبين فى جوفه

that loves creatures."[84]

"The lover becomes the beloved once he has purified his heart of anything other than Allāh that he would not wish to leave Him for the sake of anyone else."[85]

". . . The person whose heart becomes sound and attached to his Lord will see as equal: gold and clay, praise and blame, sickness and good health, affluence and poverty, good fortune and bad fortune in this world. . . ."[86]

"The Lovers feel no rest in their hearts even if they enter a million paradises until they see their Beloved. They do not wish for a created thing but they wish for the Creator[87] . . . when someone loves Allāh he loses his will because the lover can have no will above the will of his Beloved.[88] . . . Woe unto you! You claim that you love Allāh, yet you do not obey Him! The love of Allāh comes about only after observing the commandment, refraining from the prohibitions, being satisfied with whatever one gets and being content with the divine decree."[89]

Jīlānī (Raḥ.'A) maintains that the lovers choose Allāh in preference to His creatures because they see the blessings that as having come from Him and not from anyone else. He regards that a false claim will be a cause for one's destruction. Love for Allāh and other than Him can't be stored in the same

---

84. Jīlānī, *Jila'ali Khaṭīr*, Eng. tr., Setha al-Dargazelli and Louoy Fatoohi, p. 21.
85. Ibid., p. 22.
86. Ibid., p. 23.
87. Ibid.
88. Ibid., p. 24.
89. Ibid., p. 25.

heart. He explains it in these words: "The lovers choose Allāh in preference to His creatures. They see the blessings that as having come from Him not from anyone else. They recognize His subtle favours, His preparations for them and His rewards for them so they love Him . . . they abandon bed and blankets, sleep and rest."[90]

Then he quotes this verse, "Their sides shun their beds."[91] The Shaikh further eleborates in these words; "Woe unto you! you claim to love Allāh yet, in fact, you love other than Him! Your claim will be a cause for your destruction. He (the lover) has a special language and special speech. He does not wish for anything in addition to his Beloved, which is one of the greatest signs of his truthfulness."[92]

"Love for Allāh and other than Allāh cannot be stored in the same heart . . . world and *ākhirah* and Creator and creatures cannot have the same abode."[93]

Criteria for Love and Hatred

In one of his discourses, the Shaikh opines that the criteria for love and hatred should be *Qur'ān* and *Sunnah*. He advises, ". . . If one happens to be dearer to these two authorities (*Qur'ān* and *Sunnah*) you should love him, but if they are hateful to him you should hate him. . . ."[94] He subscribes to this fact that one's safety lies in strictly adhering to the injunctions to the *Qur'ān* and the *Sunnah* of Prophet

90. Jīlānī, *Jila'ali Khaṭīr*. Eng. tr., Setha al-Dargazelli and Louoy Fatoohi p. 21.
91. Holy Qur'ān, XXXII: 16. تتجافى جنوبهم عن المضاجع
92. Jīlānī, *Jila'ali Khaṭīr*, p.28.
93. Jīlānī, *Fath-i-Rubbānī*, Discourse no. 24, also cf. Discourse no. 59.
94. Ibid., Discourse no. 31.

Muḥammad (SAW). He preaches, "And safety lies in the Book of Allāh and the practice of the holy Prophet (SAW), and destruction in what is besides them and with the help of these two (*Qur'ān* and *Sunnah*) the servant of Allāh gets promoted towards the state of *wilāyat, badaliyyat* and *ghawthiyyat*."[95]

He regards the obedience to Allāh as the primary thing under which other things should come. He says; Make obedience to Allāh the primary thing under which every other thing should come and make it the guiding factor and make whatever is besides this as of secondary and subordinate consideration."[96]

Striving against the Lower Self

The Shaikh (Raḥ.'A) while commenting on this theme says that one should clean both his clothes (of dirt) and heart (of sins). To create a barrier between oneself and lustful desires one should keep the grave and death in view. The seeker of success, according to him, must teach his lower-self the self-renunciation. He affirms:

"Do not occupy yourself with washing the clothes of your body yet leave the clothes of your heart dirty . . . combine both acts of washing, both acts of purification. Wash your clothes clean of dirt and wash your heart clean of sins."[97]

". . . Stick to the door of His mercy, build a barrier of iron between yourself and the lustful desires, keep the grave and death under the eyes of your head and your heart. . . ."[98]

---

95. Jīlānī, *Fath-i-Rubbānī*, Discourse no. 36.
96. Ibid., no. 59.
97. Jīlānī, *Jila'ali Khaṭīr*, p. 62.
98. Ibid.

"The person who seeks success must exhort his lower self, teach it renunciation and strive against it."[99]

"Give up the lustful desires, for in this lies healing and pure serenity of the hearts. Gratifying the desire to unlawful things blinds and intoxicates the heart, so what is the benefit of satisfying the desire to unlawful things?"[100]

The Shaikh (Raḥ.'A) treats purification of heart as an obligatory duty. The lower-self being ignorant, needs proper education, training and discipline. He compares it with an unruly horse. He holds:

"Work on purifying your heart first, for this is an obligatory duty, and then move to the acquisition of knowingness. Because if you miss the root, your engrossment in the branch would not be accepted of you."[101]

"The lower-self is ignorant, so educate it. It lacks polite behaviour, so teach it that. It is unable to distinguish between the disease and the medicine, between what is lawful and what is unlawful and between what mends and what ruins. It keeps on disputing with its Lord."[102]

"O people acquire faith and strike your lowerselves with the stick of striving. Hand it over to the trainer of faith. It is an unreliable horse. Your lower selves are untamed, untrained and full of ignorance and pride."[103]

"The believer must strive against his lower self in order

---

99. Jīlānī, *Jila'ali Khaṭīr*, p. 63.
100. Ibid., p. 64.
101. Ibid.
102. Ibid., p. 68.
103. Ibid., p. 69.

to improve his behaviour and force it to adhere to good manners."[104]

The Shaikh (Raḥ.'A) exclaims how one could wish for nearness to Allāh when he is inclined towards lustful desires and pleasures. He advises to fight against *nafs* (self), whims and the will in the hope of *nuṣrat* (victory) from Allāh which is then sure to come. He affirms:

"Make it binding on your lower selves to behave with humility towards Allāh and the believers among His creatures."[105]

". . . How could you wish for nearness to Allāh when prohibited things have infiltrated your body through your food and drink, when your lower self is in control of you, when your passion is guiding you, when you are inclined towards lustful desires and pleasures. . . ."[106]

". . . Do not forget your commitment. Fight against your *nafs* (self), your whims, devil, your will and your world and don't lose hope so far as His *nuṣrat* (victory) is concerned because that is due to come to your rescue."[107]

In his discourses Jīlānī (Raḥ.'A) warns about the ill effects of the *nafs* (self). He holds, ". . . *nafs* (self) of man entertains presumptions wherefrom arise false hopes and passions and sensual pleasure."[108] In the same sermon he says that *khaer* (good) lies in fighting against one's own *nafs* (self) in all conditions. He speaks, ". . . all good lies in fighting one's self

104. Jīlānī, *Jila'ali Khaṭīr*, p. 69.

105. Ibid., pp. 69-70.

106. Jīlānī, *Jila'ali Khaṭīr*, p. 73.

107. Jīlānī, *Fath-i-Rubbānī*, Discourse no. 11.

108. Jīlānī, *Futūḥ al-Ghaib*, Discourse no. 10.

in everything and in all conditions of life."[109] In order to make one understand the wisdom of disobeying one's low desires of *nafs* (self) he quotes this verse of holy *Qur'ān*: ". . . Do not follow your low desires because they will lead you astray from the path of Allāh. . . ."[110]

Shaikh correlates the state of reality with the state of *wilāyat* (saintliness) and he advises to retain this state by way of opposing one's passions (of *nafs*) and obeying the commandments of Allāh. He comments in these words: "And if you are in the state of reality and it is the state of *wilāyat* (saintliness), then stand opposed to your passions and obey the commandments (of Allāh) fully."[111] While elaborating his precise statement, Shaikh adds, "An obedience to commandments (of Allāh) is of two kinds. One is that you should take from world the means of subsistence to the extent of the just demands of yourself and that you should avoid indulging in sensual pleasures and sins, open and secret. And the second kind relates to the hidden commandments."[112]

Treating attainment of different states of spirituality as a consequence of striving against the lower self, the Shaikh (Raḥ.'A) asserts: "And where there is not (even) this hidden commandment, and is just an act of Allāh, it entails a state of resignation. And if you have attained the realization of Truth which is otherwise called the state of *mahw* (immersion) or *fanā* (annihilation), it is the state of *abdāl* — who are broken-hearted on account of Him, a state belonging to pure

109. Jīlānī, *Futūḥ al-Ghaib*, Discourse no. 10.
110. Holy Qur'ān, XXXVIII: 26.
111. Jīlānī, *Futūḥ al-Ghaib*, Discourse no. 10.
112. Idem.

monotheists, to men of spiritual enlightenment, to men of knowledge and (higher) intelligence.[113]

Refuge of the Broken-hearted

In the time of Jīlānī (Raḥ.'A) the Muslim society could be broadly divided into two classes. The first of these comprised the men of substance who were deficient in faith and virtuous behaviour. As against this, there was another class, poverty-stricken and downtrodden, but endowed with faith and a spirit of righteousness, moral strength and uprightness. These people, sometimes, feeling disconcerted and broken-hearted, viewed the affluent with jealousy and mistrust, and regarded themselves as discarded and deprived. Jīlānī (Raḥ.'A) holds out hope and cheer to these poeple in one of his sermons. He preaches:

"O empty-handed beggarly fellows, the world would appear to be at loggerheads with you; you are barefooted, unclothed and unfed, broken-hearted and ill-starred, evicted from every place and deprived of your longings and fancies. But do not say that Allāh has reduced you to poverty, turned the world against you, abandoned, maligned or persecuted you, did not assign the portion of earthly pleasures due to you, or did not bestow honour and fame upon you. Nor it is proper for you to complain that Allāh has granted his favours to others, made them reputed and honoured, although they belong to the same faith as you do and are the progeny of Adam and Eve like you." The Shaikh (Raḥ.'A) adds:

"It is really so because you are like fertile land on which Allāh is sending down the rains consisting of endurance and resignation, conviction and faith, knowledge and grace. The

113. Jīlānī, *Futūḥ al-Ghaib*, Discourse no. 10.

tree of your faith is taking roots, sprouting forth its branches, its shade closing over you, pushing out new shoots and fruits, getting higher and bigger without your providing any fertilizer to it. Allāh Almighty knows what you really need. He has, therefore, assigned a befitting place for you in the Hereafter. He has made you a lord in the life-to-come where His bounties are countless, inconceivable and unheard of. As Allāh has said, nobody knows what delights have been stored for your eyes in the Paradise. This shall be your recompense for the faithful performance of what has been enjoined unto you, and your endurance, resignation and submission to the will of Allāh."

Jīlānī (Raḥ.'A) continues: "As for those who have been well-afforded in this world, they have been placed in easy circumstances for they are like a barren land, rocky and sandy, which neither stores nor absorbs the rains, and it is difficult to implant the tree of faith in it. It has, therefore, to be provided with fertilizers so that the weak saplings of their faith may get nourishment and push out the shoots of righteous action. Thus, if the wealth, honour and fame are taken away from them, the tree of their faith shall waste away and its leaves and fruits shall wither although Allāh intends to make it strong. Therefore, my poor brethren, you ought to know that the faith of the wealthy does not have deeper roots, it lacks that strength which has been endowed to you, and it needs the riches and earthly prizes for its nourishment. If these gifts were to be taken away from them, their faith will give place to blasphemy and they shall join the ranks of infidels, apostates and hypocrites, unless, of course, Allāh bestows on them spiritual light and enlightenment, endurance and resignation to strengthen their faith."[114]

---

114. Jīlānī, *Futūḥ al-Ghaib*, Discourse no. 25.

The Shaikh (Murshid/Preceptor) and the Murīd (Novice) Relationship

Jīlānī (Raḥ.'A) explains the purpose of having *murshid* (preceptor) in these words, "with everyone among the prophets and the *awliyā* (saints) of Allāh is to be found a secret which cannot be known by any other person . . . and sometimes the Shaikh holds a secret which is not known to the *murīd* (novice) . . . when the *murīd* reaches the spiritual state of the Shaikh, he is made to separate himself from the Shaikh . . . the Shaikh is needed by him (*murīd*) so long as he is infested with low desires and purposes which have to be crushed."[115]

'Abdu'l Qādir (Raḥ.'A) also prescribes certain conditions for a devotee before his inclusion in the company of spiritual beings. He says, "Do not expect to be included in the company of spiritual people unless you have become an enemy of your whole self and have become absolutely separated from all the organs of your body and all your limbs and have cut off all your connections with your existence, with your movements and restful conditions, with your hearing and seeing, with your speaking and holding, with your effort and action, with your action and your intelligence and with everything that proceeds from you before your spiritual existence comes into being in you, and that will be found in you after the spiritual existence is breathed into you because all these things constitute a screen between you and your Lord."[116] In his another discourse Jīlānī (Raḥ.'A) comments on the company of the Shaikhs in these words, "And you should keep company with the *dervish*es (saints) with humility and good manners and kill your self till you regain your life in spirituality."[117]

115. Jīlānī, *Futūḥ al-Ghaib*, Discourse no. 17.
116. Ibid., no. 40.
117. Ibid., no. 76.

Dervish (saint), according to Jīlānī (Raḥ.'A), is he who is indifferent to everything besides Allāh.[118] He also advises a *walī* (saint) to keep on remembering Allāh in all conditions and to adhere to the covenant of Allāh. He advises thus, "O *walī*! it devolves on you to keep on remembering Allāh in all conditions because it brings together all the good things and it is also your duty to adhere to the covenant of Allāh because it wards off all injurious things.[119]

Jīlānī (Raḥ.'A) opines that Shaikh's function is only temporary and that he becomes like a wet nurse who has stopped suckling the baby after two years of lactation period. The Shaikh is needed by him so long as he is infested with low desires and purposes which have to be crushed. But after the disappearance of these weaknesses of the flesh there remains no need of the Shaikh.

While commenting upon the desired qualification of the *murshid* (preceptor), Jīlānī (Raḥ.'A) also warns about the pretenders in these words: ". . . Beware of the person (pretender) who speaks about wisdom but does not act according to it, who has got a tongue, but no heart. He abhors defects in others but who himself persists in similar defects. He shows to others his piety but contends with Allāh by committing major sins. And when he is alone he is like a wolf in sheep's clothes. He is a person against whom the prophet (SAW) has also warned."[120]

Thus, Jīlānī's (Raḥ.'A) *taṣawwuf* is dynamic and not passive and self-deluding. His spiritual culture aimed at and led people

---

118. Jīlānī, *Futūḥ al-Ghaib*, Discourse no. 76.

119. Ibid.

120. Ibid., Discourse no. 17 and 33.

to noble deeds and righteous conduct in life and to rebel against all dishonest means and methods.

Behaviour in the Company of the Shaikh (Preceptor)

Jīlānī (Raḥ.'A) sets a criteria about the recognition of his true novice in these words:

"No one loves me but one who is knowledgeable of Allāh, given to much action and little talk. The sincere person loves me (the preceptor), while the hypocrite hates me. One who follows the *Sunnah*[121] loves me while one who follows false innovations[122] hates me."[123]

'Abdu'l Qādir (Raḥ.'A) in his discourses, points out the weaknesses of hermits, recluses, Ṣūfīs and novices and advises and guides them to live a life in conformity with Islam. He imparts guidance to them in these words:

". . . Woe unto you, the majority of you are in illusion, worshipping creatures in your cells . . . woe unto you! Walk in search of knowledge and knowledgeable persons until no further walking can be done."[124]

"Woe unto you! O you who associate creatures with Allāh! How often you knock on doors behind which there is none to answer you, and how often you knock on iron without fire."[125]

121. The Arabic word *sunnah* generally means "way," "method" or "law." Specifically *sunnah* refers to the behaviour of the Prophet Muḥammad (SAW), his sayings and doings.

122. The term "false innovations" (*bid'a*) refers to any idea or practice that is introduced into religion, yet it is not a genuine part of the religion.

123. Jīlānī, *Jila'alī Khaṭīr*, p. 1.

124. Ibid., p. 2.

125. Ibid., p. 3.

"When faith has become certitude, certitude has become knowingness, and knowingness has become knowledge, you will become an expert in distinguishing between the good and the bad in the service of Allāh."[126]

The Shaikh (Raḥ.'A) imparts further instructions on *murshid* (preceptor) and *murīd* (novice) relationship in these words:

"If you come to me here but do not put my teachings into practice you will only be a nuisance to the audience."[127]

"When the company of the seeker with the Shaikh has become sound, the Shaikh will feed and nourish him from his heart with the food of knowingness and its drink."[128]

"Refined behaviour is as much an obligatory duty on the part of knower as is repentance for a disobedient person . . . refined behaviour in the company of Allāh is essential."[129]

"O people, love your Lord and make His creatures recognize that He is worthy of all love. Love Him and guide the creatures to Him so that they join you in loving Him."[130]

"O you who waste your time in your houses and cells in the company of the lower self, natural inclination, passion and scarcity of knowledge! You have to accompany the Shaikhs who have to put their knowledge into practice. Obey them and follow their footsteps."[131]

The Shaikh comments upon the influence of *ṣuḥbat* (companionship) in these words:

---

126. Jīlānī, *Jila'ali Khaṭīr*, p. 1.
127. Ibid., p. 2.
128. Ibid., p. 4.
129. Ibid.
130. Ibid., p. 7.
131. Ibid., p. 8.

"Accompany the people of Allāh, for one of their attributes is that if they look at a person and direct towards him their spiritual influence they will love him even if the person they looked at was a Jew, Christian or Zoroastrian. And if he was a Muslim, his faith, his certitude and his steadfastness would increase."[132]

The 'Ilm (knowledge) of Saints and its Effects

The true believers (saints), according to 'Abdu'l Qādir (Raḥ.'A), possess the eye of the heart and the eye of the innermost besides the eye of the head. It is they who have understood this world and Hereafter properly. They put their knowledge into practice and act with sincerity. They are absolutely devoted to the goodness of the creatures, and the Creator (Allāh) supports them. He maintains:

"The (true) believer has three eyes; the eye of the head with which he looks at this world, the eye of the heart with which he looks at the Hereafter, and the eye of the innermost being which remains with the True one (Allāh) in this world and in the Hereafter because it is focused on Him in this world and in the Hereafter."[133]

"It is the people of Allāh who are those with sound reason. They have properly understood this world so they renounced it. Then they understood the Hereafter so they entered into it."[134]

"The people of Allāh (saints) have faith and belief and they put their knowledge into practice, act with sincerity and spend their money in the service of the righteous."[135]

---

132. Jīlānī, *Jila'ali Khaṭīr*, p. 11.

133. Ibid., pp. 84-85.

134. Ibid., p. 89.

135. Ibid., p. 97.

"The people of Allāh totally belong to the True One (Allāh). They are wholly devoted to the goodness of the creatures and the Creator (Allāh) supports them."[136]

The Shaikh (Raḥ.'A) says that when true believers respond to Allāh, He shows them the way to Him. The one who is content with Allāh to the exclusion of all creatures has really accomplished servitude. In fact, the saints have inherited the spiritual imprints of the Prophets. One who is not among the saints should render the service to them (saints). He affirms:

". . . When the believer hears the private conversation of the True one (Allāh), he responds to Him, wanders searching for Him and longs for Him. He awakens the hearts and shows them the way to Him."[137]

"The servant who has really accomplished servitude is he who is content with his Lord to the exclusion of all creatures, content with his spiritual state to the exclusion of the spiritual states of others and content with His Prophet (SAW) to the exclusion of all others."[138]

"The people of Allāh have inherited the inprints of the spiritual states and spiritual stations of the Prophets. They have also inherited the qualities and virtues that the Prophets possessed."[139]

"If you are not among the people of Allāh, serve them, accompany them, sit in their presence, draw near to them, make your money available for their use and follow them."[140]

---

136. Jīlānī, *Jila'ali Khaṭīr*, p. 98.
137. Ibid., p. 100.
138. Ibid., p. 101.
139. Ibid., p. 104.
140. Ibid., p. 106.

The Shaikh (Raḥ.'A) says that austerity is imposed on the lower selves of sincere people. One is rewarded according to his behaviour. He holds:

"As for those who are sincere in their belief in the oneness of Allāh, their cells are their hearts. Their austerity is imposed on their lower selves, passions and natural inclination."[141]

"If you learn for the sake of this world you will end up working for this world, and if you learn for the sake of the Hereafter you will end up working for the Hereafter. The branch is based on the root. You will be rewarded according to your behaviour. Every vessel exudes its own contents."[142]

Relation Between 'Ilm (Knowledge) and 'Amal (Practice)

Jīlānī (Raḥ.'A) advises to acquire knowledge and put it into practice. Mere memorization of knowledge will be an evidence against oneself. To him, knowledge is not goal in itself but the aim is its fruit. He forbids one to attend the lessons of such scholars who do not put their knowledge to practice. They are like laymen who, according to him, do not fear Allāh and have no hope in Him (Allāh). He maintains:

"Acquire knowledge for there is much good in it. Acquire knowledge and put it into practice in order to derive benefit from it. Knowledge is like the sword and action is like the hand."[143]

"How diverse your knowledge is, yet how few are your deeds! You have restricted your share of knowledge to memorizing and relating stories and narrations. It would not

141. Jīlānī, *Jila'ali Khaṭīr*, pp. 106-07.

142. Ibid., p. 108.

143. Ibid., p. 124.

benefit you at all to memorize certain utterances and not put a single letter of it into practice. This will be evidence against you and not in your favour."[144]

"O you who claim to possess what you do not have, you will sooner or later know the punishment for your claim! O learned scholars, O learners, knowledge is not in itself the goal but the aim is its fruit!"[145]

"Woe unto you! Do not attend the sessions of those scholars who do not put their knowledge into practice. . . . These scholars are like laymen in comparison to those who act on their knowledge. The scholar who does not put his knowledge into practice is a layman, even if he has memorized all kinds of knowledge. . . . Everybody who does not fear Allāh and does not have hope in Him is a layman."[146]

Conditions to Become Vessel of the Divine Knowledge

The Shaikh (Raḥ.'A) prescribes three conditions for a believer so as to be capable and competent to retain the knowledge of Allāh. He preaches, "Vanish from the people by the command of Allāh and from your desire by His order and from your will by His action, so that you may become fit to be the vessel of the knowledge of Allāh."[147] The Shaikh not only points towards the necessary conditions to hold the divine knowledge but he also explains the ways as to how to qualify for this job. He holds that sign of one's vanishing from the people is that he should make his mind free from all expectations for what is in the (people's) control. The sign of

---

144. Jīlānī, *Jila'ali Khaṭīr*, p. 128.
145. Ibid., p. 128.
146. Ibid., p. 132.
147. Jīlānī, *Futūḥ al-Ghaib*, Discourse no. 6.

one's vanishing from his desires, according to the Shaikh, is that he should entrust all the affairs to Allāh, because He (Allāh) had the charge of it in the beginning and so He (Allāh) would have it till the end. The sign of one's vanishing from his will by the action of Allāh is that he should never entertain any resolve and should not have any objective other than the one of Allāh and instead the action of Allāh will be manifested in him. He adds, "So Allāh the exalted will not be with you unless all your desires and will are smashed."[148]

In the same discourse Jīlānī (Raḥ.'A) comments that when a person is in the state of *fanā* (self annihilation), he will be in no expectation of any *khair* (good) from *makhlūq* (people), nor fear any evil from them. He affirms, "*fanā* is the aim and objective and the final base of the journey of the saints."[149] He holds that all the previous saints had been asking for persistent efforts for changing their will to the will of Allāh and that these personages regarded it a sin to associate their own will with the will of Allāh.

Fruits of Knowledge

A knowledgeable person, according to the Shaikh (Raḥ.'A), does not knock at the door of *sulṭāns* for worldly shares; instead he knocks at the door of Almighty Allāh. An ignorant person being blinded by his passions has no right to guide others. Jīlānī (Raḥ.'A) holds that a person whose actions do not conform to his claim, has no right to speak. He affirms:

"O knowledgeable person! If you were in possession of the fruit and blessing of knowledge you would not go to the doors of *sulṭāns* for seeking shares for your lower self and

148. Jīlānī, *Futūḥ al-Ghaib*, Discourse no. 06.

149. Ibid.

lustful desires. The knowledgeable person has no legs with which he goes to the doors of creatures and the ascetic has no hands with which he takes people's properties."[150]

"How can you guide others when you are blinded by your passion, your natural inclination and your pursuit of lower self, and your love for this world for your superiority and for lustful desires?"[151]

"If you borrow another person's words and utter them, pretending that they are your own, the hearts of the righteous people will hate you. If you do not have actions that match these words, you do not have the right to speak. Apparently, the matter is wholly about action."[152]

Not to Complain Against Allāh

Shaikh 'Abdu'l Qādir (Raḥ.'A) advises that one should never complain against Allāh even if one's flesh be cut into pieces by means of scissors. He shows his concern in these words: ". . . You should never complain about any mishap . . . you should rather give publicity to what good happens to be with you."[153] He quotes a verse from the *Qur'ān* in this regard, ". . . And if you count the blessings of Allāh you will not be able to enumerate them. . . ."[154] He adds, "Therefore, beware of complaint with utmost effort even if your flesh be cut into pieces by means of scissors. Save yourself! Fear Allāh! Fear Allāh! Fear Allāh! Make good your escape! Make good your

---

150. Jīlānī, *Jila'al Khaṭīr*, p. 174.
151. Ibid., p. 175.
152. Ibid., p. 176.
153. Jīlānī, *Futūḥ al-Ghaib*, Discourse no. 18.
154. Holy Qur'ān, XIV: 34.

escape! Beware! Beware![155]

The Shaikh (Raḥ.'A) holds that one should not be angry with Allāh and should not attempt to find fault with Allāh because for every course of events there is an appointed time and for every calamity there is a point of consummation. Neither it can be made earlier nor deferred. Instead, one should stick to silence, patience and cheerful submission and reconcilement with Allāh. Jīlānī (Raḥ.'A) asserts that Allāh does not do anything without any meaning and that He does not create anything without any purpose and in a playful manner. He advises that one should not ask for a thing untimely. The least of one's spiritual state should be remembering Allāh, adhering strictly to one's faith in His unity while asking anything from Him and that one should not ask from anybody else and not carry one's need to anybody excepting Allāh.[156]

The Shaikh gives observation about a believer that, at all times, during night or day, in health or illness, in adversity or prosperity, in difficulty or ease, a believer either refrains from asking and remains satisfied and reconciled and surrendered to the act of Allāh like a dead body or he supplicates before Allāh with prayer, and humble entreaties regarding Him as great, and being obedient to His orders.[157]

In his another discourse Jīlānī (Raḥ.'A) regards that blaming Allāh leads to *kufr* (unbelief) and one should rather be at war with his own self for the sake of Allāh. He remarks:

---

155. Jīlānī; *Futūḥ al-Ghaib*, Discourse no. 18. He also quotes a *ḥadīth* in this connection. "Allāh is more merciful towards His servants than a mother is towards her son."

156. Jīlānī, *Futūḥ al-Ghaib*, Discourse no. 34.

157. Ibid.

"And if you are blaming Him (Allāh) in this matter, you are an unbeliever on account of your finding fault with Him because thereby you are ascribing to Him injustice whereas He is not unjust to His servants . . . and if it is unavoidable that you should blame and be lacking in confidence at all cost, then to blame your ownself which by its very nature commands evil and disobedience to its Lord. . . . Be at war with your ownself for the sake of Allāh."[158]

No Argument with Allāh

"Argument with Allāh about one's *taqdīr* (destiny)," according to Jīlānī (Raḥ.'A), "is death of basic requirements of faith. He affirms, "Argument with Allāh, when one's *taqdīr* (destiny) is framed is death of religion, *tawḥīd* (oneness of Allāh), *tawwakul* (trust), and *ikhlāṣ* (sincerity)."[159]

"If you want to win the pleasure of Allāh then be absorbed in obeying Him, observing patience and being satisfied with your *taqdīr* (destiny).[160]

"Woe unto you! Do not be an idiot, disputing with Allāh and arguing with Him with your foolishness and your ignorance. . . . You behave with impudence with Allāh for the sake of your own benefit."[161]

Critique of the Kings

The Shaikh did not admonish and sermonize the populace alone; he boldly denounced such actions and policies of the officials, nobles and kings which were not in conformity with

---

158. Jīlānī, *Futūḥ al-Ghaib*, Discourse no. 65.
159. Jīlānī, *Fath-i-Rubbānī*, Majlis no. 1.
160. Ibid.
161. Jīlānī, *Jila'ali Khaṭīr*, p. 32.

the *sharī'ah*. Without the slightest consideration of their power and position, he bitterly criticized the misdeeds of the great ones. Hafiz 'Imām ud-din ibn Kaṯhir, a historian of his time, mentions this approach of Jīlānī in these words:

"He admonished all — the caliphs, viziers, kings, jurists, elīte and the laity — to adopt the righteous course and to forsake the things forbidden. He openly criticized, unsparingly, everyone to his face in his discourse.

"He used to denouce the authorities sternly if any tyrant was appointed to a public office by them. He never cared for anyone if he saw the commandments of God being overstepped."[162]

Ibn Kathīr writes that when Abu'l Wafa' Yaḥyā, a man notorious for his cruelty, was appointed as Qāḍī by the Caliph al-Muqtafi l'Amr Illah, 'Abdu'l Qādir (Raḥ.'A) admonished the caliph in these words:

"You have appointed a man notorious as the "most tyrant" to rule over the Muslims. What would your answer be tomorrow on the Day of Judgement, before the Lord of the Worlds, the Most Merciful?"[163]

Ibn Kathīr says that when the caliph came to know of the admonition of Jīlānī he burst into tears and without any delay dismissed Abū'l Wafā Yaḥyā from his office.

Jīlānī (Raḥ.'A) vigorously condemns this-worldliness of those saints, jurists and scholars who were prepared to accept an office or encouraged the rulers. He holds this class responsible for the waywardness of the rulers. In one of his addresses he rebukes these people thus:

162. Ibn Kathir, *al-Bidaya wa an Nihāya*, vol. XII, p. 252.

163. Ibid.

"Ah, you are the fellows who have misused the knowledge and wisdom. What have you to do with your predecessors? You are enemies of Allāh and His Apostle; you are no less than the robbers, tyrants and hypocrites! How long will you persist in your pious fraud? How long will you continue to don this shroud of assumed piety for the sake of your kings and rulers? How long will you remain a slave of power and position, passions and desires? Verily, you and most of your kings are tyrants and traitors unto God and his bondsmen. O! God, our Lord, either degrade these transgressors and humiliate them or make them repent for their sins; either mortify the tyrants and efface them from Thy earth or let them mend their ways."[164]

On another occasion, Jīlānī (Raḥ.'A) addresses a religious scholar in these words:

"Are you not ashamed that your avarice has forced you to serve these tyrants and crave for the emoluments declared unlawful and prohibited by the *sharī'ah*! How long shall you hold on to your mean pursuits? The kingdom of the rulers to whom you are playing a second fiddle shall shortly be no more and then you shall be presented before God Almighty who is Eternal, Omnipotent."[165]

The Deeds of Heart

The heart, according to the Shaikh (Raḥ.'A), differentiates between *ḥaqq* (truth) and *bāṭil* (falsehood) only when it acts in accordance with the Book (*Qur'ān*) and the *Sunnah* (the way of prophet SAW). The hardness of heart is among the signs of wretchedness of the servant. He holds:

---

164. Jīlānī, *Fatḥ-i-Rubbānī*, Discourse no. 51.

165. Ibid., no. 52.

"When the heart acts in accordance with the Book and the *Sunnah*, it will draw near. Once it has drawn close, it will come to know and see its credits and faults, what belongs to Allāh and what belongs to others, what belongs to the *ḥaqq* (truth) and what belongs to the *bāṭil* (falsehood)."[166]

"Among the signs of wretchedness of the servants is the hardness of the heart . . . the person with a hard heart does not show mercy towards anyone and his eyes never turn moist with tears in times of happiness or in times of sadness, for the dryness of his eyes is due to the hardness of his heart."[167]

Jīlānī (Raḥ.'A) says that the heart with the belief of oneness of Allāh keeps on growing bigger and higher till it sees none but Allāh. The soundness of heart is determined by its forgetfulness about all except Allāh. He elaborates:

"The heart inside which the belief in the oneness of Allāh has developed, keeps on growing bigger daily. As it grows bigger, greater and higher, it will no more see on the face of the earth and in heaven other than Allāh."[168]

The Shaikh (Raḥ.'A) adds:

"When the heart becomes sound, it forgets everything apart from the True one, the one whose existence has no beginning, the Perpetual one, the Eternal one . . . the heart will speak to the innermost being, the innermost being to the private life, the private life to the essence, the essence to the kernel, the kernel to the consciousness."[169]

---

166. Jīlānī, *Jila'ali Khaṭīr*, p. 79.
167. Ibid., p. 81.
168. Ibid., p. 82.
169. Ibid., p. 83.

Allāh Monopolizes the Heart of Believer

Jīlānī (Raḥ.'A) holds that Allāh monopolizes the heart of His servants for His ownself to the exclusion of all others. He says, "He (Allāh) destroys His partner and annihilates it in order to monopolize the heart of His servant for His ownself to the exclusion of all others. . . ."[170] He explains that if one has any wealth or children whom he loves, his love for His Lord becomes divided, then it becomes diminished and scattered, as it is distributed between Allāh and others, Allāh does not brook any partner. He is powerful over all things and predominant over all.

In one of his discourses the Shaikh (Raḥ.'A) preaches about the purging of one's heart of objects other than Allāh in these words, "Save yourself so that Allāh does not find anyone in your heart other than Himself. . . . Purge your heart of all that is other than Allāh. Don't attribute your gains and losses to anyone other than Allāh."[171]

Apprehensions of the Heart

'Abdu'l Qādir (Raḥ.'A) opines that there arise six types of apprehensions in the man's heart from six things[172] namely, *nafs* (self), *saṭān* (devil), *rūḥ* (soul), *firishta* (angels), *'aql* (sense) and *yaqīn* (belief).

One's *nafs* (self) motivates him towards his own whims and sexual urge . . . *saṭān* (devil) endangers faith and motivates towards *kufr* (infidelity) and *shirk* (polytheism) . . . common people are subjected to these two. . . . The dangers which arise on account of *rūḥ* (soul) and angels motivate towards

170. Jīlānī, *Futūḥ al-Ghaib*, Discourse no. 42.

171. Jīlānī, *Fath-i-Rubbānī*, Discourse no. 20.

172. Jīlānī, *Ghuniyāt at-Ṭālibīn*, pp. 670-72.

the obedience of Allāh. . . . Both of these are good in nature and never vanish from the hearts of selected people.

So far as the apprehension of *'aql* (sense) is concerned it sometimes leads to virtues and sometimes to vices. The apprehension of *yaqīn* (belief) is inevitable for the beloved ones of Allāh — those who are annihilated in His majesty and hidden from the people.[173]

Trials and Tests

Jīlānī (Raḥ.'A) holds that Allāh tries His believing servants in proportion to their faith and these trials are restrainers of hearts, and they strengthen the heart and certainty and establish the faith and patience. While elaborating his statements he comments, "It is a practice of Allāh to try His believing servant in proportion to his faith. . . . Everyone is tried according to his faith and certainty. . . . Allāh keeps the trials in continuance for these honourable leaders *Rasūl, Nabī, Abdāl Walī* according to their grade. . . . Trials are restrainers of their hearts and a kind of imprisonment for their souls. . . . Trials and calamity strengthen the heart and certainty and establish the faith and patience and weaken the animal self and its desire."[174] To substantiate his view, the Shaikh quotes this *ḥadīth*, "We prophets are beset with the greatest number of trials among people, then others and still others according to rank."[175]

While discussing the *ḥikma* (wisdom) behind the trials of man, the Shaikh comments: "And as for the trial of man — sometimes it comes as a punishment for any violation of law and any sin which has been committed; at others it comes

173. Jīlānī, *Ghuniyāt at-Ṭālibīn*, pp. 220-21.

174. Jīlānī, *Futūḥ al-Ghaib*, Discourse no. 22.

175. Ibid., no. 27.

with the object of removing the defects and refining the nature of man, and at still others it comes to raise a man in spiritual rank and to take him to higher stages where he may join the people of spiritual knowledge who have experience of different states and positions."[176]

When Allāh, according to the Shaikh (Raḥ.'A) selects a person for His own purpose, He, Almighty subjects him to trials and tests. He affirms: ". . . when Allāh wishes to choose and select a believer for His own purpose, He makes him pass through various spiritual conditions and tries him with various kinds of struggles and calamities."[177]

Jīlānī (Raḥ.'A) opines that at the time of calamity when it befalls upon a believer, he should protect his heart from being inclined towards the worldly interests and should behave like a dead body in front of a man who gives it a funeral bath. He explains it as:

"And protect your heart from being inclined towards what you have renounced of people and desires and wishes and option and effort and from losing patience and harmony and pleasure with Allāh at the time of the befalling of calamity, but throw yourself before Him in the manner of a ball before a polo-player who makes it to revive by his stick or like a dead body in front of a man who gives it a funeral bath or like a sucking baby in the lap of mother or nurse."[178]

Again, while commenting upon the *ḥikma* (wisdom) behind the trials and tests to which believers are subjected, the Shaikh (Raḥ.'A) maintains:

---

176. Jīlānī, *Futūḥ al-Ghaib*, Discourse no. 45.
177. Jīlānī, *Futūḥ al-Ghaib*, Discourse no. 46.
178. Ibid., no. 50.

"Certainly Allāh tries a party from the believers who are His friends and who hold friendly relations with Him and spiritual knowledge in their possession in order that they may be turned, through the trial, towards prayer to Him and He loves to receive prayers from them."[179]

He adds, "Tests and trials are necessary especially upon those who claim (to be sincere believers). If there would have been no tests and trials then most people would have laid a claim for *wilāyat* (saintship)."[180]

Enduring Afflictions

Jīlānī (Raḥ.'A) advises that when affliction comes one's way he should receive it with faith, patience and submission. According to him nothing turns one away from the obedience to Allāh other than one's sins and ignorance. The wisdom behind tribulations and afflictions is that these cleanse the remnants of sins. He elaborates:

"A few individuals have on them remnants of sins of which they are cleansed by tribulations and afflictions which turn into degrees that they have in the Hereafter. You have to be satisfied with the divine decree, observe the law and perform righteous deeds under all circumstances."[181]

"Nothing turns you away from His obedience and from the belief in His oneness other than your sins, your ignorance and the ruinous state of your homes and your sanctuaries."[182]

"O young man, when affliction comes your way, receive

---

179. Jīlānī, *Futūḥ al-Ghaib*, Discourse no. 52.
180. Jīlānī, *Fatḥ-i-Rubbāni*, Discourse no. 53.
181. Jīlānī, *Jila'ali Khaṭīr*, p. 217.
182. Ibid., p. 218.

it with faith, patience, submission and a smile. . . !"[183]

"O young man, when Allāh causes you any harm or affliction, no one will be able to remove it except He."[184]

The Shaikh (Raḥ.'A) says that both imposing and removal of afflictions is in the hands of Allāh. Afflictions, according to him, guide to the door of Allāh and make faith, knowingness and knowledge to become apparent and also promote one's spiritual degrees. He affirms:

"Affliction and removal of affliction are both in the hands of Allāh. It is He who has sent down the disease and the remedy. He afflicts you with tribulations to make you come to know Him through affliction. . . ."[185]

"Afflictions show the way to the door of Allāh and knock on it. They bring the heart and the True one together. They promote the status."[186]

The Shaikh (Raḥ.'A) advises:

". . . Do not escape from affliction but endure it with patience."[187]

"The afflictions come to the hearts of truthful persons, salute them and intercede on their behalf."[188]

"Be patient with your Lord for He removes your affliction and promotes your spiritual degrees in His eyes as a reward

---

183. Jīlānī, *Jila'ali Khaṭīr*, p. 219.
184. Jīlānī, *Jila'ali Khaṭīr*, p. 220.
185. Ibid., p. 221.
186. Ibid.
187. Ibid., pp. 221-22
188. Ibid., p. 223.

for your patience."[189]

"He afflicts you with tribulations to see how you act."[190]

"Afflictions and tribulations make faith, knowingness and knowledge to become apparent."[191]

On Death

Man, according to Jīlānī (Raḥ.'A), should treat good health and leisure time as the blessings of Allāh and thereby utilize in the obedience to Allāh. Death can overtake any person unawares so everyone should be prepared for it, he adds. Remembering of death is remedy for disease of the lower self. He maintains:

"Use your good health and your leisure time in obedience to Allāh before the approach to you of an illness that spoils your good health and business that takes away your leisure time."[192]

"(Death) is watching you while you are unaware. You have forgotten to wait for it despite the fact that it is standing in front of you."[193]

"O people, die before you die. Die as far as your lowerselves and your wills are concerned. Remember death frequently and prepare for it before its arrival and then you will have died before you die."[194]

---

189. Ibid.
190. Jīlānī, *Jila'ali Khaṭīr*, p. 224.
191. Ibid., p. 226.
192. Ibid., p. 210.
193. Ibid., p. 211.
194. Ibid.

"The sensible among you is one who remembers death and is satisfied with whatever destiny brings . . . focus your reflection on matters related to your religion, instead of reflecting on lustful desires and pleasure. . . ."[195]

"Remembering death is remedy for the disease of the lower self and a benefit over its head."[196]

"O you who are in the company of their wordly goods and their great expectations! The appointed time of death will soon come and separate you from your hopes."[197]

The Shaikh (Raḥ.'A) advises to find faults with one's own self and not to find faults with others. He preaches:

"Preparing for that which lies after death is of concern to you, striving against your lower self is of concern to you, paying attention to your faults is of concern to you, but attending to the faults of other people does not concern you."[198]

Death Without Life and Life Without Death

One day a certain matter had kept Jīlānī's mind very disturbed. His inner self was agitated under its burden and was asking for ease and comfort and a way out. On being asked what he wanted, he said, "I want death which has life in it and a life which has no death in it." Then he explained his statement in these words; "The death that has no life in it is my death from my own species so that I do not see them either in benefit or in harm, and my death from my own self and my own desire and my own purpose and my own wishes in my worldly life

---

195. Jīlānī, *Jila'ali Khaṭīr*, p. 210.
196. Ibid.
197. Ibid., p. 212.
198. Ibid., p. 213.

as well as in my life after death, so much so that I do not live in any of these and am not found in them. And as for the life that has no death in it, it is my life with the act of my Lord in such a manner that I have no existence in it and my death in it is my existence with Him. Since I have attained understanding this has been the most precious of all purposes of mine."[199]

Fate of Following Desires / Fate of Violation

In one of his discourses Jīlānī (Raḥ.'A) preaches that negligence towards Allāh, *shirk* (polytheism) and sin are the consequences of following one's desires. He says, "And when the *nafs* (self) of the man moves the heart in search of any object of desire and any enjoyment, and the heart responds to this demand for the object and this without any command from Allāh, and His permission, the result is negligence towards Allāh, and polytheism and sin."[200]

The Shaikh (Raḥ.'A) warns the unbelievers, hypocrites and sinners, of the hell fire on account of their following their desires and associating themselves with *saṭān* (devil). He elaborates his statement as: "But as for the unbelievers, hypocrites and the sinners when they have left the struggle with their own selves and their desires in this world and made alliance with the devil and became mixed with the various kinds of sins of unbelief and polytheism and such like things till death comes to them without their having adopted Islam and repented, Allāh will make them enter the fire which is prepared for the unbelievers as is indicated in His words:"[201]

---

199. Jīlānī, *Futūḥ al-Ghaib*, Discourse no. 64.

200. Ibid., Discourse no. 22.

201. Ibid., Discourse no. 67.

". . . Then be on your guard against the fire of which man and the stones are the fuel; it is prepared for the unbeliever."[202]

Kinds of Men

Jīlānī (Raḥ.'A) classifies people into four divisions. The first group consists of those people, "who do not count with Allāh and who have nothing good in them." He compares them with chaff. He regards them as the people of chastisement and wrath and anger of Allāh and says that they are the inhabitants of fire and its inmates. Such people, according to Shaikh, have neither tongue nor heart.

The other kind of person, according to Jīlānī (Raḥ.'A) has got a tongue but no heart. Such a person speaks on wisdom but does not act according to it. He calls people to Allāh but himself flees from Him. He shows to others his piety and contends with Allāh by committing major sins. Jīlānī (Raḥ.'A) compares him with a wolf in sheep's clothing.

The third kind of man, according to Shaikh, has a heart but no tongue and he calls him a believer. This man is a friend of Allāh in His secrets, protected, possessing safety and plenty of intelligence, companion of the Beneficent Allāh, blessed with His favours and as for good, everything good is with him. Shaikh (Raḥ.'A) advises to keep company with such a man and mix with him and render him service and endear to him by fulfilling the needs which he may feel, and providing him with things which will give ease and comfort.

The fourth kind of man, Shaikh holds, is one who is invited to the world invisible and clothed in dignity. He is possessed of the knowledge of Allāh and His signs and his heart is made the repository of the rare things of His knowledge and He

202. Holy *Qur'ān*, II: 24.

intimates to him such secrets as He has kept hidden from others and He has selected him and drawn him towards Himself and guided him and raised him towards Himself and expanded his heart for the acceptance of these secrets and points of knowledge.

This man, Shaikh holds, is the end and culminating point of mankind and there is no station above this, excepting that of Prophethood.[203]

Jīlānī (Raḥ.'A) also classifies men of spirituality as *awliyā* and *abdāl.* While making a comparison of saints and *abdāl*, Shaikh (Raḥ.'A) says that the saints are protected from their worldly desires and the *abdāl* from the impurity of will. He holds, "of course, the saints are protected from their desires of the flesh and the *abdāl* from the impurity of will of motive."[204]

At another place he makes a difference between *awliyā* and *abdāl* in this way. "The *aḥwāl* (states of spiritual changes) belong to the *awliyā* (ordinary saints) whereas *maqāmāt* (stations of spiritual establishment) to *abdāl* (advanced saints)."[205]

Commenting upon the manifestation of acts Shaikh (Raḥ.'A) holds: "Such acts of Allāh are manifested to the *awliyā* and the *abdāl* in the course of *kashf* (spiritual vision) and *mushāhadah* (spiritual experience) and overwhelm the reasoning power of man and shatter into pieces all habits and customs."

Jīlānī (Raḥ.'A) classifies these manifestations into two types, in these words, "This manifestaion is of two kinds — one of them is called *jalāl* (majesty and glory), and the other *jamāl* (gracefulness)."[206]

203. Jīlānī, *Futūḥ al-Ghaib*, Discourse no. 33.

204. Ibid., Discourse no. 06.

205. Ibid.

206. Ibid.

Denouncing Nifāq (Hypocrisy)

Jīlānī (Raḥ.'A) holds that in order to denounce hypocrisy one should return to Islam and perform *tawbah* (repentance). The tongue of the hypocrite, according to him, is in front of his mind and heart while that of a believer is behind his mind and heart. He maintains that hypocrite's actions are totally dedicated to creatures and he undermines his relationships with the Creator. 'Abdu'l Qādir (Raḥ.'A) warns the hypocrites that they should do something (to return to Allāh) before death overtakes them suddenly.

He affirms:

"Woe unto you! Hypocrisy has become firmly stuck to your heart, so you need Islam, repentance and cutting the (disbeliever's) waistband (that you wear). Be sensible, you will see when the dust has cleared."[207]

"As for the hypocrite, he has a clever tongue and a clumsy heart. All his knowledge is in his tongue. This is why the Prophet (SAW) said, The most that I fear for my *ummah* is a hypocrite with a clever tongue."[208]

"It is the habit of the believers to reflect first and then speak, while the hypocrite speaks first and then reflects. The tongue of the believer is behind his mind and heart, while the tongue of the hypocrite is in front of his mind and heart."[209]

". . . O hypocrite! how many you are! your efforts are totally dedicated to cultivating your relationships with creatures and undermining your relationships with the Creator."[210]

---

207. Jīlānī, *Jila'ali Khaṭīr*, p. 177.
208. Ibid.
209. Ibid., p. 178.
210. Ibid.

"Do something before death surprises you, before you are overtaken suddenly and end up in regret when regret is of no good at all."[211]

Curses of (Ḥasd) Envying

Jīlānī (Raḥ.'A) holds that envying one's neighbours weakens his faith and causes him to fall in the eyes of his Master and makes him loathsome to Him. He quotes a saying of Prophet (SAW) in this regard, "Verily envy eats up the virtues as fire eats up the fuel." Addressing an envying person Jīlānī (Raḥ.'A) says, "Then who will be more unjust than yourself and the more miserly and more foolish and stupid? and if you envy him on account of your portion, then you have betrayed utmost of ignorance, because your portion will not be given to anybody else and will not be transferred from you to anybody else. Allāh is free from such injustice."[212]

The Shaikh (Raḥ.'A) warns about the ill effects of *ḥasd* (envying) in these words:

". . . Beware of envy for it is a bad companion. It was envy that wrecked the house of *Iblīs*, destroyed him, rendered him one of the people of the fire and made him cursed by Allāh. . . ."[213]

"How long will it be before you give up envying your brothers and hoping to obtain what they have? Woe unto you! you envy your Muslim brother for his wife, his children, his house and his worldly possessions, although all those are already created to be his and you have no share in them."[214]

---

211. Jīlānī, *Jila'ali Khaṭīr*, p. 182.

212. Jīlānī, *Futūḥ al-Ghaib*, Discourse no. 37.

213. Jīlānī, *Jila'ali Khaṭīr*, p. 206.

214. Ibid.

Nūr — Spiritual Light of the Believer

According to the Shaikh (Raḥ.'A), Allāh gives a special *nūr* (light) to a true believer after he masters the light of the knowledge. In fact, when someone puts his knowledge (of Truth) into practice both flint and fuel come to his heart. He affirms:

"The truthful person sees by the light of Allāh, not by the light of his eye nor by the light of the sun and the moon. This is the general light of Allāh and he is given a special light. Allāh has given him this light after mastering the second light of knowledge."[215]

"When someone acquires knowledge and puts it into practice with sincerity, both the flint and the fuel will come to be in his heart. In his heart will come the light of Allāh which he and others use for enlightenment."[216]

The Shaikh (Raḥ.'A) adds: "O Young man, when someone does righteous deeds, his deeds will become a light in front of him and a riding animal beneath him."[217]

"The real light is the light of the hearts and the real cleanness is the cleanness of the hearts."[218]

About Life Hereafter

According to Jīlānī (Raḥ.'A) the only real life is the life Hereafter. He holds, "When an intelligent man takes a critical view of the matter (i.e. reality of life), if of course he possesses a certain knowledge of reality, he will understand that there

215. Jīlānī, *Jila'ali Khaṭīr*, p. 151.

216. Ibid.

217. Ibid., p. 152.

218. Ibid.

is no real life excepting the life Hereafter."[219] He is, however, of the opinion that without the mercy of Allāh no one can enter the paradise. He states: ". . . No one will enter the paradise in the life Hereafter through his good deeds alone but by the mercy of Allāh."[220]

'Abdu'l Qādir (Raḥ.'A) regards the worldly life as a cultivation ground of the life Hereafter. He says, "The worldly life is a cultivation ground of the life Hereafter and the good deeds of the prophets and *awliyā* (saints) after the performance of commandments and prohibitions consist in patience and pleasure and reconcilement in the midst of trials."[221]

The Shaikh also advises that in order to succeed in both the worlds one should prefer life Hereafter to the worldly life. He affirms, "Prefer life Hereafter to the worldly life so that you succeed in both the worlds."[222]

Hope and Fear, Two Wings of a Bird

'Abdu'l Qādir (Raḥ.'A) in one of his sermons reveals that every spiritual state has fear and hope attached to it. He also warns that there are numerous chances of *shirk* (polytheism) in every state, step and station of a spiritual pilgrim. He affirms, ". . . There is no spiritual state nor any spiritual step nor any spiritual station but has fear and hope attached to it. These two are like two wings of a bird, but for which no flight can be perfect

---

219. Jīlānī, *Futūḥ al-Ghaib,* Discourse no. 17. Jīlānī (Raḥ.'A) quotes these two *Aḥādīth* to substantiate his statement. "There is no life excepting the life in the Hereafter." "The world is a prison for the believer and a heaven for the unbeliever."

220. Jīlānī, *Futūḥ al-Ghaib,* Discourse no. 68.

221. Ibid., no. 71.

222. Jīlānī, *Fatḥ-i-Rubbāni,* Discourse no. 13.

. . . and there are numerous chances of *shirk* (polytheism) in every state, step and station of a spiritual pilgrim."[223]

One is Either Seeker or the Object Sought For

'Abdu'l Qādir (Raḥ.'A) regards one either in the position of a seeker or one sought for. He maintains:

"You are either a seeker or the object sought for. If you are a seeker or a disciple you must be burdened and be a carrier of burden carrying everything difficult and heavy. . . . But if you are the thing sought for, then do not blame Allāh if He made a calamity befall you and you should by no means entertain doubt with regard to your position and rank with Him. . . ."[224]

About Sins

In one of his discourses 'Abdu'l Qādir (Raḥ.'A) regards that sins render the man unworthy of the company of Allāh. He elaborates: ". . . In the *nafs* (self) of man there are various kinds of sins and faults and blemishes on account of which he is unworthy of the company of Allāh, unless he becomes purged of impurities of sins."[225] He holds this view that one should prefer to ask from Allāh the forgiveness of sins. He explains, "Do not ask from Allāh, the Mighty, the Glorious, anything other than the forgiveness of past sins and protection from sins in the present and the future and the power of goodly obedience. . . ."[226]

---

223. Jīlānī, *Futūḥ al-Ghaib*, Discourse no. 44.

224. Ibid., Discourse no. 71.

225. Ibid., Discourse no. 18.

226. Ibid., Discourse no. 69.

Gratefulness

Jīlānī (Raḥ.'A) regards gratefulness towards Allāh as the best course and advises to ascribe one's all achievements to Allāh only. He says, "The best course for you is to give thanks and to praise the Helper (Allāh) and to praise Him continuously and to ascribe your achievements to Him in all conditions of your life unless it be the evil and sins and blames."[227] The Shaikh quotes this verse of holy *Qur'ān* to substantiate his viewpoint, "If you are grateful, I would certainly give you more and if you are ungrateful, My chastisement is truly severe."[228]

According to Shaikh (Raḥ.'A) the reality of *shukr* (gratefulness) lies in the fact that one accepts the One to whom he is grateful with full submission and loyalty. *Shukr* can be reciprocated by *shukr* only.

Shukr, according to Jīlānī (Raḥ.'A), can be expressed in three ways. It can be expressed by uttering the words of gratefulness through one's tongue, by admitting the blessings (of Allāh) with perfect submission, by fulfilment of commitment, worship, and obedience.[229]

On Truthfulness

The Shaikh (Raḥ.'A) holds that a person who is truthful in his belief with regard to the oneness of Allāh, never backslides on the advice of his lower self. He does not like to look at anyone other than his beloved (Allāh). The Shaikh (Raḥ.'A) affirms:

"O servants of Allāh, be truthful and then you will succeed! The truthful person never backslides. The person who is

227. Jīlānī, *Futūḥ al-Ghaib*, Discourse no. 70.
228. Holy *Qur'ān*, XIV: 7.
229. Jīlānī, *Ghuniyat ul Ṭālibin*, p. 681.

truthful in his belief in the oneness of Allāh never backslides on the advice of his lower self, his passion or his devil."[230]

"If the truthful person meets all creatures he would not like to look at anyone apart from his Beloved."[231]

A truthful person, according to Jīlānī (Raḥ.'A), plunges into dangers. He maintains, "The lover who is truthful in his love always plunges into dangers in the quest for his Beloved."[232]

Ṣabr (Patience)

Jīlānī (Raḥ.'A) advises to hold patience in these words, "You should thus hold your patience and oppose your desire and hold fast to the commandment of the Law."[233] The Shaikh regards patience as one of the trials and tests. He quotes this Qur'ānic verse to substantiate his statement, "And most certainly we will try you until we have known those among you who exert themselves hard and the patient and made your case manifest."[234] Jīlānī (Raḥ.'A) holds that at the time of calamity even if one becomes exhausted he should but exhibit patience. He says, "Exhibit patience at the time of calamity even if you become exhausted by patience."[235] The Shaikh quotes a Qur'ānic verse which reads:

"Fighting is enjoined on you and it is an object of dislike to you; and it may be that you dislike a thing while it is good

230. Jīlānī, *Jila'ali Khaṭīr*, p. 55.
231. Ibid.
232. Ibid.
233. Jīlānī, *Futūḥ al-Ghaib*, Discourse no. 11.
234. Holy *Qur'ān*, XLVII: 31.
235. Jīlānī, *Futūḥ al-Ghaib*, Discourse no. 18.

for you and it may be that you love a thing while it is bad for you, and Allāh knows and you do not know."[236]

Jīlānī (Raḥ.'A) quotes these verses of Holy *Qur'ān* to explain the different dimensions of patience.

"O you who believe, be patient and excel in patience and remain steadfast and be careful of your duty to Allāh."[237]

"Verily the patient will be given their reward without any measure."[238]

Jīlānī (Raḥ.'A) correlates patience with *tawwakul* (trust in Allāh) in these words, "And remain in your patience with those who trust in Allāh till the way out comes to you because Allāh has promised you sufficiency in His words."[239] Then, he quotes a Qur'ānic verse to substantiate his viewpoint. "And whoever trusts in Allāh, He is sufficient for him."[240]

'Abdu'l Qādir (Raḥ.'A) holds that *ṣabr* (patience) is the source of safety in this world and in the *ākhirah* (life Hereafter). It is also, according to him, the source of all virtues. He says, "The *ṣabr* (patience) is the source of all virtues and all kinds of safety in this world and in the *ākhirah* (life Hereafter) and through it the believer rises to the will of Allāh and then attains the state of merging in the acts of Allāh which is the state of *badaliyyat*."[241]

Patience, according to the Shaikh (Raḥ.'A), leads to many extraordinary experiences as in the case of Haḍrat Yūsuf (A.S.),

236. Holy *Qur'ān*, II: 216.
237. Ibid., III: 200.
238. Ibid., XXXIX: 10.
239. Jīlānī, *Futūḥ al-Ghaib*, Discourse no. 30.
240. Holy *Qur'ān*, LXV: 3.
241. Jīlānī, *Futūḥ al-Ghaib*, Discourse no. 30.

when he observed it. He maintains, "If you observe patience for the sake of Allāh you will come across through many extraordinary experiences. When Haḍrat Yūsuf (A.S.) exhibited extraordinary patience on being arrested, enslaved, imprisoned and humiliated for the sake of Allāh, he became the extolled and dignified one."[242]

Speaking about the effects of patience the Shaikh (Raḥ.'A) affirms, "If you wish to be a man of *taqwā* (piety) and absolute trust then exhibit patience as it is the basis of all virtues. When you stand sincere in your exhibition of patience you will achieve *qurbat* (nearness) to Allāh."[243]

In one of his discourses Jīlānī (Raḥ.'A) compares the patience and faith with head and body. He affirms, "How can you lay claim to faith when you have no patience? . . . If you do not have patience, then your faith is without head and hence its body is worthless."[244]

The Shaikh (Raḥ.'A) holds that *ṣabr* can be exemplified in three ways: "One for the sake of Allāh only. Here, one fulfils his duties towards Allāh and remains disassociated with the unlawful deeds. The second way is that one shows his contentment with his *taqdīr* (destiny). The third way is that one awaits the fulfilment of commitments on the part of Allāh with regard to means of livelihood, help and reciprocation in *ākhirah*."[245]

Fanā (Annihilation)

While explaining the state of *fanā* (annihilation) Jīlānī (Raḥ.'A)

242. Jīlānī, *Fatḥ-i-Rubbāni*, Discourse no. 38.

243. Ibid., Discourse no. 42.

244. Jīlānī, *Jila'ali Khaṭīr*, p. 48.

245. Jīlānī, *Ghuniyat ul-Ṭālibīn*, p. 683.

says, "When you are united with Allāh and you attain His nearness by His attraction and help, . . . so, this is the state of *fanā* (annihilation).[246] At another place he holds that adoption of Islam and then submission to the decree of Allāh leads to *fanā*. He explains it as, "O you man! the *fanā* (self-effacement) is to deny all creations and transform your nature into the nature of the angels. . . . If you want this stage you should adopt Islam and the submission to the decree of Allāh, and then acquire knowledge of Allāh and then realize Him and then exist in Him, and then you get such an existence that you wholly belong to Him."[247]

The wrong notion of *fanā* led to self-elation at the expense of social relationships and social obligations and developed a peculiar type of hallucination which makes even the meanest intellect fancy that he is the select and chosen by Allāh.

Let us examine the Shaikh's views on the subject. He says: "When you have become one with Allāh and you attain to His *qurbat* (nearness) by His attraction and help; the meaning of Union with Allāh is your going out of the creation, desire and purpose and becoming established in His action and His pleasure, without there being any more unity in you or through you in His creation unless it be with His order and action and command. So, that is the state of *fanā* (annihilation) by which is meant union with Allāh. But Union with Allāh the Mighty, the Glorious, is not like union with anything in His creation in an understandable and appointed manner."[248]

So, the state of *fanā* (annihilation), according to the Shaikh, is a conscious state, above excitement of the spiritual

246. Jīlānī, *Futūḥ al-Ghaib*, Discourse no. 17.

247. Ibid., Discourse no. 76.

248. Ibid., 55.

experience, when the person becomes a divine instrument and carries out Allāh's work. His ego is then completely surrendered to His purpose and he himself has no desires, no urges of his own. When he reaches that state, he absorbs himself in some work and takes to life's noble activities with a zest.

According to the Shaikh (Raḥ.'A), "There are four stages on this path (*fanā*): the first stage is that of the urges of nature and this is unlawful; the second is that of the law; and the third stage is that of inner commandment which is the state of *wilāyat* and discarding of desires. And the fourth stage is that of divine favour and this is the state of disappearance of purpose and of being the Divine objective and this is the state of *m'arifat* (gnosis) and of being possessed with the quality of righteousness."[249] That is the state of *fanā*. It can only manifest itself by the quality of man, by the quality of righteousness, by noble deeds and work.

Extent of Allāh's Mercy

'Abdu'l Qādir (Raḥ.'A) describes the extent of Allāh's mercy in these words, "Glory be to Him, how generous and merciful of Him! He ascribes the actions to them and says that their entry into paradise is on account of their deeds whereas these deeds owe their existence to His help and mercy."[250] The Shaikh then quotes a *ḥadīth* in this connection which reads as: "No one enters paradise on account of his deeds alone." Prophet (SAW) was asked "And even not you, O Prophet of Allāh!" He replied, "Yes, not even me unless Allāh covers me with His mercy."

---

249. Jīlānī, *Futūḥ al-Ghaib*, Discourse nos. 17, 33, 55.

250. Ibid., 28, 68.

Tawbah (Repentance/Return to Allāh)

Ṣūfīs are divided on the interpretation of the term *tawbah*. Some regard it as repentance while some others regard it رجوع الى الله (return to Allāh). The Shaikh (Raḥ.'A) treats *tawbah* both as repentance as well as return to Allāh. He holds, ". . . and do not delay repentance and return to Him (Allāh)."[251] In one of his sermons he regards it as the best of all the (*aḥwāl*) states. He affirms, ". . . the best of all states in a servant is the state of seeking protection and of turning to Allāh."[252]

Commenting about the *ḥikma* (wisdom) of *tawbah* (repentance) he holds that *tawbah* is acknowledgement of one's sin and fault and thereby reflecting the heritage from Ādam (A.S.).

Jīlānī (Raḥ.'A) regards *tawbah* as the root of every goodness due to which no righteous person abandons it under any circumstances. The reality of his *tawbah* lies in maintaining the commandments of Allāh in all one's affairs. He elaborates it in these words:

"The key to the fear of Allāh is *tawbah* and sticking to it is the key to the nearness to Allāh. *Tawbah* is the root and branch of every goodness, that is why the righteous persons never abandon it under any circumstances. . . .[253] If you keep to repentance and proper reflection you will give up all interests in worldly things and become occupied with those (which are) relevant to the Hereafter."[254]

"When will you repent, O black sliders, O disobedient

---

251. Cf. Holy *Qur'ān*, يا ايها الذين آمنو توبو الى الله توبة نصوحا LXVI:08.

252. Jīlānī, *Futūḥ al-Ghaib*, Discourse no. 7.

253. Jīlānī, *Jila'ali Khaṭīr*, p. 13.

254. Ibid., p. 16.

ones? Be reconciled with your Lord by means of *tawbah.*[255] . . . O disobedient ones, repent disobedience, for your Lord is forgiving, Merciful! He accepts repentance from His servants, covers their sins and erases them."[256]

"Repent, do you not see that Allāh tests you so that you can repent but you continue to disobey Him. . . .[257] The reality of *tawbah* is that one cares for the sanctity of doctrines of Allāh in all his affairs."[258]

According to Jīlānī (Raḥ.'A) *tawbah* means relinquishing of vices and diversion towards pious deeds. He quotes various verses of the Qur'ān in connection with *tawbah.*[259] He, however, differentiates between the *tawbah* of common people and that of the select ones. The former's *tawbah* is from vices and the latter's from *ghaflat* (negligence) and that of the highest among select ones is aimed at purging their heart of all other than Allāh.[260]

The Shaikh (Raḥ.'A) puts forward three conditions for *tawbah* (repentance/return): "One should regret upon his deed committed against the will of Allāh. He should avoid sinful acts in all circumstances and should not resume sinful acts."[261]

Cheerful Submission

'Abdu'l Qādir (Raḥ.'A) opines that cheerful submission to the will of Allāh by carrying out His orders and observing His

---

255. Jīlānī, *Jila'ali Khaṭīr,* p. 14.
256. Ibid., p. 15.
257. Jīlānī, *Fatḥ-i-Rubbānī,* Sermon no. 12.
258. Ibid., Sermon no. 23.
259. Holy *Qur'ān,* LXXI: 10-12; II: 286; III: 08.
260. Jīlānī, *Ghuniyat ul-Ṭālibin,* p. 248.
261. Jīlānī, *Ghuniyat ul-Ṭālibin,* p. 225.

prohibitions is always better and proper for the servants of Allāh. He holds:

". . . It is better and proper for the servants to be in a state of cheerful submission and resignation and to be engaged in service to Him by carrying out His orders and observing His prohibitions and being resigned to His allotment and by discarding such occupations as pertaining to the nourishment of the creation — because this privilege is the source of all allotments and the point of their coming into force and their basis; and to be silent on why, how and when (of happenings) and to refrain from ascribing fault to Allāh in all His actions and inactions is desirable."[262]

In his another discourse the Shaikh states the sin these words: "You should surrender yourself in everything so that He may do His work through you."[263]

At another place the Shaikh (Raḥ.'A) opines that cultivation of *ṣabr* (patience), cheerful submission and avoiding complaining against people stand guarantee for safety in the world and *ākhirah*. He says,

". . . Whoever desires safety in the world's life and in the Hereafter should cultivate patience and cheeful submission and avoid complaining against people and obtain all his necessities from His Lord, the Mighty, the Glorious, and make it an obligation to obey Him and should wait for ease and be exclusively devoted to Him, the Mighty, the Glorious. He in any case is better than those besides Him in the whole of His creation."[264]

---

262. Jīlānī, *Futūḥ al-Ghaib,* Discourse no. 42.
263. Ibid., 13.
264. Ibid., 42.

Shaikh further says, ". . . His (Allāh's) punishment is a blessing, His calamity a remedy, His promise a cash. His credit is existing state. His word is a deed."[265]

The unfailing and penetrating vision into the *tawḥīd* or Unity of God had conferred upon 'Abdu'l Qādir (Raḥ.'A) that sublime piety which produces an absolute resignation in the will of God. He explains the state of resignation in these words:

"When a man finds himself in a trouble, he first endeavours to get rid of it. If he fails, he seeks the help of others, such as kings, officials, grandees or the rich, or, physician in the case of an illness; when this effort also fails him he turns to Allāh with invocations and praises, and not unoften with tears and lamentations. In other words, he does not look for the assistance of others so long as he can obtain the requisite help from his own self; similarly, he does not implore Allāh if he can get the help from His creatures; and, finally, when he does not get any help from that source too, he surrenders completely to Allāh Almighty. It is only at this stage that man seeks the help of Allāh with prayers and invocations, lamentations and tears but Allāh does not accept his entreaties till he gets tired of these too. Then, being completely dejected and broken-hearted, he is permeated by an enlightenment of spirit which makes him indifferent to the causes and effects. Now he has a sublimated soul, unconscious of everything save the Divine Being and aware of the true content of *tawḥīd* (unity). He has now a certitude of knowledge that save Allāh nothing has any power to move a thing or keep it stationary, to promote or debase, to benefit or harm, to give life or bring death, to give honour or indignity, or to make affluent or

265. Jīlānī, *Futūḥ al-Ghaib,* Discourse no. 42.

indigent. The man is now like a ball in the hands of a player, or a child in the lap of a nurse, or else a corpse in the hands of those who bathe it; for, these are completely at the mercy of those who possess them. Likewise, the man thus loses his identity in the will of his Master; immersed in his higher-self he has no comprehension of anything save the acts of his Lord, nor does he witness or hear or think of anything else. If he seeks anything, it is the craftsmanship of the Supreme Creator; if he hears, it is His voice; if he comprehends, it is by the knowledge vouchsafed by Him; and if he is enlivened, it is only by His nearness. Thus, in the state of total absorption, he gets peace only through the grace and blessings of Allāh; he detests to depend on anything save his Lord; he surrenders himself completely before the will of Allāh; acquires the knowledge of mysteries hidden from the senses through intuition and enlightenment of heart; and overflows with the gratitude of the Lord for His countless blessings."[266]

Renunciation

In one of his discourses, the Shaikh (Raḥ.'A) maintains that the reality of renunciation is giving up everything other than the Lord of creatures because He is the final destination. He asserts:

"The reality of renunciation is giving up this world, giving up the Hereafter, giving up all the lustful desires and pleasures, giving up one's very existence, giving up seeking spiritual states, rankings, miracles and spiritual stations, and giving up everything other than the Lord of the creatures so that no one remains other than the Creator. He is the final destination and He is the ultimate aim of all hopes. To Him all affairs belong."[267]

---

266. Jīlānī, *Futūḥ al-Ghaib,* Discourse no. 3.

267. Jīlānī, *Jila'ali Khaṭīr*, p. 35.

While discussing various stages of renunciation, 'Abdu'l Qādir (Raḥ.'A) affirms:

"Renunciation means giving up those things that are prohibited, then giving up those things that are legally dubious, then giving up those things that are permissible, and then giving up those things that are absolutely lawful under all circumstances, to the extent that absolutely nothing to be given up remains."[268]

'Abdu'l Qādir (Raḥ.'A) regards renunciation as a source of comfort for the hearts and a means of benefit for the creatures. He, however, warns against the outwardly renunciation which, according to him, is hypocrisy. He maintains:

"Renunciation is a source of comfort for the hearts of the obedient ones, the ascetics."[269]

"When someone has genuinely renounced the creatures, they will become genuinely interested in him and derive benefit from listening to his words. . . ."[270]

"Woe unto you! It is the heart that practises renunciation, not the body. O you who are ascetic only outwardly, your renunciation is returned to you! . . . You have opened your shop to sell hypocrisy."[271]

Ikhlāṣ (Sincerity)

Jīlānī (Raḥ.'A) advises to work sincerely for Allāh in one's all the deeds. He asks to run away from the association of partners

268. Jīlānī, *Jila'ali Khaṭīr*, p. 63.

269. Ibid., p. 35.

270. Ibid., p. 36.

271. Ibid., p. 37.

with Allāh as a token of sincerity. To him absolute sincerity means to be with none but Allāh. He asserts:

". . . You must work sincerely for Allāh in your prayers, fasting, pilgrimage, giving obligatory alms and in all your deeds."[272]

"O Sincere one, run away from the association of partners with Allāh to the door of your Lord."[273]

"Absolute sincerity means to be with none but Allāh. You won't succeed until you have an iota of worldly love."[274]

Taqwā the Only Noble Pedigree

'Abdu'l Qādir (Raḥ.'A) regards *taqwā* as the only noble pedigree. He asks his novices to approach him on the basis of *taqwā* and not that of mere pedigree. He holds, "O you who have such a noble pedigree! Forget about your pedigree and come here. The truly noble pedigree is the fear of Allāh. . . . Do not come to me on the feet of your pedigree but rather come to me on the feet of your fear of Allāh. Be sensible that which Allāh has, would not fall into your hand only by virtue of your ancestral pedigree, but rather until you deserve the pedigree by the fear of Allāh."[275]

While discussing the qualities of those who are God-fearing, the Shaikh (Raḥ.'A) holds that such people fear Him both in their public and private lives. They give up acts of disobedience, sins and their own will in favour of His will. He affirms:

---

272. Jīlānī, *Jila'ali Khaṭīr*, p. 50.
273. Ibid., p. 50
274. Jīlānī, *Fatḥ-i-Rubbānī*, Sermon no. 17.
275. Jīlānī, *Jila'ali Khaṭīr*, p. 61.

"The God-fearing ones are those who fear Allāh in their public and private lives and watch for Him under all circumstances."[276]

"The God-fearing ones are those who give up acts of disobedience and sins, both the apparent and hidden ones. They also give up dissimulation, hypocrisy and working for the sake of creatures and worldly purposes."[277]

"Give up your wish in favour of His wish, your preference in favour of His preference, your decision in favour of His decision and your will in favour of His will. He is doer of what He wills."[278]

Jīlānī (Raḥ.'A) compares the heart of a person who does not have fear of Allāh to a herd of sheep without a shepherd who are, therefore, doomed to be food for wolves. He advises that one should be afraid of Allāh only as He possesses the power to subject to the eternal punishment. He elaborates as:

"Every heart that has no fear (of Allāh) is like a town without trees or sheep without a shepherd. Such a town is nothing but ruins and such sheep are doomed to be food for the wolves."[279]

". . . You claim that you fear Allāh but actually you fear others. Don't be afraid of any *jinn* (ghost), any being, any angel, any animal. . . . You should rather fear one who subjects to the eternal punishment."[280]

---

276. Jīlānī, *Jila'ali Khaṭīr*, p. 40.
277. Ibid., p. 41.
278. Ibid., p. 42.
279. Ibid., p. 43.
280. Jīlānī, *Fatḥ-i-Rubbānī*, Sermon no. 27.

The Shaikh (Raḥ.'A) prescribes ten characteristics for the perfection of *taqwā* (piety).[281] These are:

1. Save oneself from backbiting. The *Qur'ān* preaches

   ولايغتب بعضكم بعضاً 282

2. Save oneself from thinking ill of others, i.e. save oneself from pessimistic mode of life

   as has been stated in the *Qur'ān*

   اجتنبوا كثيرًا من الظن ان بعض الظن اثم 283

3. Save onself from making fun of others. The Almighty Allāh states:

   لا يسخر قومٌ من قوم 284

4. Keep one's eyes shut from unlawful things. The holy *Qur'ān* preaches:

   قل للمومنين يغضوا من ابصارهم 285

5. One speaks the truth based on *'adl* (justice). The *Qur'ān* guides:

   واذا قلتم فاعدلوا

6. Admits the beneficiary nature of Allāh and does not feel proud of himself. The *Qur'ān* preaches:

   بل الله يمن عليكم ان هدا لكم للايمان

7. Spends his wealth lawfully. Allāh praises such believers at one of the places in *Qur'ān* as:

   والذين اذاانفقوالم يُسرِفوا ولم يقتروا 286

---

281. Jīlānī, *Ghuniyat ul-Ṭālibīn*, pp. 275-76.

282. Holy *Qur'ān*, IL: 12.

283. Ibid.

284. Ibid., IL: 11.

285. Ibid., XXIV: 30.

286. Ibid., XXV: 67.

8. One doesn't become over-ambitious. The Allāh affirms:
تلك الدار الأخرة نجعلها للذين لا يريدون علو فى الارض و لافسادا [287]

9. One offers *Ṣalāh* five times (obligatory) strictly and seriously. Allāh the Almighty maintains:
حافظوا على الصلوٰت والصلواةِ الوسطىٰ و قوموا لله قٰنتين [288]

10. Follows strictly the *Sunnah* (way) of Prophet Muhammad (SAW) and remains (united) with the rest of the Muslim *ummah*. Allāh affirms:
و ان هٰذا صراطى مستقيما فاتبعوه ولا تتبعو السبل فتفرق بكم عن سبـ [289]

The Blessing of dhikr (Remembrance of Allāh)

The Shaikh (Raḥ.'A) preaches that regular remembering of Allāh helps to ward off the devil as it destroys and defeats him and disperses his soldiers. One who remembers Allāh in his heart, is (real) *dhākir*. He affirms:

". . . Keep on remembering your Lord (Allāh), reciting His Book and the Traditions of His Messenger."[290]

"Constant *dhikr* of Allāh is a means for the contribution of good in this world and in the Hereafter."[291]

". . . Ward him (*saṭān*) off and force him to escape from your vicinity by continuously performing *dhikr*, for *dhikr* destroys him (*saṭān*), defeats him and disperses his soldiers."[292] One who remembers Allāh in his heart is (real) *dhākir*."[293]

---

287. Holy Qur'ān, XXVIII: 83.
288. Ibid., II: 238.
289. Ibid., VI: 153.
290. Jīlānī, *Jila'ali Khaṭīr*, p. 75.
291. Ibid., p. 78.
292. Ibid., p. 77.
293. Jīlānī, *Fatḥ-i-Rubbānī*, Discourse no. 23.

The Shaikh (Raḥ.'A) prescribes the following ways of *dhikr* so as to get rid of *saṭān*.

"Seek help in defeating *saṭān* by saying: There is no might nor strength but by Allāh, the High, the Great (*la hawla wa la quwwatan illa billahi al-'aliyal-'aẓīm*). What Allāh wills will happen (*masha'a allāh kana*). There is no God save Allāh, the King, the Manifest True one (*la ilaha illa allāh al-malik al-haqq al-mubīn*).

Glory be to Allāh and praise be to Him, Glory be to Allāh, the Great, and praise be to Him, (*subhan, allāh wa bi ḥamdi hī, subhan allāh al-aẓīm wa bihamdi hī*). Thus, he (*saṭān*) will be overthrown, his power will be broken and his soldiers will be defeated."[294]

Moderate View about Jabr and Qadr

Shaikh adopts a moderate view about the problem of *jabr* (جبر) and *qadr* (قدر). He holds this view that actions belong to Allāh in the point of creation and to man in the point of effort. He gives due weightage to the human effort without violating the sanctity of the divine power. He elaborates his statement in these words; "And do not forget at the same time the position of human efforts so as not to fall a victim to the creed of *jabariyya* (fatalists), and believe that no action attains its fulfilment but in Allāh, the exalted. You should not therefore, worship them and thus forget Allāh nor should you say that the actions of men do not proceed from anything but from Allāh, because if you say so you will become an unbeliever and belong to the category of people known as *Qadiriyya* (believers in the doctrine that men have absolute control over the origin and cause of actions). You should rather say that

294. Jīlānī, *Jila'ali Khaṭīr*, p. 77.

actions belong to Allāh in the point of *takhlīq* (creation) and to man in the point of *kasb* (effort)."[295]

Limits of Taqlīd

Jīlānī (Raḥ.'A) regards the *taqlīd* of pious as a decree of Allāh and at the same time he seems to be conscious about the limits of *taqlīd* prescribed by the *Qur'ān* and the *Sunnah* (way) of Prophet Muhammad (SAW). He clarifies it in these words: "And your being with them (pious men) is a decree of Allāh and this decree of Allāh is in darkness, so enter this darkness with a lamp which is also the judge and this is the Book of Allāh (*Qur'ān*) and the *Sunnah* (way) of His holy Prophet (SAW). Do not go beyond these two."[296]

'Ulamā'-i-Sū

The Shaikh (Raḥ.'A) was greatly shocked to notice contradiction in the claims and deeds of scholars of his time. He points out their weaknesses and warns them about the ill consequences of such a state of affairs. He addresses these *'ulamā-i-sū* (ill-fated scholars) in these words:

"O man! who claims to be an *'ālim* (scholar) and asks the worldly persons (for help) and bows before them; listen, you are misled despite being a scholar."[297]

"O! those who commit *khayāna* (misappropriation) of *'ilm* (knowledge) and *'amāl* (deeds)! How are you related to them (Allāh and His Messenger). O! enemies of Allāh and His Messenger; O! dacoits of people; you are openly involved in

295. Jīlānī, *Futūḥ al-Ghaib*, Discourse no. 10.

296. Ibid.

297. Jīlānī, *Fatḥ-i-Rubbānī*, Discourse no. 29.

brutality and hypocrisy. How long will (your) hypocrisy flourish! . . .

O *'ulamā'* (scholars) and *zāhid* (one who undergoes austerity)! How long would you live as hypocrites for the sake of *salāṭīn* and monarchs to enjoy the luxuries of life. You and most of the monarchs (of this period) are cruel and misappropriators in relation to the bounty of Allāh and His slaves."[298]

"How long would you continue to gain knowledge without following it? Close your chapter (book) of knowledge and open your chapter of action with sincerity, otherwise you would'nt be successful."[299]

"O *'ālim* (scholar), do not pollute your knowledge by adopting the company of worldly persons. Do not exchange a honorific thing for a disrespectful one. Knowledge is honourable and their world is condemnable."[300]

Tawwakul (Absolute Trust in Allāh)

While giving his interpretation of *tawwakul* the Shaikh (Raḥ.'A) says, "the reality of *tawwakul* lies in the fact that one entrusts his whole affairs to Allāh. . . . One believes that *taqdīr* (destiny) does not undergo any drastic change. . . ."[301]

The Shaikh (Raḥ.'A) holds that *tawwakul* (trust), *taslım* (absolute submission) and *tafwīd* (surrender) are three stages of absolute *tawwakul*. According to him *mutawwakil* (one who trusts) remains satisfied on account of the commitments of

---

298. Jīlānī, *Fatḥ-i-Rubbānī*, Discourse no. 51.

299. Ibid., Discourse no. 58.

300. Ibid.

301. Jīlānī, *Ghuniyat ul-Ṭālibīn*, p. 674.

Allāh, the man of *taslīm* remains satisfied on account of the *'ilm* (knowledge) of Allāh and the man of *tafwīd* remains pleased in the pleasure of Allāh. *Tawwakul* is the beginning, *taslīm* the middle and the *tafwīd* is the highest of all the positions. *Tawwakul* is the quality of *mu'min* (believer), *taslīm* that of *awliyā ullāh* and *tafwīd* that of *muwwāḥid* (those who believe in extreme *tawḥīd*). Also it can be said that *tawwakul* is the quality of common people, *taslīm* that of select ones and *tafwīd* that of highest among select ones.[302]

302. Jīlānī, *Ghuniyat ul-Ṭālibīn*, p. 674.

5

Impact of Shaikh 'Abdu'l Qādir Jīlānī's Thought on the Subcontinent

Thought-provoking and impressive sermons of Shaikh 'Abdu'l Qādir Jīlānī (Raḥ.'A) served as a source of inspiration for thousands of people. These enabled numerous people to offer *tawbah* (earnest repentance) for their sins. But in order to build up a movement aimed at a widespread and permanent reform of the moral, social and spiritual life of the people, it was necessary to find out a way whereby more durable relations could be fostered between the mentor and the disciples and, at the same time, arrangements could be made for the religious education and training of the latter.

Religious seminaries and educational institutions too could not provide an answer to the problem because of the vast population of Muslims and the mundane pre-occupations of the people. The problem of making arrangements for a continued and effective effort for the education and training of the people in religious tenets and practices, and infusing a breath of new life in the vast numbers, spread over far off lands, defied a solution in the absence of a real Islamic state. The then Muslim states were extremely allergic to any movement or criticism which could pose a threat to their political supremacy. Thus, these governments being suspicious of all efforts made for the resurgence of Islamic spirit, and, erroneously taking these as movements designed to build-up political leadership, lost no time in crushing them.

In these circumstances there was no way left to revivify the religious spirit and fill the people with zeal, enthusiasm and self-confidence for re-introduction of the precepts of religion in their life. The only possible alternative left was to call upon the people to take an oath of allegiance for the purpose. Following the way of the Prophet (SAW), it had become imperative that a spiritual guide of high ethical excellence should obtain an oath of allegiance, or the *bai'at*, from the people to lead a virtuous life in accordance with the directions of their preceptor.[1] The mentor had to infuse the spirit of moral uprightness and correct ethical behaviour, following the teachings of Islam, to the illumination of the pupil's soul. This was, in truth, what the *bai'at* meant and by which the inspired souls tried to infuse into their disciples, through preaching and personal example, loving care and unalloyed sincerity, an inner vitality of spirit and strength of moral integrity. The reformers and renovators of faith succeeded in revivifying the true faith and tapping new sources of popular strength in their own times, through this tried and infallible method which just copied the procedure and technique followed by the Prophet (SAW) of Islam. Innumerable persons have been provided with an opportunity of not only adopting a virtuous life through this method but have also been led to attain even the stage of "Divine Acquaintance" and "Love" by the inspired preceptors and teachers, of whom the mentor *par excellence* was Shaikh Muhiyud-din 'Abdu'l Qādir Jīlānī (Raḥ.'A). Islamic history

1. Most of the Ṣūfīs attempt to derive the origin of *bai'at* from the Holy Qur'ān, XLVIII: 10.

bears witness to the fact that no guide, after the period of Jāba'īyn, with an enlightened soul had been more successful than Sayyid 'Abdu'l Qādir in bringing about a revival and resurgence of the true Islamic spirit. At the same time, the method followed by him is still the most viable and most effective way of filling the people with faith and enthusiasm aiming at the reformation of their lives in accordance with the tenets of Islam.

With his profound knowledge, intellectual gifts, charming and loving personality and above all spiritual excellence, Sayyid 'Abdu'l Qādir renovated the system of *bai'at*. He elaborated and systematized the mystic practices, made these more wide-based and harmonious with the principles of the *sharī'ah*.

The moral and spiritual excellence of 'Abdu'l Qādir, his unflinching devotion to Allāh, the efficacy of his sermons, the inspiring and regenerating influence exercised by him over the people in his own time and the upright character and moral rectitude of those who have had an opportunity to be instructed by him, mark him as one of the most eminent men, born in Islam. He was not only a worker of incessant *karāmāt* (miracles), as the chroniclers of his time report, but his miracle of miracles lay in his inspiring and impressive teachings which made thousands to turn away from the lust of power and wealth and to inculcate the real spirit of faith through self-correction and purification of the soul.

Countless people were guided through this path of self-discipline, devotion to Allāh and virtuous living during the lifetime of Sayyid 'Abdu'l Qādir, and after him, his disciples[2]

2. Among the disciples of 'Abdu'l Qādir who devoted their life to the cause of preaching and inviting people through their precepts and example in spiritual and moral purification, the most notable →

propagated the teaching of Qādiriyya order in almost every Muslim country. The branches of the order were formulated in Yemen, Hadhramaut, India, Indonesia and in the countries of Africa where it helped innumerable people to come back to the path of loyalty and obedience to Allāh and His Messenger.

There is, however, difference of opinion about the real founder of Qādiriyya *silsilā* (order) in the Indian subcontinent.[3]

→ was Sheikh Shihab al din Suhrawardī (AH 593-632), the spiritual successor and nephew of Sheikh Abu Najib Suhrawardi. He was the founder of another Ṣūfī order known as Suhrawardiyya. He also wrote a very popular work entitled *'Awārifal–Ma'ārif*. Ibn Khallikān writes that during his old age he was the greatest mystic of Baghdad and there was none so pious and popular as he. (Ibn Khallikān, *Wafayat al-A'yan*, vol. III, p. 119). Another writer Ibn al Najjar has left records about his immense popularity and preaching (*Mir'at ul-Jinan*, vol. IV, p. 81). Ibn Khallikān writes that mystics from far off places visited him for guidance and spiritual light. Ibn Khallikān adds that his sermons were very efficacious. (Ibn Khallikān, ibid., pp. 119-20), *'Awarif al-Ma-ārif*, written by Shihab-ud-din Suhrawardī, has a pride of place among the mystic works. One of its distinguishing features is that unlike the mystic writings of the earlier Ṣūfīs, it upholds the tenets of the orthodox school and cleanses the *shariah* of all innovations.

Shihab-ud-din Suhrawardī too was fortunate in having some very notable personages among his disciples. One of these, Bahā ud-din Zakariya Multānī was a well-known and eminent saint of his time in India.

3. Khalīq Ahmad Niẓāmī holds that in the middle of fifteenth century CE Qādiriyya and Shaṭariyya *silsilā*s (orders) were introduced in India. Qādiriyya *silsilā* was introduced in India by Shah Niamatullah Qādirī. Sayyid Muhammad Ghawth Gilani, Makhdum Shaikh 'Abdu'l Qādir second, Sayyid Mūsā and Shaikh 'Abdu'l Ḥaqq Muhadith Dehlawī propagated Qādiriyya *silsilā* during the period of Mughal regime. (*Tarikh-i Mash'aikh Chisht*, p. 134). Also see, monthly magazine, *Zouq-i Naẓr* (Ghawth-i A'zam Number), February and March, 1985, p. 73. And Shaikh Ikram, *Roud-i Kawthar*, p. 63.

Chroniclers have mentioned Shah Ni'amatullāh Qādirī, Shah Ni'amatullāh Firozābādī,[4] Sayyid Muḥammad Ghawth Gīlānī,[5] Sayyid Muḥammad Gwaliyārī,[6] Haḍrat Sayyid Muḥammad Qādirī Amjhari,[7] Pīr Shah 'Ata'ullāh Baghdādi,[8] Sayyid Abul Ḥayāt Qādirī,[9] Sayyid Bahau'd Dīn Qādirī[10] and Mīr Sayyid Ismāīl Qādirī[11] among the early founders of Qādiriyya *silsilā* (order) in the Indian subcontinent.

Maqbool Rahim Muftī, the author of *Tadhkira Qādiriyya* opines that Qādiriyya *silsilā* (order) was introduced in the Indian subcontinent during the lifetime of Shaikh 'Abdu'l Qādir Jīlānī by his eldest son, Shaikh 'Abdu'l Razāq Jīlānī (Raḥ.'A). Ghulam Yahya Anjum has done a paintaking research

---

4. *Firozeābādī*, according to Shaikh Ikram, introduced Qādiriyya *silsilā* in Bengal (*Roud-i-Kawthar*, p. 513).
5. Mirza Ahmad Akhtar, *Tadhkirah-Awliya-i-Hind*, vol. III, p. 18.

   Mirza claims that Sulṭān Sikandar Lodhi also entered into the oath of allegiance with Gīlānī and that the latter was the first to introduce Qādiriyya *silsilā* in India. Also see, Saffi Haidar, *Taṣawwuf oor Sha'iri*, p. 88. Ya'qub 'Umar, *Muṭā'la Islāmiyat*, p. 144.
6. Muftī Ghulam Sarwar, *Khazīnatu'l Āṣfiya*, p. 333.
7. Faḍalu'l Ḥaqq, *Sayyidu'l Hind oor Apka Islāmi Mission*, pp. 14, 73. Also Shaikh 'Ali Shirāzī, *Manaqib-i-Muhammadiyya*, p. 72. Tayyib Abdāli; *Jada'h Irfān*, p. 210.
8. Baghdādi became the influential personality in preaching the Qādiriyya doctrines particularly in Bihar, India. *M'arif*, vol. VI, *Bihar Kay Ṣūfiya-i Kirām*, p. 454.
9. Muftī Ghulam Sarwar, *Hadīqatu'l Awliyya*, p. 40.
10. Maulana Ahmad Raḍā Qādirī, *Hadayaq Bakhshish*, vol. II, p. 40.
11. Shaikh 'Abdu'l Ḥaqq Dehlawi, *Akhbāru'l Akhyār*, Delhi, 1914, p. 439.

in this direction.[12] His findings partially substantiate the view of Muftī. According to this theory Mu'inud Din Chistī spent some months under the guidance of Shaikh 'Abdu'l Qādir Jīlānī (Raḥ.'A) and on his (Chistī's) second sojourn to India the eldest son of Jīlānī, 'Abdu'l Wahhab accompanied him to India.[13] Abdul Wahhāb finally got settled at Nāgaur in Rajasthan.

The Qādiriyyas in Delhi and Agra Regions

Shaikh Abul Fatah bin Jamalu'd-Din Makki 'Abbasi Qādirī was the earliest Ṣūfī to settle in Agra on the invitation of Sulṭān Sikandar Lodhi (894/1489–923/1517). Abul Fataḥ was originally from Shīrwān[14] and on account of his long sojourn in Makkah became known as Makki. Having inherited the *khirqa* of Shaikh 'Abdu'l Qādir Jīlānī (Raḥ.'A) from one of the

---

12. Dr Gh. Yaḥyā Anjum has worked on the *Development of* Qādiriyya *Silsilā in India*, under Young Careers Award sponsored by UGC India. Dr Anjum submitted a three-volume research project on this theme to UGC, India.

13. Muhammad Hasan Ṣābirī, *Haqiqat-i-Gulzār-i-Ṣābirī*, Rampur, 1957, pp. 67, 380; Muhammad Hafizullah, *Badī Swāneh Umrī*, p. 6, Delhi, 1904; Sharif Ahmad Murād, *Kufristan-i-Hind Kay Teen Walī*, p. 45, Delhi, n.d.; Shah, M. Ali Haider Qalandar, *Tadhkirah Hussaini*, p. 296, Lucknow, 1360 AH. Intizamulah Shihabi, *Maḥtāb-i-Ajmīr*, pp. 12-13, Agra, n.d., Muftī Gh. Sarwar, *Khazinatul Asfiya*, vol. 1, p. 257, vol. II, p. 234. Lahore, AH 1284; Dārā Shukoh, *Safīnatul Awliya*, Agra, 1853, p. 158; Ghawthi Shaṭarī, *Gulzār-i Abrār*, p. 28, Lahore AH 1395; Hadratu'l Hadya Chistī, *Siru'l Aqtab*, pp. 106, 124, Lucknow, 1913; Jamali bin Fadlulah Suhrawardi, *Sirul Arifin*, Delhi, n.d., p. 4, Shaikh Muhammad Ikram, *Iqtibāsul'l Anwār*, Lahore, n.d., pp. 134-35; Yusuf, *Jawāhirul Aamal*, p. 504; M. Sidiq Latifi Qadiri, *Mahbūbul Mani*, p. 537; Khādim Hasan Zubairi, *Muinul Arwah*, Agra, 1953, pp. 36, 43.

14. A province along the Caspian sea with the famous port called Darband.

latter's descendants, he led an independent life sheltered from the intrigues surrounding the Sulṭān and his nobles. Abul Fatah, however, deserted Ibrahim Lodi (923/1517-932/1526), when he set out from Delhi to repel the invasion of the Emperor Bābur. In fact, Ibrāhīm was accompanied by many eminent Ṣūfīs and *'ulamā'*, including Shaikh 'Abdu'l Qadūs Gangohi[15] and Shaikh Abul Fatah. Abul Fatah fled back to Agra where he lived until his death in *Sha'ban* 953/September–October, 1546.[16]

Sayyid Shah Muhammad Firozābādī who claimed direct descent from Jīlānī (Raḥ.'A), migrated from Deccan to Agra during the reign of Sulṭān Ibrahim Lodi. After Bābur had seized the throne of Delhi, he allowed the Sayyid to stay in the palaces of Firozabad Fort, near Delhi and the Sayyid was even honoured by Humāyūn, the successor of Babur. The Sayyid reached the height of his fame during the reign of Islam Shah Sūrī, and was treated with exaggerated deference, even the *sulṭān* and his nobility waiting on him slavishly.

Mīr Sayyid Shamsu'd-Din[17] and Sayyid Abū Ṭālib were two other Sayyids who migrated to northern India from Iraq or Iran. After a brief stay, the two Sayyids, however, were found murdered in the house of their host, Sayyid Shah Muhammad Firozabadi in about 955/1548.[18]

---

15. A.A. Rizvi, *History of Ṣūfism in India*, I, Delhi, 1986, pp. 345-46.
16. M. Ghawthi Shatarī, *Gulzār-i-Abrār*, Ms, p. 254b.
17. Mīr had lived for a long time in Kabul and was deeply respected by the Emperor Humāyūn, also.
18. An agitation mounted over their death. An enquiry by two high ranking government officials was initiated. A joint assembly of the *'ulamā'* of Lahore, Delhi, Jaunpur and Bihar was convened by Islam Shah Sūrī. The accused Muhammad Shah, their host, eventually died in prison. Abdul Ḥaqq Muhaddith Dehlawī, *Akhbāru'l Akhyār*, Delhi, 1914, pp. 208-10.

Shaikh 'Abdu'llah Baghdādi (d. 10 Rabi'i 1037/19 November, CE 1627),[19] was another notable descendant of Jīlānī (Raḥ.'A) who migrated to Delhi and settled there. He initiated a large number of disciples into Qādiriyya *silsilā* (order).

Shaikh Muhammad Hasan, the eldest son of Shaikh Hasan Ṭāhir[20] was initiated into Qādiriyya *silsilā* in Yemen while he was on his holy pilgrimage to Makkah. After his return from Arabia he first settled at Agra and then at Delhi. Apparently the Shaikh composed some of his mystical thoughts, he, unfortunately, later destroyed the drafts. Some of his letters, however, were put into book form and a number of his treatises, all compiled by his disciples, survived until the end of the sixteenth century. From one such letter, quoted by Shaikh 'Abdu'l Ḥaqq, we learn of Shaikh Muhammad Hasan's exuberant enthusiasm for the *Waḥdat al wujūd*. Muhammad Ḥasan passed away on 27th *Rajab* 944/30 December, 1537. Shaikh Faḍlullāh also known as Shaikh Manjhu[21] and Shah 'Abdur Razzāq of Thanjhana were outstanding disciples of the Shaikh. During the second half of the sixteenth century Shah 'Abdur Razzaq (d. 949/1543) was regarded as one of the leading exponents of Ibn-i 'Arabi's philosophy by Indian scholars and Ṣūfīs.

Shaikh Ḥāji[22] of Delhi, Shaikh Yūsuf and Sayyid 'Ali were favourite disciples of Shah 'Abdur Razzāq. Among them, Ḥāji succeeded the Shaikh and Yūsuf compiled the Shaikh's *malfūẓāt*.

19. Dārā Shukoh, *Safinatu'l Awliya*, Kanpur, 1900, pp. 69-70.
20. A.A. Rizvi, *History of Sufism in India*, vol. I, Delhi, 1986, pp. 265-66.
21. He was an uncle of Shaikh 'Abdu'l Ḥaqq. Also see, Dehlawi, *Akhbāru'l Akhyār*, pp. 235-37.
22. Muhammad Sadiq Kashmiri Hamdani, *Kalimatu's Sadiq*, MS. (Mashhad), p. 237.

Sayyid 'Ali later decided to settle at Ludhiana.[23]

Mīr Sayyid 'Abdu'l Awwal was another eminent Qādiriyya saint who lived in Delhi. Sayyid remained in Gujarat until 947/1540-41 and then travelled to Makkah and Madīnah. On his return to Ahmedabad, he was invited by the Khan-i Khānān Bairam Khan to move to Delhi, where he finally died at the end of 968/1561.[24] Earlier in 941/1534 he compiled an abridged version of a book on *Ḥadīth* by Majdu'd-Din Muhamad bin Ya'qūb al-Firozābādī (b. 729/1329 at Kazirun, and d. 817/1414 at Zabid). The title of the original was *Safar al-Sa'ada* or *al-Sirāṭ al-Mustaqīm*. 'Abdu'l Awwal also wrote commentaries on various works. *Faiḍ al-Bārī*,[25] *Ma'rifat-i Nafs*,[26] *al-Sair wa'l Sulūk*[27] are some of his famous works. His commentary on *Futūḥāt al-Makkiya*[28] simplified the complex theories of Ibn-i 'Arabī.

Mīr Sayyid Ibrahim (d. 953/1546-47) buried in the complex of the tomb of Shaikh Niẓāmuddin Awliya,[29] was a Qādiriyya Ṣūfī of some repute. He received initiation into a few other orders also. He was passionately fond of books and it has been claimed that Shaikh Bahāuddin Shaṭṭarī compiled the

23. Dehlawi, *Akhbāru'i Akhyār*, p. 237.

24. Dehlawi, *Akhbāru'i Akhyār*, pp. 253-54, *Gulzār-i-Abrār*, p. 159b.

25. It is a commentary on the celebrated work *Ṣaḥiḥ al-Bukhārī*. The *Ṣaḥiḥ* was compiled by Muhammad bin Isma'jil al-Bukhārī (b. 194/810, d. 256/870), who travelled extensively to collect the *'Ahādith* of Prophet Muhammad (SAW), working on this work for not less than sixteen years.

26. It is a treatise written by him on the soul.

27. It is a treatise on Ṣūfism.

28. It is originally written by Muhyu'd-Din Ibn al-'Arabi in which he discusses various aspects of *Waḥdat al-Wajūd* (unity of Being).

29. Dehlawi, *Akhbāru'i Akhyār*, pp. 250-51.

Risāla-i-Shaṭṭariyya for Mīr Sayyid Ibrahīm. He was humble enough to learn from the *'ulamā,'* who periodically visited him to sharpen their own religious perception.

Shaikh Amānullah Pānipatī (d. 11 *Rabi*-II, 957/29 April 1550) was one of the most outstanding Ṣūfīs of Qādirriyya *silsilā* and an exponent of the *Waḥdat al-Wujūd*. He was introduced to *Fuṣūṣ al-Ḥikam* and several other works on *Waḥdat al-Wujūd* by his preceptor Muhammad Mawdūd Lārī,[30] who himself delivered extempore lectures on the unity of Being. Panīpatī was an author of a number of treatises on *taṣawwuf* and the theory of *Waḥdat al-Wujūd*. In his *Ithbat al-Ahādiyya* he meaningfully reinterpreted the Universality of Reality and its process of encompassing the essence of phenomenal existence and embodying what was beyond existence. Tracing the history of the controversy over the *Waḥdat al-Wujūd* in his above quoted work, the Shaikh quotes the Persian Ṣūfī and Poet, Mawlana Jalalud'Din Rūmī (d. 672/1273), who in his *Sharḥ-i-Rubāi'yat* has clarified the most basic attacks on the *Waḥdat al-Wujūd* by its detractors.[31]

Amānullāh also wrote a detailed commentary on the *Lawa'ih* of Maulana 'Abdu'r Rahman Jāmī. In this work he

---

30. Mawdūd originally hailed from Agra but in his old age migrated to Panipat, where he breathed his last. Dehlawi, *Akhbāru'i Akhyār* p. 234.

31. Rūmī asserted that some unenlightened interpreters of Ṣūfī aphorism believed that Divine Reality was infused into all existences. Such a fallacy, holds the Shaikh, had arisen from a rationalization that the whole exists only in sections, which meant it was believed that God existed through His creations, depending Himself on their existence and that His attributes also depended on the attributes of created beings. To Ṣūfīs like Shaikh Amān or Rūmī such a view was founded on total ignorance of the truth, and was also a sheer heresy.

stressed that the perfection of a *dervish* depended on refinement of morals, coupled with an intense devotion to the family of the Prophet Muhammad (SAW). Before his death, Panipati conducted the *'urs* of Jīlānī (Raḥ.'A) and then dispersed food to the people of Delhi. He was buried near the grave of his preceptor, Shaikh Muhammad Mawdūd.[32]

Despite the unwillingness of Shaikh Amānullāh to enrol disciples, he left a good number of them by the time of his death. The most outstanding among his disciples was Shaikh Taju'd-Din Zakariyya Ajodhānī. 'Abdu'l Ḥaqq highly praises Ajodhānī for his excellent personal qualities, as well as for his extensive knowledge on Ṣūfism and *Waḥdat al-Wujūd*.[33] Badāyūnī, however, is highly critical towards Ajodhānī for the latter subscribed to the view, held by a considerable number of Akbar's courtiers, that the Emperor was the perfect man (as devised by the followers of Ibn-i 'Arabi).[34] But, this could not alter the profound respect of 'Abdu'l Ḥaqq for Ajodhani.

Shaikh Saifud-Din (b. 920/1514), father of 'Abdu'l Ḥaqq Dehlawi, was another prominent disciple of Shaikh Aman. When asked to express his own feelings towards *taṣawwuf*, Shaikh Saifud-Din replied to his preceptor that he often felt the whole universe encircling him and that he in turn encircled it. Shaikh Amān decided that an understanding of the unity of Being was already germinating in his new disciple.[35] The serene and pious environment of Shaikh Saifud-Din's home

---

32. Dehlawi, *Akhbāru'i Akhyār*, pp. 241-42.
33. Dehlawi, *Akhbāru'i Akhyār*, pp. 241-42.
34. 'Abdu'l Qādir Badāyūnī, *Muntakhabu't Tawārikh*, vol. II, Eng. tr. W.H. Lowe, Calcutta, 1884-98, p. 258.
35. Dehlawi, *Akhbāru'l-Akhyār*, p. 243.

made him meditative and introspective, his ears echoed with the mystical verses of Amīr Khusrau.[36] The egocentric brawling and the intriguing of the *'ulamā'* at Akbar's court weighed heavily on the Shaikh's mind and he expressed his gratefulness to Allāh that he was neither a scholar nor a theologian.[37]

Shaikh Saifud-Din, while lecturing, used a number of analogies to persuade other mystics to see One in the many and many in the One. *Ta'ayyunat* (self-determination) of the Absolute which was divided into *māhiyya* (quiddities), according to the Shaikh, was not a process in which reason could comprehend, using the analogy of the division of physical objects. Similarly the Absolute, despite His *ta'ayyunat* (self-determination) retained His primordial Oneness.

The allegations of jurists that *samā'* bred hypocrisy was strongly refuted by the Shaikh on the ground that the listener who has lost his consciousness of his own individual existence could not be guilty of hypocrisy. He was an ardent listener to Persian verses especially that of 'Umar al-Khayyām[38] (*c.* 412/1021-22–515 or 516/1122).

The lectures of Saifud-Din were so expressive and emotional that his listeners would often beg him to deliberate on subjects, which really moved them, like divine love, the longing for Allāh and the pangs of separation. Before his death on 27th *Sha'ban* 990/16 September 1582,[39] the Shaikh performed

36. A.A. Rizvi, *History of Ṣūfism in India*, vol. I, Delhi, 1986, pp. 168-74.

37. Dehlawi, *Akhbāru'l-Akhyār*, p. 302.

38. This *ruba'i* of Umar Khayyam would reduce him to tears:

    In its early life this jug was madly in love,
    Crazed by the curling locks of its sweetheart.
    The handle you see at its neck,
    Had been the hand around the neck of its beloved.

39. Dehlawi; *Akhbāru'l Akhyār*, pp. 308-09.

pās-i-anfas[40] for he believed this was possible for Ṣūfīs even after the limbs had ceased to function.

The Shaikh was a poet with *Saifi* as his pen-name, but his verses survive no longer. His son, 'Abdu'l Ḥaqq, however, reproduced a *qaṣīdah* in praise of Shaikh Aman Panipati and another two *ghazal*s by him which in the traditional mystical style eulogize Divine love and ascetic poverty. The theme of *Waḥdat al-Wujūd* is quite evident in what has survived.[41] A short extract from a treatise entitled the *Kashifat* preserved in *Akhbāru'l Akhyār* points out the different forms of perception of the manifestations of the Absolute and re-emphasizes the reality of man as seen by the scholars of the *Waḥdat al-Wujūd.*[42]

Saifud-Din graced a good number of disciples by his instructions. He, however, paid special attention to the education and *tarbiat* (training) of his son, 'Abdu'l Ḥaqq (b. *Muhammram* 958/January 1551 – d. 21 *Rabi'i* 1052/19 June 1642). Besides extreme seriousness in education, learning and training, 'Abdu'l Ḥaqq pursued a rigorous schedule of prayer and fasting. At the age of twenty-two the Shaikh began to teach advanced theological scholars.

Saifud-Din had awakened in his son a passionate interest in the Qādiriyya order as well as the *Wahdat al-Wujūd*. Later, he advised him to become a disciple of the most illustrious living Qādiriyya *pīr*, Shaikh Mūsa and the latter initiated him

---

40. Breath-Control, cf. Rizvi, *History of Ṣūfism in India*, pp. 272, 341, 353.

41. To the scholarly *gnostic* it is authoritatively known that He is the *'Ayn* (Essence) of the universe but is distant from it. Sometimes He, like a newly wedded bride, hides His face behind. Sometimes He is seen producing confusion, rioting and the tearing of clothes. Dehlawi, *Akhbāru'l-Akhyār*, p. 304.

42. Dehlawi, *Akhbāru'l-Akhyār*, pp. 306-7.

into Qādiriyya *silsilā* on 6 *Shawwal* 985/17 December 1577.

In September 1578 when Emperor Akbar resumed second round of religious debates in the *'Ibādat-Khāna* and Anup Tala's (Tank) at Fatehpur Sīkrī, Shaikh 'Abdu'n-Nabi and Makhdumu'l Muluk emerged as leading rivals to each other. During this period also, the *'ulamā'* signed the *mahzar*. 'Abdu'l Ḥaqq came in touch with Abu'l Faḍal and Faiḍī and also became friendly with other dignitaries of the Akbar's court. The electric trend in the new religious developments designated the Shaikh and he withdrew to Delhi. 'Abdu'l Ḥaqq refused to take part in the war which was waged by the *'ulamā'* and he was, therefore, regarded as being neutral to the new imperial policies. Early in 995/1586-87, Shaikh 'Abdu'l Ḥaqq travelled through Malwa and Gujarat. At Mandu he was the guest of Shaikh Ghauthī Shaṭṭarī, the author of the *Gulzār-i Abrār*. He learnt Qādiriyya *dhikr* under the guidance of Shaikh Wajihu'd-Din.

'Abdu'l Ḥaqq reached Makkah in 996/1588 and became proficient in such outstanding *ḥadīth* works as the *Ṣaḥīḥ Muslim* and *Ṣaḥīḥ al-Bukhāri* and studied under Shaikh 'Abdu'l-Wahhab Muttaqi al-Qādirī al-Shazilī.[43]

On his return from Makkah in 1000/1592[44] Dehlawi stood by his decision to dissociate himself from the court, turning

43. Abdul Wahhab was a disciple and successor of celebrated *Ṣūfī* Shaikh 'Ali Muttaqi (d. 975/1567). Wahhab, probably born in 943/1536-37 in Mandu (India), stayed for some time in Ceylon and then he went to Makkah after having perfected himself in religious education. Besides, he was an expert calligrapher in Persian *nasta'liq* and Arabic *naskh*. The Shaikh continued to lecture on *fiqh*, *ḥadīth* and Arabic lexicography close to the Ka'aba. His teachings were reintroduced into the Indian subcontinent by his talented disciple, Shaikh 'Abdu'l Ḥaqq Muhaddith Dehlawi.

44. Dehlawi, *Zadu'l Muttaqīn*, MS. Rampur, pp. 36b, 37a.

to teaching and compiling works on *ḥadīth*.[45] After the death of Emperor Akbar on 16 October 1605, Dehlawi corresponded with the members of nobility including Murtaza Khan and Khan-i-Khānān with the hope that the powerful dignitaries, friendly to him, might succeed in replacing Akbar's policy of "peace with all" by strict Sunnī rule as envisaged by Ghazālī. He wrote a letter to Murtaza Khan suggesting that in the discharge of his worldly duties he should never neglect the faith of the *sharī'ah*. Similarly, when a courtier informed Dehlawi of Jahāngir's interest in the *ḥadīth*, he wrote a short political treatise, the *Nūriyya-i Sulṭāniyya*. The Shaikh's main concern, however, remained teaching, writing, preaching and undergoing Ṣūfī practices.[46] His *khānqāh* in Delhi, which he built sometime before CE 1611 and where he spent most of his time, was known as the *Khānqāh-i-Qādiriyya*.

Dehlawi developed friendly relations with Khwaja Bāqī Billāh, when the latter established a Naqshbandiyya *khānqāh* at Delhi in 1008/1599. The intimacy became so cemented that an authority suggests that Dehlawi became a disciple of Bāqi Billāh.[47] After the death of khawājā, his disciple Khawājā Husāmu'd-Din remained in close contact with Dehlawi. 'Abūl-Ma'ali Qādirī was another intimate friend and guide of 'Abdu'l Ḥaqq.

In 1619-20 Emperor Jahāṅgīr rewarded Shaikh 'Abdu'l Ḥaqq with lavish honours and gifts when he invited the latter to his court.[48]

45. A.A. Rizvi, *Religious and Intellected History of the Muslims in Akbar's Reign*, Delhi, 1975, pp. 327-33.
46. A.A. Rizvi, *A History of Ṣūfism in India*, vol. II, Delhi, rpt. 1992, pp. 86-87.
47. Muhammad Sadiq Kashmiri Hamadani, *Kalimatu'-Ṣādiqīn*, MS., AMU, p. 245.
48. Jahāṅgīr, *Tuzuk-i Jahāṅgīr*, Ghazipur and Aligarh, 1863-64, Eng. →

Shaikh 'Abdu'l Ḥaqq died at the age of ninety-four[49] and was buried at the Hauz-i Shamsi.[50] A lengthy account of his life and activities inscribed on his gravestone mentions that the Shaikh had written 100 books. In a list of his works, however, the Shaikh mentions 49 titles to which were added another 11. The Shaikh, therefore, wrote some 60 treatises. His works on *ḥadīth* include *Ashi'āt al-Lama'āt,*[51] *Lama'at al-*

→ tr. A. Rogers, ed. H. Beveridge, London 1909-14, rpt., New Delhi, 1978, p. 283.

Just prior to his death, Jahāṅgīr's attitude towards Shaikh 'Abdu'l Ḥaqq, his son Nur'ul-Ḥaqq, and Shaikh Husāmu'd-Din turned hostile. According to Dārā Shukoh people made unjust allegations against the Shaikh and his son. It would seem that Nur'ul Ḥaqq who was Qāḍī of Agra, was accused of friendship with prince Khurram who later ascended the throne as Shāhjahān. The Prince had rebelled against his father in CE 1622 waging war against him until his surrender in March 1626. His young sons (Dārā, then aged ten and Aurangzeb aged eight) were sent as hostage to the Emperor's court. Nevertheless he remained a potential threat to the throne. Jahāṅgīr's rapidly declining health precipitated the traditional Mughal war of succession. The interest of Nuru'l-Ḥaqq in Prince Khurram prompted the retribution meted out to those whom Jahāṅgīr considered a threat to his throne, and caused Nuru'l Haqq's exile to Kabul. After the accession of Shāhjahān to the throne, both Shaikh 'Abdu'l Ḥaqq and his son Nur'ul Ḥaqq were allowed to return to Delhi and the latter was re-appointed as Qāḍī in Agra.

Cf. K.A. Niẓāmī, *Hayāt-i Shaikh 'Abdu'l Ḥaqq Muhaddith Dihlawi*, Delhi, 1953, pp. 148-49.

49. His death took place on 21 *Rabi-I* 1052/19 June 1642.

50. A prestigious cemetery which had the reputation of being a place of rest for the pious.

51. It is a Persian commentary on the *Mishkāt al-Masābih*. The commentary was started by the Shaikh on 13 *Zu'lhijja* 1019/26 February 1611 and completed on 24 *Rabi II*, 1025/11 May 1616.

Tanqīh,[52] *Jama'al-Barakāt* and a book on *Asmā'al-Rijāl*.[53]

'Abdu'l Ḥaqq wrote a Persian commentary on the *Safar al-Sa'ada* or *al-Sirāt al-Mustaqīm* by Majdud-Din Muhammad bin Ya'qūb al-Firozābādī (b. 729/1329, d. 817/1414).[54] *Madārijun-Nubūwwa* asserts the importance of the execution of miracles by the Prophet Muhammad (SAW) and offers a detailed analysis of the prophethood in relation to these miracles. *Mat abata Bi's-Sunnah* is a rejection of the suspicious beliefs and practices of Muslims regarding different lunar months.[55] *Faḍā'il A'imma Ithnā 'Ashr*[56] is a book about twelve Shi'i *imāms*. *Takmilu'l-Īmān* gives detailed guidance in controversial matters of the fundamental aspects of Sunnī beliefs and advocates the adoption of a moderate path.[57] Writings of Dehlawi on Ṣūfism

---

52. It is an Arabic commentary on certain subtle points of the *Mishkāt* which he had not found expedient to explain to the less educated Muslims. This commentary was completed on 24 *Rajab* 1025/7 August 1616.

53. The work contains the list of the narrators of *Aḥādīth* in the *Mishkāt*.

54. Firozabadi was also the author of an Arabic dictionary *al-Qāmūs*. The *Safar al-Sa'ada* contains many traditions relating to the practices of the Prophet Muhammad (SAW) including; ablution, prayers, fasting, pilgrimages, invocations, etc. The commentary is entitled *al-Ṭarīq al-Qawim Fi Sharh al-Sirāt al-Mustaqim*.

55. It refers more particularly to the tenth day of Muharram on which Imām Husain was martyred at Karbala (AH 61/10 October CE 680).

56. It was an attempt to counter misconceptions that Sunnīs might develop from reading Shi'i works eulogizing their leading *imāms*. It was also intended to discourage some of the hostilities of extremist Sunnīs towards the family and descendants of Ḥaḍrat Ali (Raḍ.'A).

57. In this work the author stresses that sinfulness and villainy did not make a *mumin* (faithful) an infidel, adding that the companions →

are generally an attempt to reconcile the *sharī'ah* with the *ṭarīqah* (Ṣūfī way); nevertheless they also assert the superiority of Shaikh 'Abdu'l Qādir Jīlānī and the theory of *Waḥdat al-Wujūd*. His famous work *Akhbāru'l-Akhyār*, relating to the Ṣūfīs of the subcontinent, is prefaced by a long biography of Shaikh 'Abdu'l Qādir Jīlānī (Raḥ.'A). It emphasizes the belief that Jīlānī was superior to all his predecessor *awliyā* (saints) and that his precedence over future generation of *awliyā* was also guaranteed. The claim of the great Shaikh, "My foot is on the neck of every great Shaikh," according to Dehlawi, was a well considered statement.[58] He also wrote a treatise in Arabic, entitled *al-Risālat fi bayān qawl qadami* in support of this assertion. In this treatise Dehlawi disagrees with Shaikh Shihab al-dīn al-Suhrawardī's contention that Jīlānī had made this statement in a state of mystical intoxication. Dehlawi opines that Jīlānī had uttered these words in a state of complete sobriety and with full understanding of their implications.[59]

One of the outstanding efforts of Dehlawi to popularize the teachings of Jīlānī is his Persian translation of *Futūḥ al-Ghaib*. Dehlawi himself considered Jīlānī's sermons to be a true facsimile of the eloquent expressions of the Prophet Muhammad (SAW).[60]

→ of the Prophet Muhammad (SAW) had joined in funeral prayers of sinners and wicked pupil. Cf. *Takmilu'l Īmān*, Delhi, 1312/1895, p. 34.

58. Dehlawi, *Akhbāru'l-Akhyār*, p. 10.

59. *Al-Risalat fi Bayān Qawl Qadamī*, MS., Raza Library, Rampur, pp. 1-10.

60. Dehlawi had first studied *Futūḥ al-Ghaib* with his *Murshid* (Preceptor) Abdul Wahhab Muttaqī. In India he acquired a copy and commenced its translation into Persian. During a short stay in Lahore in 1023/1614-15 in Shah Abu'l Ma ali's *khānqāh*, he completed it under the title *Miftāḥ-i Futūḥ*.

Marj al-Bahrain fi'l-Jamma' bain al-Ṭarīqain is another treatise by Dehlawi in which he has attempted to place *ṭarīqah* (Sūfic way) within the framework of the *sharī'ah*. In this treatise the author also attempts to remind that the pursuit of philosophy was the principal reason for the deviation from the path of orthodoxy and sanctity.[61]

Dehlawi's unshakable faith in the *Waḥdat al-Wujūd* is clearly depicted in his letters to *Mujadid*,[62] and a treatise entitled the *Wujūdiyya*. His letters give an unambiguous explanation of his own views on Ṣūfism and the mystical life. His Ṣūfism was impregnated with an unceasing desire to reconcile the "exoteric" with the "esoteric," the *sharī'ah* with the *ṭarīqah* and *fiqh* with *taṣawwuf*.[63]

The Qādirī ideal of a perfect life in the world, according to Dehlawi, was firstly to adhere to the laws of the *sharī'ah* and the teachings of the *faqīh* (jurists) and then to follow the Sūfī path. Those who chose to become mystics without obtaining mastery over *fiqh* had strayed from the straight path. The Shaikh recommends to be a *Faqīh-Ṣūfī* and not a *Ṣūfī-Faqīh*.[64]

The corner-stone of Dehlawi's teachings was the maxim of Jīlānī that those aspects of the *ḥaqīqat* which the *shari'at* rejected, were heresy.

Like Jīlānī, Dehlawi adopts a moderate attitude with

---

61. Dehlawī, *Marj al-Bahrain*, Rampur, MS, p. 3.
62. The most important of Dehlawi's letters was one addressed to Shaikh Ahmad Sirhindi popularly known as Mujadid alf-i Thānī, shortly before 1031/1621-22. Naturally, it is not included in the *Kitāb al-Makātib*, and has been reproduced by Abdullah Khweshgi Qasūri in his *Ma'ariju'l Wilāyat*.
63. Dehlawi, *Kitāb al-Makātib wa'r-Rasā'il*, p. 307.
64. Ibid., pp. 126-27.

regard to both the Jabariyya[65] and Qadariyya[66] and holds that these are extremists. Dehlawi was highly critical towards those who violated the *shari'at* in the name of *tawhīd* (*Waḥdat al-Wujūd*). These impostors, according to him, cried *hama ust* (all is He), while their souls were foul and vicious. To them the unity of Being was an excuse for unrestrained behaviour. So audacious were they that they even went to the extent of hurling abuse at those Ṣūfīs who were truly virtuous.[67]

Dehlawi endorsed his father's interpretation of the phrases *hama ust* and *hama az ust* which he considered essentially identical. Only the true sense of *tawḥīd* (*Waḥdat al-Wujūd*) explained the significance of the many in One, and as long as a man became entangled in linguistic gymnastics he was unable to understand *tawḥīd*.

The sons and disciples of Dehlawi were strict adherents to the traditions of the Qādiriyya *k͟hānqāh* and were mystics as well as scholars. One of his three sons, Shaikh 'Ali Muhammad wrote treatises on the teachings and the biographies of Chistiyya Ṣūfīs, a biography of Shaikh 'Abdu'l Qādir Jīlānī (Raḥ.'A) and a dictionary of Arabic, Persian and Turkish words.

Shaikh Nūru'l Ḥaqq (b. 983/1575-76 – d. 1073/1663), the eldest son and successor of 'Abdu'l Ḥaqq, wrote a history of

---

65. A group of Muslim thinkers who believed that man was not endowed with *qadr* (free will) and that all human acts were predestined and that human beings were helpless and God was responsible for all their actions.

66. In opposition to Jabariyya, they assert a belief in "Free will" and predestination. Qadariyya maintained that men were responsible for their own actions, ignoring the Divine will.

67. Dehlawi, *Kitāb al-Makātib wa'r-Rasā'il*, pp. 36-40.

India from the earlier times to the accession of Jahāṅgīr[68] (1014/1605). There are many other works to his credit.[69] Shaikh Nūru'llāh, the only son of Nūru'l Ḥaqq, had little impact in Delhi as scholar. Two of the former's four sons, however, emerged as influential scholars. Shaikh Saifu'llāh also translated the *Shamā'il an-Nabi* of Tirmidhī into Persian and dedicated it to the Emperor Aurangzeb. Shaikh Muhibullāh wrote a Persian commentary on the *Ṣaḥīḥ* of Muslim which was later edited by Muibu'llāh's eldest son, Ḥafīẓ Muhammad Fakhru'd-Dīn. This work was entitled *Manab'al-'ilm fi Sharḥ-i Ṣaḥiḥ Muslim.* Ḥāfiẓ's son, Shaikh Islam Muhammad, was also a scholar of *Ḥadīth* and made a further translation of the *Ṣaḥiḥ* of Bukhāri. Shaikh Salamu'llah (d. 1229/1813 or 1233/1817), the son of Shaikh Islam Muhammad, migrated to Rāmpūr from Delhi. From the end of the eighteenth century through to the nineteenth century, Rampur emerged as centre of the work of the grandsons of 'Abdu'l Ḥaqq.

A modern scholar[70] gives an account of the activities of twenty disciples of 'Abdu'l Ḥaqq and Nūrul Ḥaqq who were scattered throughout India. Among them Maulana Sulaiman Kurd was intensely devoted to Shaikh 'Abdu'l Qādir Jīlānī (Raḥ.'A). He wrote a Persian *Mathnavi* entitled *Manba'al-Khairāt*

---

68. A.A. Rizwi, *Muslim Revivalist Moments in Northern India in the Sixteenth and Seventeenth Centuries*, Agra, 1965, pp. 296-98.

69. Nūrul Ḥaqq also wrote a Persian commentary on *Qiranus-Sa 'dain*, of Amir Khusrau Dihlawi (b. 651/1253, d. 725/1325) and entitled it *Nūr al-'Ain fi Sharh Qiranus-Sa'dain*. His works on *ḥadīth* include a Persian commentary on the *Ṣaḥīḥ* of *al-Bukhāri* under the title *Taisir al-Qārī fi Sharh Ṣaḥīḥ al-Bukhāri* and a Persian translation of *Shama'il an Nabī of al-Tirmidhī* (d. 279/892-93).

70. Muhammad Saleem Akhtar, *Shaikh 'Abdu'l-Ḥaqq Muhaddith Dihlawi ka silsilā-i Talāmidha*, Oriental College Magazine, Lahore, March and June, 1972, pp. 309-51.

eulogizing the great Jīlānī. Some other leading disciples of 'Abdu'l Ḥaqq who popularized Qādiriyya *silsilā* in the Indian subcontinent include Shaikh Muhammad Yaḥyā (a son of Mujadid), Muhamad Sādiq Kashmiri Hamadānī (the author of the *Kalimatiu's-Ṣādiqin* and the *Ṭabaqāt-i-Shāh Jahāni*), who was also a disciple of Naqshbandī, Bāqi Billāh. Maulana Sulaiman migrated to Ahmedabad where he founded a seminary. His son, Maulana Ahmad (d. 21 *Jumada* II, 1112/2 December 1700), was both a teacher and a scholar of some repute. His disciple, Maulana Nūrud-Dīn Ahmad Abadi (b. 10 *Jamad* I 1063/8 April 1653, d. 9 *Sha'ban* 1155/9 October 1742) made the seminary of Maulana Sulaiman Kurd popular in Ahmedabad. He also contributed commentaries on several chapters of the *Qur'ān*, on the *Ṣaḥiḥ* by al-Bukhāri and also on the *Fuṣūṣ al-Ḥikam* of Ibn-i 'Arabi.[71]

The disciples of 'Abdu'l Ḥaqq were also spread in Banaras, Bihar and Jaunpur. Among them Shaikh Taiyib from Banaras was a Ṣūfī as well as a scholar, who is credited with the spread of Qādiriyya order in that region. His disciple Shaikh Yāsīn (b. 1022/1613-14) popularized the order in Jaunpur, Banaras and Kora. Among his works, *Manāqibu'l-'Ārifin*, a biographical dictionary is of great significance.[72]

Shaikh Muhammad Rashid 'Uthmani bin Muhammad Mustafa (b. 1000/1592) was the most famous disciple of Shaikh Taiyib. He also studied with 'Abdu'l Ḥaqq and after being initiated into Qādiriyya *silsilā* became greatly interested in it and enthusiastically propagated its teachings. In order to convince the *'ulamā,'* of the true significance of Ibn-i 'Arabi's works, he wrote a commentary on certain controversial

71. Mirza M. Hasan bin 'Ali, *Mir'at-i-Ahmadi,* I, Baroda, 1930, p. 67.

72. Abdul Ha'i, *Nuzhat al-Khawātīr*, V, Hyderabad, 1955-57, p. 434.

passages contained in them.[73] Shaikh Rashid also wrote a guide for theological polemics, known as the *Rashīdiyya*. The Shaikh was an *'ālim* and a *Ṣūfī* of high repute and was known by his titles, Shamsu'l Ḥaqq Faiyaz Diwān and Diwān Shaikh 'Abdur-Rashid. On his death[74] he was survived by his four sons. Shaikh Muhammad Hamid (b. 1037/1627 d. 1086/1675), the eldest son of the Shaikh, compiled a collection of his father's verses entitled the *Dīwān-i-Shamsī*.

Muhammad Arshad (b.1041/1631-32), the son and successor of Shaikh Rashid, was inclined towards scholarly pursuits and he wrote a book on Arabic syntax entitled the *Hidāyat al-Naḥw*. He initiated a significant number of people into Qādiriyya *silsilā* and was a staunch follower of the *Waḥdat al-Wajūd*.[75] On his death (on 24 *Jumad* II, 1113/26 November 1701) the Shaikh was succeeded by his grandson, Shaikh Abū'l Faiyaz Qamaru'l Ḥaqq Ghulam Rashid (b. 8 Rabi'i, 1096/12 February 1685).[76] Shaikh Ghulam Rashid wrote a commentary on his grandfather's *Hidāyat al-Naḥw* and a Persian commentary on a well known Arabic Qaṣīdah, the *Qaṣīdah Ghawthiyya*, devoted to eulogise Shaikh 'Abdu'l Qādir Jīlānī (Raḥ.'A). Shaikh Ghulam Rashid also taught through the use of parables and anecdotes.

Ghulam Sharafu'd-Din succeeded Shaikh Ghulam Rashid

---

73. Gulam Sharafu'd Din, *Ganj-I Faiyazi*, MS., AMU, pp. 112a-13a.

74. He died on 9 *Ramaḍān* 1083/29 December, 1672. Gulam Sharafu'd Din, Ibid., p. 126.2

75. He divided *Tawḥīd* or *Waḥdat al-Wujūd* into three categories: *Tawḥīd-i-Af'āl* (Unity of Action), *Tawḥīd-i-Siffatī* (Unity of Attributes) and *Tawḥīd-i-dhāt* (Unity of Essence). For details see Shaikh Abū'l-Faiyaz Qamaru'l Haqq Ghulam Rashid, *Ganj-i-Arshidī*, MS., AMU., p. 105b.

76. Ghulam Sharafu'd-Din, *Ganj-I Faiyazī*, MS., AMU, pp. 112a–113a.

when the latter died on 5 *Ṣafar* 1167/2 December 1753. Sharfu'd Din was a scholar and *Ṣūfī* and considerably contributed to the popularization of Qādiriyya teachings in India.

A *Ṣūfī* of some repute who was initiated as a Qādiriyya in the *khānqāh* of Shaikh Rashid was Sayyid Hasan Rusūl-Numa. For fourteen years he studied in Jaunpur. His devotion to Ṣūfism was so intense that even his teacher would ask him questions on *taṣawwuf*. After his fourteen years of study and privation the Sayyid returned to his native land Nārnaul. He then moved to Delhi where for some time he was closely associated with Khawājā Khwund, the son of Khawājā Muhammad Bāqī. By the time of Aurangzeb's departure from Delhi for Marwar in September 1679, the Sayyid was famous for asceticism and piety. According to the author of *Safinatu'l-'Ārifin* he even refused to allow Aurangzeb to visit him.[77] According to Khwafī Khan, Sayyid was one of the leading Ṣūfīs of Aurangzeb's reign and his knowledge of Qur'ānic exegesis and *ḥadīth* was both extensive and perceptive.[78] Before his death in 1103/1692 he initiated many sincere devotees into Qādiriyya *silsilā*. His tomb in Delhi continues to be a centre of devotion even today.

Despite the fact that Shaikh 'Abdu'l Ḥaqq and his successors led a twofold role both as Ṣūfīs and *'ulamā'* we find that a unique legacy of mystical sensitivity and devotional exuberance was handed down to posterity by Miyān Mīr[79]

77. Muhammad Aman b. Muhamad Rahim, *Safinatu'l-Ārifin*, India Office, Delhi, Persian, p. 92b.

78. Muhammad Hashim Khan, *Muntakhabu'l-Lubāb*, I, Calcutta, 1860-74, pp. 552-53. Also cf. *Safinatu'l Ārifin*, *Tadhkira-i-Jāmi* and *Auliya-i Dihli*, India Office, Delhi, Persian, MS., p. 78a.

79. Miyān Mīr (Mīr Muhammad) was born in 938/1531-32. His ancestors came from Siwistan in Sindh. Both his parents were from families of *Qāḍīs*.

and his disciples. Most of them (in later part of their lives) abandoned their careers as theologians and scholars and preferred to live as mystics. Shaikh Khiḍr[80] was the preceptor of Miyān Mīr. In about 963/1555-56 when Mīr was released from Shaikh's tutelage, he (Mīr) began staying in the *masājid* at Lahore. During this period he attended the lectures of Maulana Sa'dullāh, an outstanding *'ālim* and scholar of Akbar's reign and his disciple Maulana Ni'matullāh and the teacher of Dārā Shukoh's tutor Mulla Mīrak Shaikh Harawi.

Miyān Mīr, after perfecting himself in formal religious education, turned to practical Ṣūfism. By about 1016/1607-08 his fame in Lahore had so much perturbed him that he migrated to Sirhind where he lived as a recluse.

After having spent about one year in Sirhind, Miyān Mīr quietly slipped back to Lahore and lived in the Muhalla Bhagbin and later Khafipura.[81]

Emperor Jahāṅgīr, in 1620, enroute to Kashmir from Sirhind, was informed about the outstanding ascetic nature of Miyān Mīr. At the Emperor's invitation Mīr visited his camp and overwhelmed Jahāṅgīr by his mystical discourse. So impressed was the Emperor with Mir's asceticism that he could not dare to present him any gift except for the skin of a white antelope to pray on.[82] Two years later when Shah 'Abbas Safawi of Iran besieged Qandahār the Emperor humbly

---

80. The Shaikh Khiḍr Qādirī lived mostly in the mountains of Siwistan in Sindh. Prefering nature to people, he loved the company of wild animals. According to legend he consumed leaves and wore nothing other than a loin cloth. Also cf. *Sakīnatu'l Awliya*, pp. 27-28.
81. Dārā Shukoh, *Sakīnatu'l Awliya*, Tehran, n.d., pp. 33-34.
82. Jahāngir, *Tuzuk-i Jahāṅgīrī*, Ghazipur, Aligarh, 1863-64, pp. 286-87.

requested Mīr to pray for him. The Emperor Shāhjahān called twice at Mir's house in Lahore.[83] Despite such attention and importance, Mīr preferred to remain aloof from worldly authorities and strongly refused human help in the form of gift or otherwise. On his death on 1 *Rabi'i*, 1045/21 August, 1635, Mīr was buried at 'Ālamganj, near Lahore.

Mīr strictly adhered to *sharī'ah* urging his disciples to do likewise. Treating *sharī'ah* as the first stage in the Ṣūfī journey, he preached that it helped to regulate worldly affairs and led to the *ṭarīqa* stage of mysticism. *Ṭariqa*, according to Mīr, was the way to purify the *nafs* (animal soul) from which evil tendencies were derived and that it was the source of a perception of the *ḥaqīqat*. Miyān Mīr held that man was constituted in the animal soul, the heart and the spirit. The first could only be reformed through obedience to the laws of the *sharī'ah*, the heart then fulfilled the obligations of the *ṭarīqa*, and the renovation of the spirit depended on observing the rules of the *ḥaqīqat*.[84]

The teachings of Qādiriyya *silsilā* were propagated by an impressive number of the disciples of Miyān Mīr. Most of them were *'ulamā'* as well as Ṣūfīs. The prominent disciples of Mīr included; Ḥājī Ni'matullāh[85] (d. 1017/1608-09), Miyān Nattha[86]

---

83. Dārā Shukoh, *Sakīnatu'l Awliya*, pp. 46-50.

84. Dārā Shukoh, *Sakinatu'l-Awliya*, p. 83.

85. During the Mir's illness at Sirhind he was so impressed by Ni'matullah's selfless devotion that he decided to make him a perfect Ṣūfī. His memory was very reverently cherished by the disciples of Miyān Mīr. For details see, Dārā Shukoh, *Sakinatu'l-Awliya*, pp. 33-35, 133.

86. Miyān-Nattha was also a native of Sirhind. He was enlisted into Miyān Mir's discipleship sometimes around 1007/1598-99. Also see Dārā Shukoh, *Sakinatu'l-Awliya*, pp. 134-40.

(d. 1027/1618-19), Ḥājī Mustafa[87] (d. 14 *Safar* 1039/3 October 1629), Mulla Ibrahim Rūḥī[88] (d. 1025/1616-17), Mulla Khawājā Kalān,[89] Mulla 'Abdu'l Ghafūr,[90] Mulla Ḥamid[91] (d. 17 *Ramadan* 1044/5 March, 1635), Hājī Ṣāliḥ Kashmiri,[92] and Mulla Khawājā Bihārī.[93] Among the few other prominent disciples of Miyān

87. Ḥājī was an inhabitant of Sirhind. He was a potter by profession whose excessive meditation had produced an ecstatic condition in which he overwhelmingly felt the presence of Allāh while offering obligatory prayers.

88. Rūḥī was an *'ālim* and a keen traveller. He became extremely popular in the areas around Mewat and Narnol, spreading the spiritual influence of Miyān Mīr in these regions. Among his disciples Safaru'd-Din and Natha Paracha were also eminent Ṣūfīs of high stature, but in order to avoid fame they indulged in trade and commerce. Cf. *Sakīnatu'l-Awliya*, p. 143.

89. Kalān came from around Lahore. His meditation had given him an insight into the condition of reward or punishment meted out to dead bodies in graves. He died before Miyān Mīr. Also see Dārā Shukoh's *Sakīnatu'l-Awliya*, pp. 144-45.

90. Abdul Ghafūr was an eminent *'ālim* and teacher in Lahore and he died during the Miyān's liftetime. Also see, Dārā Shukoh, *Sakīnatu'l-Awliya*, pp. 148-49.

91. Before Hamid became a *Ṣūfī* he was also one of the famous teachers at Lahore and at the height of his career his main preoccupation had been with accumulating wealth and criticizing Miyān Mīr. He, however, experienced a sudden inward change, and decided to renounce the world, his family and teaching to adopt the *Ṣūfī* life under the Miyān, Ibid., p. 142.

92. His more spiritual training was entrusted by Miyān Mīr to his distinguished disciple, Mulla Shah.

93. Bihari hailed from Hajipur (Patna). The quest for higher learning had brought him to Lahore. In accordance with Miyān Mir's traditions, most of his ascetic experiences were gained by him in the jungle and his other moments were devoted to becoming a compendium of esoteric knowledge and practices. Also see *Sakinatu'l-Awliya*, pp. 205-06.

Mīr, responsible for the spread of Qādiriyya *silsilā* in the Indian subcontinent mention may be made of Shaikh Muhammad Lahori,[94] Miyān Hājī Muhammad Banyani[95] (d. 7 *Ramadan* 1054/7 November 1644), Shaikh Ahmad[96] (d. 11 *Sha'bān* 1059/20 August 1649), Miyān Abu'l-Ma'ali',[97] Shaikh

94. Lahori was student of Mulla 'Abdu's-Salam Muftī of Lahore and a classmate of Dārā Shukoh's teacher, Shaikh Mirak. He was a teacher of great fame in Lahore with almost perfect knowledge of the exoteric sciences. Mysticism prompted Shaikh Muhammad to relinquish his career as an *'ālim*, dispose of his book collection and seek Miyān Mīr as his preceptor. Also see, Dārā Shukoh's *Sakinatu'l-Awliya*, pp. 209-11.

95. Banyani had been a soldier as well as a petty *manṣabdār*. After approaching Miyān Mīr for guidance he began accompanying his *pīr* and his disciples to the surrounding graves. As a mystical poet, he expressed his ideas with great sensitivity and emotion.

96. Ahmad from Sunnam, Punjab, was an *'ālim* of some repute. Adopting the life of Indian *Faqīrs*, he withdrew into the forests and refused offerings of food from visitors. Only food offered from his *pīr* was acceptable to him. Also see: Dārā Shukoh's *Sakinatu'l-Awliya*, pp. 216-17.

97. In order to conceal his spiritual attainments, Ma'ali recklessly violated the laws of the *sharī'ah*. He left his home for Lahore for receiving mystical instruction. At occasions Miyān would expound certain subtle points of the *tawḥīd* and the Absolute. As a poet he was specialized in verses of the emotional, ecstatic genre and also wrote a commentary on some twenty verses of Rumi's *Mathnavi*. In this commentary Abu'l-Ma'ali also dealt with the significance of divine love. Of one thousand names of Allāh, a lone word is *dhāt* (essence), while the rest are grouped under either *jamāl* (beauty) or *jalāl* (majesty). The holy and unknowable essence is interlinked with both *jamāl* and *jalāl*. Abu'l Ma'alī quotes some of Rumi's verses which challenged the belief of the *Mu-'atazila* sect that a vision of the Absolute was impossible.

Abū'l Ma'alī concludes his commentary by underlining the importance of divine love. He states that both Fir'aun (Pharaoh)

→

'Abdu'l Ghani[98] (d.17 *Dhulḥijja* 1057/13 Jan 1648), Miyān Muhammad Murād,[99] Abdur Rahman Mirza Madārī,[100] Shah Muhammad, generally known as Mulla Shah,[101] Mulla

---

→ and al-Hallāj cried Ana'l-Ḥaqq (I am truth). The former's cry was not founded on divine love while that of the latter was uttered in a genuine state of ecstasy and spiritual intoxication in *tawhid* (*Waḥdat al-Wujūd*), a mysterious spiritual state leading to the union of a spark of light with primordial light cf. Dārā Shukoh's *Sakinatu'l-Awliya*, pp. 220-34.

98. The Shaikh was a senior disciple of Mīr. He built a small cell near his preceptor's tomb so that he could care for it with great devotion and served as guide to those visiting it. Whenever Dārā Shukoh visited the tomb of Miyān Mīr, the Shaikh would discuss spiritual matters with the prince. Ibid., p. 235.

99. Murād was the son of celebrated Mulla 'Abdu's-Salam. He resigned his post as *Qāḍī* while he was overpowered by a desire to become a disciple of Miyān-Mīr. Enthusiastically he performed difficult devotional exercises.

100. Madārī was among the favourite disciples of Miyān Mīr, serving his pir for fourteen years. According to him, Mīr encouraged his disciples to visit other spiritualists and to learn from their teachings. Cf. Dārā Shukoh, op. cit., pp. 238-39.

101. His friends also called him *Ḥaḍrat Akhwūnd* (Revered Teacher). His disciples also believed that he had received from Allāh the title *Lisanu'llah* (Tongue of Allāh). Born in 992/1584 at Arkasa'i, a suburb of Rustaq in Badakhshan, Akhwund got elementary education in his own village and then at the age of twenty-one he migrated to Balkh for training in theology and to acquire further knowledge of Arabic. Then he moved to Srinagar, Kashmir where he stayed for three years. During this time he became more and more interested in mysticism. About 1023/1614-15 he returned to Lahore where he settled permanently, finding in Miyān Mīr his perfect *pīr*. Mīr instructed him in a series of mystical exercises. The disciple now expressed a sudden urge to write poetry.

In 1038/1628-29 Mulla Shah moved to Srinagar to reside at Hari Parbat fort. From this time he spent his summers in Srinagar and →

Muhammad Sharif,[102] Mulla Abū Bakr,[103] Mulla Īsā Siyalkoti[104]

→ winters in Lahore. During this period Shah was engrossed in the *Waḥdat al-Wujūd* to such an extent that his utterances while in ecstatic states began to match those of Bāyazīd and Hallāj. Miyān Mīr was singularly proud of Mulla Shah and prophesied that the Qādiriyya order and his own brand of spiritual discipline would gain fame through Mulla Shah.

In a letter to Dārā Shukoh's elder sister, Jahan-Āra, which was also intended for the Prince, Mulla gave a detailed explanation of the unity of Being. In 1057/1647-48 Mulla Shah composed a commentary in Persian entitled *Shāh-i-Tafsir* on chapters I, II, III and XII of the holy *Qur'ān*. His deep sensitivity about what he thought of as real infidelity was reflected in his voluminous *mathanavis*, *ghazal*s and *ruba'is*. He did not deal with those subjects in conventional poetic language but thoughtfully explained them in the *ruba'is* contained in his own commentaries. In 1049/1639-40 the Emperor Shāhjahān visited Srinagar and invited Mulla Shah, who reluctantly approved the invitation and imparted to the Emperor a definition of the *'ilm al-yaqin*, *'aynal-yaqin* and *ḥaqq al-yaqin* through an analogy. The same year prince Dārā Shukoh and his sister, Jahan-Ara became Mulla Shah's disciples.

In 1056/1646-47, at the Emperor's invitation Mulla Shah visited Lahore as a royal guest. In 1057/1647-48 Jahān Ārā ordered a *masjid* and a *khānqāh* built for Mulla Shah at the foot of Kohi Mārān hills in Srinagar.

The Mulla died in Lahore on 15 *Safar* 1072/10 October 1661. Jahān-Ārā had a red stone tomb erected over the *pīr*'s grave, enlarged the site and annexed a beautiful garden. For details about life, thought and impact of Mulla Shah see: (1) Dārā Shukoh, *Sakinatu'l Awliya*; (2) Tawwakul Beg Kaulabi, *Nuskha-i Aḥwāl-i Shahi*, MS. (AMU & British Musuem); (3) Sher Khan Lodi, *Mir'atul-Khayāl*, Bombay, 1324/1906, pp. 199–201; (4) Mulla Shah, *Shah-i Tafsir* and (5) Mathnawi Mulla Shah (Indian Office MS).

102. Dārā Shukoh, *Sakīnatu'l Awliya*, p. 242.

103. Ibid., p. 243.

104. Ibid., p. 244.

and Sayyid Ashraf.[105]

Among the prominent disciples of Mulla Shah, who propagated Qādiriyya teachings in the Indian subcontinent mention may be made of Khawājā 'Abdu'l Wahhāb,[106] Tawakkul-Beg,[107] Ḥafīẓ Ṭariq 'Ali,[108] Ḥakīm Masihu'z-Zaman,[109] Banwali Daswali[110] and Dārā Shukoh.

---

105. Ibid., p. 245. Among these Mulla Muhammad Sharif and Mulla Isa Siyalkoti were initiated by Miyān Mīr on the same day. Both habitually visited their *pīr* together and later acquired a degree of ascetic perfection. Mulla Muhammad Sharief settled in Ruhtas, on the road to Kabul, and Mulla Īsā Siyalkoti lived alternately in Lahore and Siyalkot.

106. Wahhāb was a descendant of Khawājā Dahbedi, an eminent Naqshbandī. He migrated from Tranoxiana to India during the reign of Shāhjahān and there he was given a *mansab* of 1,500. Tawakkul Beg Kaulabi, *Nuskha-i-Aḥwāl Shāh-i*, pp. 33b-34a. MS, British Museum, and AMU.

107. He became Mullā Shah's disciple in about 1031/1622 and their association continued for forty years. Around 1053/1643-44 he was employed by Shāh Shuja. In 1054/1644 Dārā Shukoh appointed him a *mansabdār* of 200 and go-between for himself and his *pīr*, Mulla Shah.

108. He was from Kabul and was an ascetic and a fine calligrapher. In his spare moments he copied the words of Mulla Shah.

109. Zamān was a Shi'i scholar who embraced Sunnism and became Mulla Shah's disciple. Also see Kaulabi, ibid., pp. 66a-b.

110. Walī was formerly a Hindu munshi (secretary) to Dārā Shukoh. He wrote a history of the Hindu *rājā*s of Delhi from the time of Yudhiṣṭhira to the invasion of Muizzu'd-Din Muhammad bin Sām, and gave a tabulated list of the subsequent Muslim rulers up to the Emperor Shāhjahān. His dīwan of *ghazal*s and *mathnavī*s was popular and has been published. He also translated a Sanskrit drama, *Prabodha Candrodaya*, into Persian called the *Gulzār-i-Hāl*. In his *mathnavi*, he sensitively poured out his heart in a eulogy of his *pīr*, Mulla Shah, and his *silsilā*. He died in the year 1085/1674-75. Also see: Kaulabi, ibid., p. 64b.

Dārā Shukoh (b. in Ajmer on 29 *Safar* 1024/30 March 1615)[111] was the eldest son of Emperor Shāhjahān from his wife Arjamand-Bānū (Mumtaz Mahal). Dara's first religious teacher was Mulla 'Abdu'l Latif (d. 1036/1626-27) from Sultanpur in the Punjab.[112] Mulla Shah who had received instructions from Miyān Mir[113] was the first to interest the young prince in Ṣūfism. On account of his deep love and appreciation for art and beauty, Dārā Shukoh also proved an excellent calligrapher.

Dārā Shukoh received his first *mansab* (12,000/6,000) in 1042/1633 and the lucrative *jāgīr* of Hisār-Firūza in the Punjab was assigned to him.[114] He was appointed as the governor of Allahabad, Punjab, Gujarat, Multan and Kabul between 1055/ 1645, and 1062/1652. Dārā Shukoh was promoted to the *mansab* of 60,000/40,000 in 1067/1657 by the Emperor Shāhjahān.

Dara's fascination for Ṣūfism and an irrevocable sense of his own destiny hindered him from more assiduously preparing himself for the challenges and hazards which his role as a heir apparent presented.[115]

111. Dārā Shukoh, *Safīnatu'l Awliya,* p. 94. On the life and career of Dārā Shukoh, see Muhammad Salih Kamboh Lahauri, *'Amāl-i-Ṣālih,* Calcutta, 1912, pp. 225-31; William Foster, *The English Factories in India,* 1624-29, Oxford; Abdul Hamid Lahauri, *Padshah Nāma,* I, Calcutta, 1866-72, p. 391; 1909, p. 247.

112. Rahman Ali says that Mulla Abdul-Latif Sultanpūrī was one of Aurangzeb's teachers and was an expert in both rational and theological sciences. Rahman Ali, *Tadhkira-i-'Ulamā'-I Hind,* 2nd edn., Lucknow, 1914, p. 132.

113. Dārā Shukoh, *Sakīnatu'l Awliya,* pp. 31, 59, 209, 236, 243.

114. Abdul Hamid Lahauri, *Padshah Nama,* p. 541.

115. Three younger brothers of Dārā Shukoh began plotting against him and when Shāhjahān fell ill on 7 *Dhilhijja* 1067/16 September 1657, the inevitable fratricidal war between Mughal siblings erupted. After two military reverses in 1068/1658 and 1069/ →

Dārā Shukoh's interest in the Qādiriyya order had first been kindled by his tutor, the revered Mulla Shah and later deepened through his association with Miyān Mīr. The interest of Miyān Mīr and other Qādiriyya *pīrs* in prince Dārā Shukoh, increasingly stimulated his interest in Ṣūfism. Gradually he came to have an obsessive belief that the Ṣūfī orders in India were the pivot on which all worldly and spiritual matters depended. He attributed his own well-being to the Qādiriyya *silsilā*.[116]

Dārā authored a number of works among which his *Safīnatu'l Awliya, Sakīnatu'l-Awliya, Risāla-i-Ḥaqq-Numā, Hasanatul 'Ārifīn* and *Iksir-i-A'zam* are the prominent ones. His mystical *rubā'is* and *ghazals* were also compiled later by Ahmad Nabi Khan under the title, *Diwān-i Dārā Shukoh.*

Dārā completed his first text on Ṣūfism, the *Safīnatu'l Awliya* on 27 *Ramadan* 1049/21 January 1640. It is a biographical dictionary which lists all the significant Ṣūfīs and is divided into eight sections. The second section is the most elaborate

---

→ 1659, at Samugarh near Agra and Deora near Ajmer respectively, Dārā, relentlessly pursued by Aurangzeb's loyal Rājpūt general, Mirza Raja Jai Singh, first fled to north of Ahmedabad and then decided to continue to Iran via Qandahar (Kandhar). In this attempt to escape to Iran he entrusted himself to Malik-Jiwan. In the hope of reward the perfidious Afghan, who controlled the fort of Dadar near the Bolan Pass, handed over the unfortunate Dārā and his younger son, Siphir Shukoh to Aurangzeb. Dārā and his son were paraded through the streets of Delhi. The exhibition of public support in favour of Dārā and his son, however, hastened Aurangzeb's decision to murder Dārā and his son. Both of them were eventually executed on 22nd *Dhuhijja* 1069/10 September 1659 on the charges of heresy and infidelity. Cf. Munshi Muhammad Kazim, *'Ālamgīr-nāma*, Calcutta, 1868, p. 432; *Muntakhabu'l Lubāb*, p. 68; Muhammad Saqī, Musta'idd Khan, *Ma'asir-i-Alamgīrī*, Calcutta, 1870-73, p. 27.

116. Dārā Shukoh, *Sakīnatu'l Awliya*, Tehran, n.d., pp. 13-17.

and deals exclusively with Qādiriyya *silsilā*. *Sakīnatu'l Awliya* gives an account of Miyān Mīr, Bībī Jamāl Khātūn and the disciples of Miyān. The work was completed in 1052/1643. In this work Dārā stresses his conviction that every Muslim should be initiated into one of the five *silsilās* (the Qādiriyya, Naqshbandiyya, Chistiyya, Kubrawiyya and Suhrawardiyya). Nevertheless he continues to press the superiority of the Qādiriyya. Shukoh holds that many eminent Ṣūfīs prior to Shaikh 'Abdu'l Qādir Jīlānī (Raḥ.'A) prophesied the spiritual prominence of the order's founder and that leading saints of the other four orders had been in contact with Jīlānī and received some form of spiritual benefit. Shaikh's claim that his foot was on the neck of every saint of Allāh was, according to Dārā, divinely inspired and therefore indicative of his eminence.[117]

In *Risāla-i-Ḥaqq-Numā*, completed in the year 1056/1647, Shukoh asserted that the form of Ṣūfism he outlined was patterned on the daily religious life of the Prophet (SAW). The treatise had been originally designed to describe firstly the four *'awālam* (spiritual realms)[118] through which mystics passed during their Sūfic journey, and secondly the Qādiriyya meditational exercises. Later, he added another two chapters on *Waḥdat al-Wujūd*.

Dārā Shukoh's growing interest in Ṣūfism and his association with Hindu mystics provided his rivals with a pretext for attack. The prince hastened to complete his *Hasanatu'l 'Ārifīn*, as a vehicle for his own defence, which gave a detailed explanation of the ecstatic utterances of mystics. The preface of the work contains a strong condemnation of

117. Dārā Shukoh, *Safīnatu'i Awliya*, Kanpur, 1900, pp. 13-20.

118. These include *'Ālam-i-Nāsūt* (Physical world), *Ālam-i Mīsāl* (World of Images), *Ālam-i-Malakūt* (angelic kingdom) and *Ālam-i-Jabarūt* (the world of absolute sovereignty).

those whom he considered so bigoted that they even taunted him with charges of infidelity and apostasy because of his interest in mysticism and the *Waḥdat al-Wujūd*. The book was commenced in 1062/1651-52 and completed at the end of *Rabi'i* 1064/February 1654.

Iksir-i-A'zam is basically a *dīwān* produced by Dārā and it consists of his *ghazals* and *rubā'is*. Using Qādirī as his *nom de plume*, his poems are fashioned after those of Shabistārī and Jāmī. Besides his favourite theme of the *Wahadat al-Wujūd*, Dara's poems glorify the Qādiriyyas and constantly challenge the mullahs for their approach.[119]

Qādiriyyas in the Deccan

Qādiriyya *silsilā* (order) was introduced into Deccan by Mīr Nuru'llah bin Shah Khalilullah, a grandson of Shah Nūrud-Din Muhamad Ni'amatullah bin 'Abdu'llah.[120]

The extent of devotion shown by the Bahmanid *sulṭān*, Shihābu'd-Din Ahmad (825/1422–839/1436) to Shah Ni'amatu'llah is worth to mention. The author of *Burhan-i-Ma'āsir* asserts that the *sulṭān*'s lack of faith in the spirituality of contemporary Deccani Ṣūfīs had forced him to approach

119. Ahmad Nabi Khan, ed., *Dīwān-i Dāra Shukoh*, Lahore, 1969, pp. 13, 54-55.

120. Ni'amatullah was well known for his copious *Ṣūfī* writings in both prose and poetry. Cf. E.G. Brown, *Literary History of Persia*, III, rpt., Cambridge, 1964, pp. 463-73. Ni'amatullah was born in Aleppo, Syria, in 730/1330. After the death of his *Murshid* (Preceptor), Abdullah al-Yāfī (b. 697/1298 – d. 768/1367), Ni'amatullah travelled through Iran, Samarqand, Herat and Yazd, finally settling in Mahan in the Kirmān province of Iran. His descendants in India could, therefore, trace their spiritual genealogy directly back to the Qādiriyyas because of the Shah's intimate relations with the Qādiriyyas of Iran.

Shah Ni'amatullah Walī, whose sanctity and miraculous power had made him somewhat prominent in the area. Moreover, in the first year of his reign the *sulṭān* had sent Shaikh Khujan, a disciple of Shah's family at his court, to Kirmān and the Shah had initiated the *sulṭān in absentia*. The Shah also reciprocated with the Ṣūfī robe and cap.[121] Soon after transferring his capital from Gulbarga to Bidar in 827/1424, Sulṭān Ahmad I urged the Shah to send to his court one of his own sons for company and spiritual guidance. The Shah deputed his grandson Mīr Nūrullah.[122] Mīr was feted by a royal welcome, and a new town, close to Bidar, was built and called Ni'amatabad in his honour. According to Firishta the Mīr was also given the title, *Malikul-Mashāi'kh,* as well as official precedence over all other Ṣūfīs in the Deccan.[123]

Sulṭān Ahmad I married his daughter to Mīr Nūru'llah. After Shah Ni'amatullah's death at Mahan in 834/1430-31, Shah Khalīlullah accompanied by his other sons, Shah Habibullah and Shah Muhibu'llah, joined his son (Mīr Nuru'llah) in Deccan. Another royal princess[124] was given in marriage to Shah Habibu'llah, and the *sulṭān*'s grand daughter became the wife of Shah Muhibu'llah. The coronation of the *sulṭān*'s successor, 'Alau'd Dīn Abū Muẓaffar Ahmad Shah II, was attended by Shah Khalīlullah in 839/1436.[125] Some sources mention that Shah Khalīlu'llah retired to Mahan, while others assert that he died

121. Ali b. Azizu'llah Tabataba'i *Burhān-i, Ma'āsir*, Hyderabad, 1355/ 1936, p. 54.

122. Ibid., p. 65.

123. Firishta, *Gulshan-i-Ibrāhim*, p. 329.

124. She was daughter of the heir-apparent, 'Alau'd-Din who ruled as 'Ala'ud-Din Ahmad II from 839/1436 to 862/1458. Tabataba'i, *Burhan-i Ma'asir*, p. 81; Firishta, *Gulshan-i-Ibrāhim*, p. 329.

125. Tabatabā'i, *Burhān-i Ma'āsir*, p. 74.

in the Deccan.[126] Nevertheless, his sons remained in Deccan where under the Bahmanid *sulṭāns* they continued to enjoy considerable power and prestige. However, at the end of the reign of Sulṭān 'Alau'd-Din Humāyūn (862/1458-865/1461) Shah Habibu'llah was executed by the *sulṭān* because of his opposition to the monarch's cruelty and the political support he had extended to prince Hasan Khan.[127] Shah Muhibu'llah died some time after 900/1494-95 in the reign of Sulṭān Shihabū'd-Din Mahmūd (887/1482–924/1518).[128]

The presence of Shah Ni'amatullah Wali's sons and grandsons in the Bahmanid sultanate during the Bidar period strengthened Irani elements in the culture of the Deccan on one hand and on the other hand it facilitated the enrolment of more and more Ṣūfīs and saints in the Qādiriyya *silsilā* (order).

The Qādiriyyas in Sindh and Punjab

In the second half of the fifteenth century a Qādiriyya *khānqāh* was established at Uch near Multan. Sheikh Muhammad al-Husaini al-Jīlānī, the founder of this *khānqāh*, was a direct descendant of Shaikh 'Abdu'l Qādir. His genealogical tree is as under.

Shaikh Muhammad Husaini b. Sayyid Shah Amir b. Sayyid 'Ali b. Sayyid Mas'ūd b. Sayyid Ahmad b. Sayyid Saifu'd Dīn b. Shaikh Saifu'd Dīn 'Abdu'l Wahhab b. Shaikh 'Abdu'l Qādir Jīlānī (Raḥ.'A).[129]

Al-Husaini was originally a native of Turkey and travelled to Khurasan, then Multan and Uch, in a grand tour of the

126. Firishta, op. cit., p. 329.

127. Tabatabā'i, op. cit., p. 94.

128. Ibid., pp. 153-55.

129. Shaikh 'Abdu'l Ḥaqq Muhadith Dehlawi, *Akhbāru'l Akhyār*, p. 429.

Islamic world. Upon deciding to settle in Uch he returned to his homeland to bring his family and a large retinue of his followers. There was a dearth of spiritual talent in Multan, so naturally the Shaikh and his followers were warmly welcomed by the Multani ruler and the Uch elite.

Shaikh Muhammad al-Husaini was also a poet who used the pen-name Qādirī. A selection of eight of his verses quoted by Shaikh 'Abdu'l Ḥaqq indicates that he used traditional Ṣūfī similies such as *qalandar*, the wine bottle, the wine cup and exuberance.[130] Al-Husaini passed away in 894/1488 and was survived by three sons: 'Abdu'l Qādir Thāni, Sayyid 'Abdu'llah and Sayyid Mubārak. Of these Sayyid 'Abdu'llah was also a great poet and it has been said by 'Abdu'l-Rahman Jāmi that Maulana Nūrud-Dīn (817/1414–898/1492) sent his own verses to him for comment.[131]

Shaikh 'Abdu'l Qādir Thāni, the eldest son of Shaikh Muhammad al-Husaini, emerged as the new leader of Qādiriyyas at Uch. According to Dārā Shukoh, Sheikh 'Abdu'l Qādir converted a large number of Hindus to Islam, as well as causing many wayward Muslims to adopt a pious life.[132]

Shaikh 'Abdur Razzaq, the eldest son of Shaikh 'Abdu'l Qādir Thānī succeeded his father in 940/1533. After a brief period he passed away in 942/1535.[133] His place was assumed by his son, Shaikh Ḥamid, who had been trained by his grandfather, Sheikh 'Abdu'l Qādir Thāni. In Uch he was showered with gifts and grants which he apparently enjoyed

130. Shaikh 'Abdu'l Ḥaqq Muhadith Dehlawi, *Akhbāru'l Akhyār*, p. 430.

131. Ibid., p. 431.

132. Muhammad Dārā Shukoh, *Safīnatu'l Awliya*, Lucknow, 1872, p. 69.

133. Dehlawi, op. cit., p. 436.

disposing of. Shaikh Ḥamīd died in the year 778/1571 and was buried in Ḥamīdpūra, a village of Multan.[134]

The issue of succession remained unresolved for several years between Shaikh 'Abdu'l Qādir and Shaikh Mūsa, the sons of Shaikh Ḥamīd. Eventually, in Uch and Multan, Shaikh 'Abdu'l Qādir was recognized as the father's successor and in Delhi and at Akbar's court scholars and Ṣūfīs honoured Shaikh Mūsa in this role. Shaikh 'Abdu'l Ḥaqq Muhaddith Dehlawi, a disciple of Shaikh Mūsa, also describes his preceptor as Shaikh Ḥamid's successor.[135] Shaikh Mūsa's life at court was fruitful as he was a loyal supporter of Akbar and a friend to the two powerful courtiers, Faiḍī and Abu'l Faḍal.[136] Shaikh Mūsa Qādirī was killed by some rebels, headed by Maḥmūd Langah, in early February CE 1602. The obituary by Abul Faḍl included these lines:

"Shaikh Mūsā Qādirī was among the turban wearers who led the life of a *khānqāh* dweller. Discipleship (*murīdī*)[137] of the Emperor enabled him to achieve the rank of an *amīr*."[138]

Shaikh Dāwūd was another outstanding disciple and successor of Shaikh Ḥamīd. He studied under eminent scholars in Multan, Uch and Lahore and devoted himself passionately to Ṣūfism. Once or twice annually on the death and birth anniversaries of Shaikh 'Abdu'l Qadir Jilānī (Raḥ.'A), some hundred thousand people would assemble near his Shergarh

---

134. Badāyūnī, *Muntakhabu't-Tawārikh*, III, p. 91; Dehlawi, op. cit., p. 437.

135. Dehlawi, op. cit., p. 437.

136. S.A.A. Rizvi, *Religious and Intellectual History of the Muslims in Akbar's Reign*, pp. 183, 185, 291, 331.

137. S.A.A. Rizvi, *Religious and Intellectual History of the Muslims in Akbar's Reign*, pp. 394-417.

138. Abūl Fazal, *AkbarNāma*, III, Calcutta, 1886, p. 802.

k͟hānqāh to share the gifts received by Shaikh Dāwūd.[139]

Mulla 'Abdu'l Qādir Badāyūnī, after hearing first-hand information of the Shaikh's fame from the Ṣūfīs travelling in Punjab, visited the Shaikh some time about 981/1573-74 at Shergarh. The celebrated author has put on record his impressions in his chronicle.[140] More particularly he describes the significant number of non-Muslims embracing Islam under the guidance of the Shaikh. Before his death in 982/1574-75 at Shergarh, the Shaikh was invited by Emperor Akbar in 981/1573-74 through Shahbaz Khan, Kamboh, an orthodox Sunnī, to attend his court. The Shaikh, however, turned down this invitation and pleaded that his secret prayers for the Emperor were sufficient for the spiritual welfare of the latter.[141]

Shaikh Abūl Ma'ālī (b. 961/1553-54), the nephew and son-in-law of Shaikh Dāwūd emerged as his successor. Owing to his considerable religious and literary background, Abūl Ma'ālī began writing poetry under the name of *Ghurbati*. Here is an example:

> How can this frozen heart be warmed by the speech of all?
> Nay, it requires the breath of Dāwūd, which can soften even iron.[142]

And again he praises Dāwūd in these verses:

> I sit on the throne of poverty, now that I have attained.
> I reign like Sulaiman (A.S), for I am heart and soul the slave of Dāwūd.

139. Badayūnī, op. cit., pp. 29-35; Abul Fazl, op. cit., p. 207.

140. Badayūnī, op. cit., pp. 35-36, Eng. tr. Wolsely Haig, III, Calcutta, 1925, pp. 57-60.

141. A.A.Rizwi, *Religious and Intellectual History of the Muslims in Akbar's Reign*, pp. 186-87.142.

142. Badāyūnī, *Muntak͟habu't-Tawārikh*, Eng. tr. W. Haig, III, p. 153.

Again he says:

> *Ghurbati* make thy life a sacrifice to Him.
> For the felicity of union with Him is not bestowed as a worthless gift.

The Shaikh died on 16 *Rabi'i* 1024/15 April 1615 and was buried in Lahore.

Shaikh 'Abdu'l Ḥaqq Muhadith Dehlawi, the author of *Akhbāru'l Akhyār*, was one among the most prominent devotees and admirers of Abūl Ma'ālī.

Shaikh Abū Isḥāq Qādirī was another leading disciple of Shaikh Dāwūd. Before his death in Lahore on 5 *Muharram* 985/25 March 1577, Abū Isḥāq lived as a very popular Ṣūfī. His place of burial turned as a central point around which the cluster of tombs of his descendants was later built.[143] Shah Sahmsu'Dīn Qādirī was the most significant disciple of Abū Isḥāq. Emperor Jahāṅgīr is said to have had great reverence for his miraculous powers.[144]

Sayyid 'Abdu'llah Rabbāni and his son Sayyid Ismā'īl Gīlānī are among the other early Qādirī Ṣūfīs of Punjab. Emperor Akbar is said to have presented 1,000 *bīghās*[145] of land in Firozpur to Gīlānī. Besides many other people, the merchants of Lahore were among his greatest followers. Both Rabbāni and Gīlānī passed away in the year 978/1570-71.[146]

Among other prominent Qādiriyyas of Punjab was Shaikh Bahlul Darya'i[147] (d. 983/1575-76) and his disciple Shaikh

---

143. Ghulam Sarwar, *Khazīnatu'l Āsfiya*, Lucknow, 1873, I, pp. 132-33.
144. Ghulam Sarwar, *Khazīnatu'l Āsfiya*, I, op. cit., p. 184.
145. A Mughal *bīghā* was approximately five-eighths (5/8) of an acre.
146. Ghulam Sarwar, op. cit., I, p. 127.
147. Ibid., pp. 131-32.

Hussain Lahori (d. 1008/1599). Husain's great grandfather, Kalas Rai had embraced Islam during Sulṭān Firūz Shah Tughluq's reign (752/1351–790/1388). During his lifetime Shaikh Husain enrolled a legion of disciples who became Qādirī ambassadors in all parts of Punjab as well as elsewhere in India.[148]

Shaikh Madho, a favourite disciple of Shaikh Husain enrolled a good number of people into Qādiriyya *silsilā*, after the death of Husain. He succeeded his preceptor as head of the *khānqāh*. Madho died in the year (1056/1646-47) and was succeeded by his disciple Shaikh Rang Balau'l. It was, however, Balau'l's disciple, Hājī 'Abdu'l Jamil (d. 1082/1671-72) who emerged as an influential Qādirī saint and achieved prominence in Lahore. Hājī is reported to have built a dome over the footprints of Prophet Muhammad (SAW) which his ancestors had brought from Hijaz.[149]

Another branch of Qādiriyya *silsilā* in Punjab flourished through Sayyid Muhammad Ghawth Bala Pir (d. 959/1551-52), a grandson of Shaikh 'Abdu'l Qādir Thāni. He travelled extensively and first settled at Uch but later migrated to Satghara in the Punjab.[150] His son and successor, Sayyid Jiwān (d. 1022/1613-14)[151] was given the prestigious title of Sayyid 'Abdu'l Qādir *Thālith* (the third) in recognition of his piety and asceticism. After his father's death, Jiwān travelled extensively throughout India and finally settled at Lahore where he founded a quarter called Rasulpūra.

Abdur Razzāq Chiragh Lahorī, one of the grandsons of Jiwan, became an eminent scholar and Ṣūfī. He was highly

148. Ghulam Sarwar, op. cit., I, pp. 141-46.

149. Ibid., I, pp. 176-77.

150. Ibid., p. 124.

151. Ibid., pp. 148-49.

respected by the Mughal Emperor Shāhjahān. He passed away in the year 1068/1657-58 in Lahore and was buried near the tombs of his father and grandfather.[152]

The successors of Shah Ma'rūf Qādirī (d. 987/1579-80), a descendant of Bābā Farīd, who were also Qādiriyyas, enjoyed considerable following in Punjab. Among them the most noteworthy was Shah Sulaiman (d. 1065/1654-55) and his most outstanding *Khalīfah* Shaikh Hājī Muhammad Qādirī (d. 1064/1654),[153] who was better known as Naushah Gani Bakhsh. His successors were known as Naushahiyyas and until modern times their founder enjoyed the most intense devotion and respect of the villagers around Lahore. Some of the many sons and grandsons of Shaikh Naushah were Ṣūfīs. Their descendants, who chose various villages around Lahore for their spiritual and meditational activities, proved a source of great strength to Muslims during the political and military upheavals and turmoil in Punjab in the eighteenth and nineteenth centuries.

Khawājā Muhammad Fuzail Naushahi (d. 1111/1699-1700) emerged as the most eminent disciple of the Shaikh. He was a native of Kabul and had served the Mughal government and resigned from the public service to become more deeply involved in *taṣawwuf*.

Shaikh Muhammad Taqī Qādirī (d. 1133/1720-21), Shaikh Pir Muhammad, Qāḍī Ruknu'd Dīn were also among the prominent disciples of the celebrated Shaikh Naushah who enrolled a significant number of people into Qādiriyya *silsilā* in Punjab and its adjacent territories.[154]

---

152. Ibid., p. 172.

153. Muhammad Iqbal Mujaddidi, *Intikhāb-i-Ganj-i Sharif,* ed. Sayyid Sharafat Naushahi, Lahore, 1975, pp. 15-17.

154. Idem.

Through the influence of Shaikh Kamāl (d. 981/1573), disciple of Shaikh Fuzail of Baghdad, the town of Pa'il and Kaithal, near Sirhind, became the centres of the Qādiriyya *silsilā*. Passionately fond of travelling, during his peregrinations in Thanesar, Shaikh Kamāl met Shaikh 'Abdu'l Ahad, the father of the famous Shaikh Ahmad Sirhindi. They developed great intimacy. Both Shaikh Kamāl and his successor and grandson Shaikh Sikandar (d. 1023/1614-15), strengthened Shaikh 'Abdu'l Ahad's interest in the Qādiriyyas although he had already obtained initiation into the Chistiyya order.[155]

Qādiriyya Silsilā in Kashmir

With Uch and Lahore as bases, branches of the Qādiriyya order were founded in Kashmir. Shaikh Ahmad Qādirī, a descendant of Shaikh Bahāu'd-Din Zakariyya, was one of the early founders in that region. Shaikh Ahmad was initiated into Qādiriyya *silsilā* by Shaikh Muhammad at Lahore. Bābā Dāwūd Khākī[156] (d. 994/1586) invited him to settle in Kashmir. Shaikh Ahmad finally died in Srinagar and was buried there in Qutbu'd-Din Pura.

Hājī Mūsā, the son and successor of Shaikh Ahmad Qādirī often sought seclusion in the jungles of Kashmir and Punjab. People became more convinced of his spiritual power after he reportedly repulsed an elephant single-handed at Lahore.[157]

155. Muhammad Hashim, *Zubdatu'l Maqāmāt*, Kanpur, 1890, pp. 104-08.

156. Bābā Dāwūd Khaki was an influential scholar and *Ṣūfī* of Kashmir and also a disciple of Shaikh Hamza Makhdūm (900/984-1494/1576) a distinguished Suhrawardiyya leader of Kashmir. Impressed by the asceticism and piety of Shaikh Ahmad, Khaki became a Qādiriyya. *Risala-i-Ghusliya, Rishi Nāma, Wirdu'l Muridin* and *Dasturu's-Sālikīn* are prominent works of Bābā Dāwūd.

157. Khawājā Muhammad A'zam Didamari, *Waqi'āt-i Kashmir*, Lahore, 1303/1886, pp. 108-09.

After the death of Mīr Nāzuk,[158] a Suhrawardiyya and a Qādiriyya, in 1022/1613-14[159] at Srinagar and then that of his son and successor, Mīr Yūsuf Qādirī,[160] the responsibility for enrolling the people into Qādiriyya *silsilā* fell upon Mīr Muhamad 'Ali Qādirī, the youngest son of Mīr Nāzuk.

Mīr Muhammad 'Ali Qādirī, while on his way to Delhi, met Shaikh Muhammad Ma'ṣūm, the son of Mujaddid 'Alifi Thānī (d. 1034/1624), in Sirhind. Both the Ṣūfīs expressed their dissatisfaction with the administration of Shah Jahān and became friendly. The Mīr died in 1070/1659-60 at Srinagar and his successors enthusiastically continued the preaching of Qādiriyya order in Kashmir.[161]

Two Kashmiri brothers, namely Khawājā Hasan and Khawājā Isḥāq, were also enrolled into Qādiriyya *silsilā* by Shaikh Ahmad Qādirī. Both of them were disciples of Shaikh Hamzah in the early period of their life. Khawājā Hasan lived in a village near Zaingiri where he was finally buried after his death. Khawājā Isḥāq preached and practised the Qādiriyya teachings for some time before his migration to Madīnah where he eventually passed away and was buried there.[162]

Shah Ni'amatullāh Qādirī and Shah Muhammad Fāḍil were two prominent Qādiriyya Ṣūfīs who migrated to Kashmir for some time in seventeenth and eighteenth centuries respectively. Shah Ni'amatullāh migrated from Punjab and

---

158. Mīr Nāzuk was originally a disciple of Bābā. He was a puritan and fiercely opposed to Sama.

159 Didamarī, op. cit., pp. 126-27.

160. Ibid., pp. 128-29.

161. Ibid., op. cit.; pp. 141, 163.

162. A.A. Rizvi, *History of Ṣūfism in India*, vol. I, Delhi, 1986, pp. 300–09; Didamari, op. cit., pp. 121-22.

initiated one Hājī Bābā, a member of Katjū merchant community of Kashmir, into Qādiriyya *silsilā*. Ni'amatullāh's activities in Kashmir strengthened Qādiriyya circles there. Before his departure from Kashmir, Ni'amatullah appointed Hājī Bābā as his spiritual successor. After the death of Hājī Bābā in 1066/1655-56, Qādiriyya *silsilā* flourished under the patronage of his son 'Uthmān Qādirī alias Bābā. 'Uthmān emerged as a widely respected and influential Qādirī saint.[163] Fāḍil[164] (d. 1117/1705) is believed to have been a descendant of Shaikh 'Abdu'l Qādir Jīlānī (Raḥ.'A). He reached Kashmir about 1090/1679-80.

Shaikh Mīrak Mīr (d. 5 *Safar* 990/1st March 1582) is mentioned as another prominent Ṣūfī of Qādirī silsilā in Kashmir. The ancestors of Mīr had migrated to Kashmir from Andrāb[165] during the late fourteenth century.[166] Shaikh Mirak, after the death of his father Shamsu'd-Din Andrābī spent most of his time in meditation at Srinagar in *Khānqāh-i-Andrabi*,[167] built originally by one of his ancestors. Under Shaikh Mirak this *khānqāh* emerged as the headquarter of Qādiriyya Ṣūfīs in Kashmir.

Sayyid Ismā'īl Shāmī was another Qādirī saint of some repute who migrated to Kashmir in 992/1581, from India.[168]

---

163. Didamari., op. cit., p. 144.
164. Ibid., pp. 201-02.
165. The city of Andrab is on the confines of Khurasan towards India.
166. Dāwūd Khākī, *Rīshī Nāma*, p. 42a; Muhammad Husain Qādirī, *Futuhat-i Qādiriya*, p. 208 b.; Dāwūd Mishkati, *Asraru'l Abrār*, p. 192a.
167. Qādirī, op. cit., p. 208 a; Mishkati, op. cit., pp. 190 a-b; Khākī, op. cit., pp. 40b-41a.
168. Mishkātī, p. 189a; Qādirī, op. cit., p. 205b; Hasan Shah, *Tārīkh-i Hasan*, III, p. 54.

Like many other Qādiriyyas, Shāmī also traced his descent from Shaikh 'Abdu'l Qādir Jīlānī (Raḥ.'A). Shāmī was initiated into the Qādirī order by one Sayyid Muhammad Qasim.[169] Sayyid Ismā'il besides patronizing the Qādiriyya *silsilā* in Kashmir developed great intimacy with some other Ṣūfīs including Bābā Dāwūd Khākī and his disciple Mīr Nazuk Niyazi. The piety and devotional zeal of Ismā'il has been extolled in many sources.[170] On his departure from Kashmir Sayyid gave *khirqa* and *ijāzat-nāma* to Mīr Nāzuk, thereby granting him permission to enrol disciples in the order.[171] Mīr breathed his last on 9 *Dhu'l Hijja*, 1022/20 January 1614, and was buried at Qadi-Kadal in Srinagar.[172] After the death of Mīr Nāzuk, the charge of his *khānqāh* at Khanyar in Srinagar, was taken up by his eldest son, Mīr Yūsuf[173] (d. 1027/1617). It was, however, Mīr Muhammad 'Ali (d. 17 *Dhu'l-Hijja*, 1070/ 24 August 1660), the third son of Mīr Nāzuk, who popularized the Qādirī order in Kashmir. This *khānqāh* at Khānyār, Srinagar continues to be a great centre of visitation and veneration. The celebration of 'Urs-i Shaikh 'Abdu'l Qādir Jīlānī every year on 11th of *Rabi'u'l Thāni*, in which thousands of *muhibbān* (devotees) of the great Shaikh participate with high enthusiasm, is a regular feature with this *khanqah*.

---

169. Didamarī, op. cit., p. 106; Shah, op. cit., p. 63; Mishkātī, op. cit., p. 190a.

170. Hasan Shah, op. cit., p. 54; Qādirī, op. cit., pp 205 a-b; Didamari, op. cit., p. 106; Mishkati, op. cit., p. 188a. Bābā Dāwūd Khākī eulogizes laudable character, spiritual achievements and simplicity of Sayyid Isma'il in a poem.

171. Miskīn, Tārīkh-i Kabīr, p. 179; Qādirī, op. cit., p. 206b; Hasan, op. cit., p. 246; Dīdamarī, op. cit., pp. 126-27.

172. Dīdamarī, op. cit., p. 127; Hasan, op. cit., p. 249; Miskīn, op. cit., p. 180.

173. Hasan Shah, *Tārīkh-i Hasan*, vol. III, p. 275; Miskīn, op. cit., p. 180.

Qādiriyya Silsilā in Gujarat and Malwa

Sayyid Jamāl Pathri, who traced his lineage back to Shaikh 'Abdu'l Qādir Jīlānī, is regarded as the founder of Qādiriyya *silsilā* in this region. His father, Sayyid Hussain had earlier migrated from Iran to Deccan and settled at Pathri near Ahmadnagar. Sayyid Jamāl, in response to an invitation given by Sulṭān Bahādur Shah (932/1526–943/1537) of Gujarat, settled in Ahmedabad in a *khānqāh* built for him by the *sulṭān*. In 971/1564. On the death of the Sayyid, Sayyid Yatīmullāh, his son succeeded to the leadership of this *khānqāh*.[174]

Sayyid Ghiyāth ud-Dīn and Shāhjī were among other Qādiriyya Ṣūfīs who claimed their descent from Shaikh 'Abdu'l Qādir Jīlānī (Raḥ.'A), and settled in Gujarat. Both of them were killed in a local war and were buried at Sarasvatī, Ahmedabad. However, Qādiriyya *silsilā* flourished under the patronage of the descendants of Ghiyath ud-Dīn and all of them enjoyed considerable respect in that region.[175]

Mīr Sayyid 'Abdu's Ṣamad and Shaikh Bahāu'd-Dīn (d. 921/1515-16)[176] were two other Qādiriyya Ṣūfīs who contributed towards the extension of the *silsilā* in the region of Gujarat and Malwa. 'Abdu's Ṣamad lived the life of an ascetic, thereby, inspiring a deep asceticism among his disciples.[177] Bahāu'd-Dīn was originally a Shaṭṭariyya and at a later stage he became a Qādiriyya.

---

174. Muhammad Ghauthi bin Hasan Shattarī, *Gulzār-i Abrār*, MS. p. 133a, 'Ali Muhammad Khan Bahadur, *Mir'at-i Ahmadi*, supplement, Baroda, 1930, p. 62.

175. Bahādur, op. cit., p. 63.

176. Dehlawi, op. cit., pp. 198–200.

177. Mulla Nizamud-Din Muhammad Sihalawi, *Malfūẓāt-i-Razzāqi*, Lucknow, 1896/1905, pp. 8-9, 22, 25.

Another Qādiriyya Ṣūfī of some prominence in this region was Qāḍī 'Abdu'l Qādir (d. 1011/1602-03), a *khalīfah* of Shah 'Abdu'r Razzaq Janijhana and a nephew and disciple of Shaikh Amanu'llāh. From time to time Abdul Qādir would accept the invitation of local officers to become a Qāḍī but then invariably he would resign.[178] In his youth he travelled extensively and visited Makkah, Madīnah and Jerusalem and after returning to India he retired to Ujjain, before settling in Sarangpur.

The Qādiriyyas in Other Parts of India

Shah Qāmūs (d. 3 *Zu'lqada* 992/November 1584) the son of Abul-Hayāt, who traced his descent from Shaikh 'Abdu'l Qādir Jīlānī (Raḥ.'A), established a Qādiriyya centre in Baghdad during sixteenth century. He later migrated to Sabūra Khizrabad in Thanesar where he settled in a *khānqāh* and enrolled a significant number of disciples. Shah was persuaded by the Mughal Emperor, Akbar, to return to Bengal where the former breathed his last.[179]

During seventeenth century many prominent disciples of Dīwān 'Abdu-Rashid of Jaunpur also established Qādiriyya centres in Bengal. Among them was Mīr Sayyid Muhammad Qādirī of Rājmahal, who was succeeded by Shah Ni'matullah. Ni'amatullāh, who originally hailed from Narnaul, settled in Bengal, where he established a *khānqāh* in the village of Firozpur, four miles from Rajmahal. Prince Shah Shuja the viceroy of Bengal, his sons and some of the Mughal nobility became Shah Ni'amatullāh's disciples. Later, Emperor Aurangzeb read some of Ni'amatullāh's writings and began

178. Shattari, *Gulzār-i Abrār*, MS. f. 261b.

179. 'Abdu'l Ḥaqq Muḥadith Dehlawī, *Akhbāru'l Akhyār*, Delhi, 1914, p. 208.

corresponding with him. Before his death in 1077/1666-67,[180] Shah had enrolled a large number of disciples who played a vital role in the spread of Qādiriyya mystical practices in Bengal. Hājī Shuhrat, one of the outstanding disciples of Ni'amatullāh received an encouraging reception at Aurangzeb's court and was assigned a village in Mathurā, where he enjoyed the bounty of imperial favours.[181]

Hājī Ibrahim Muhadith Qādirī (d. 19 Dhul hijja 1001/16 September 1593),[182] born at Manikpur, Allahabad made frequent trips to Egypt and Arabia. He got education and *tarbiah* (training) from Shaikh Shamsud-Din 'Alqami (a disciple of the famous *ḥadīth* scholar, Shaikh Jalalu'd-Din Suyūtī) and Shaikh Muhammad Bakri Shafi'i in different branches of learning. At Makkah he was also taught *ḥadīth* by Shaikh 'Ali Muttaqi. He associated with many saints in Syria. After staying for more than 24 years abroad he returned to India. He remained chiefly occupied in lecturing on *ḥadīth*, *fiqh* and *taṣawwuf*.

On account of the efforts of the dynamic Shah 'Abdu'r Razzāq (b. 1046/1636-37 and d. 1136/1724)[183] of Basa the Qādiriyya order won many followers during late seventeenth and early eighteenth centuries around Lucknow. The Shah was deeply interested in the dissemination of the teachings of

---

180. Sher Khan Lodhi, *Miratul-Khayāl*, Calcutta, 1831, pp. 142-45; M. Baqa, *Miratul-'Alam* (AMU, MS.), p. 184a.

181. Muhammad Baqā, *Mira't-i Jahan Numa* (AMU MS.) p. 323a.

182. Shaṭṭari, *Gulzār-i Abrār*, MS., p. 242a.

183. Early in his career he had been forced to serve as a common soldier both in the Deccan and Delhi. He was initiated into Qādiriyya order at Gujarat by Mīr Sayyid 'Abdu's-Ṣamad Khiḍr Numa. In Delhi, in compliance to his *pīr*'s instructions, he visited Sayyid Hasan Rasul-Numa, Muhammad Khan Razzaqi, *Malfuz-i Razzāqi*, Lucknow, 1313/1896, pp. 4-6, 23.

the *Fuṣūṣ al-Ḥikam* and delivered regular lectures on it.[184]

Mulla Nizāmu'd-Din Muhammad Sihalwi (d. 1161/1748), a scholar of high repute, was one of the leading disciples of the Shah. The Mulla paid his debts to his *pīr* by writing a biographical and anecdotal account of Shah 'Abdu'r-Razzāq. In this account, entitled as *Manaqib al-Razzāqiyya* and the *Malfūẓ-i Razzāqi* the Shah has been depicted as a friend of both Hindus and Muslims, Sunnīs and Shi'as and the spiritual supporter of many, whom the local administrators, moneylenders and *ẓamīndārs* had oppressed.

On account of the energetic efforts of Mīr Sayyid Ṭāhā Qutbu'd-Din Qādirī (d. 12 *Rabi II* 1084/27 July 1673), of Kattana during the middle of seventeenth and eighteenth centuries, the Qādiriyya order progressed from one success to another in the area, between Kattana and Muzaffarnagar and as far as Ambala.[185]

Sayyid Ṭāhā left innumerable disciples who preached Qādiriyya teachings in different parts of the world. Twenty-four among them, however, were regarded to be perfect *khullafā*.' Among these, Shah 'Abdu'l-Wahid lived in Madīnah, Shah Shafi in Istanbul, Shah Fatah in Qandahar, Shah 'Abdu'llah Ṣālih in Ceylon and Shah Allāh Bakhsh in Baghdad. Shah Muḥibullah and Ḥājī Shah Fatah Muhammad Qādirī were two distinguished Indian *khullāfā'* of Sayyid Taha.[186]

Shah Fatah visited Makkah and Egypt where he was also initiated into Qādiriyya *silsilā* by Shaikh Yaḥyā and Shah

---

184. Razzaqī, op. cit., pp. 105-06.
185. Muhammad 'Abdu'r Rashid, *Tahā'if-i Rashīdiya*, f. 152a.
186. *Tahā'if-i Rashīdiya*, Ms (AMU) f. 160a.

Badru'd-Din Qādirī respectively. He returned to India in 1108/1696-97 and settled at Kairana, 31 miles south-west of Muzaffarnagar, in Uttar Pradesh. There he established a Qādirī *khānqāh*. After his death on 29 *Rabi'I-i* 1130/2 March 1718,[187] Qādiriyya teachings and practices were popularized in Uttar Pradesh mainly through the disciples of his nephew and son-in-law, Naẓar Muhammad Qādirī Kairanawi and the latter's son, Muhammad 'Abdu'r Rashid.

187. Ibid., f. 176a.

Conclusion

After Prophet Muḥammad (SAW) *Ṣaḥāba* (companions) was the title adopted by the Muslims of that period. They needed no other title, for it was unanimously regarded to be the highest and the best one. Those who associated with the *ṣaḥāba* were called in their own times *tāba 'yīn* (followers). *Taba tāba 'yīn* (followers of followers) was the title conferred upon those who associated themselves with *tāba 'yīn* (followers).

In fact, right from first century AH there were powerful ascetic tendencies within Islam. An exaggerated consciousness of sin and an overwhelming dread of divine retribution appear as two chief factors in this early asceticism. The movement proceeded on orthodox lines, and with the passage of time asceticism passed into mysticism. People like Hasan of Basrah (CE 642-728) and Rabi'ah al-Adawiyyah (d. 185/801) were not satisfied with only formal acts of devotion. The ascetics of this type were, in fact, forerunners of Ṣūfism. The term *ṣūfī*, however, came into use before the end of second century AH and it was first applied to Abū Hāshim of Kūfa (d. AH 150). The Ṣūfism of the ascetic type, such as we find in the sayings of Ibrahim bin Adham (d. AH 161), Dā'ūd al-Ṭā'I (d. AH 165), Fuḍayl ibn 'lyāḍ (d. AH 187) and Shaqīq of Bulkh (d. AH 194) was by and large the native product of Islam. The raptures of later Ṣūfism were unknown to them as were its daring speculations.

With the dawn of third century AH Ṣūfism assumes an entirely new character. Passing over to Bishrul-Ḥāfi (d. 227/841) who described the *'ārifīn* (gnostics) as the peculiar favourites of Allāh, we come to Dhul Nūn al-Miṣrī (d. 246/861), the man who deserves to be called the founder of "theosophical Ṣūfism." His right to this honour is acknowledged by oriental biographers and historians. In fact, the development of Ṣūfism down to the end of third century AH took place in two ways. On one hand the existing doctrine was amplified, elaborated and systematized, and on the other hand new doctrines and practices were introduced.

Ṣūfism which was first a form of religious life adopted by individuals, and communicated only to a comparatively small circle of *aṣḥāb* (companions) gradually became an organized system, a school of saints, with rules of discipline and devotion which the *murīd* (novice) learned from his *pīr, ustād* (spiritual director), to whose guidance he submitted himself absolutely.

The Ṣūfis of the third and fourth centuries AH worked out a complete theory and practice of mystical mode of religion. Ṣūfism became an organized system with teachers, pupils, and rules of discipleship, and continual efforts were made to show that it was based on the *Qur'ān* and the Traditions of the Prophet (SAW).

It is to this period that the great Shaikhs including Shaikh Sayyid Abdu'l Qādir Jīlānī (Raḥ.'A), Shaikh Abū Najib Suhrawardī (Raḥ.'A), Shaikh Shihab-u'd-Din Suhrawardi (Raḥ.'A) and Mu'inu'd-Din Chistī (Raḥ.'A) belonged. They preached their teachings in a more elaborate and systematic way. Shaikh Abdul Qādir Jīlānī (Raḥ.'A), however, emerged as the most influential preacher of the period. He preached at Baghdad, the capital city of the Abbāsid caliphate, where he had come from Jīlān.

The Shaikh (Raḥ.'A) did not sermonize and admonish the populace alone; he fearlessly performed the duty of enjoining the right and forbidding the wrong, made incumbent by the *shari'at*. The caliph and his ministers too attended his sermons along with the rank and file and used to sit in a corner without any fanfare.

Notwithstanding the implicit reverence cherished for Jīlānī (Raḥ.'A) by the people, he was always modest, humble and unpretentious. He would boil with indignation if the Divine Commandments were overstepped but remained listless to the wrongs and ill-treatments of his own person. The love of humanity, in general, and the affection for the *ummah* in particular, was symptomatic of his sublimated soul and indicative of his close affinity to the Prophet (SAW) and the rightly-guided caliphs.

His was a striking example of the innate power of Islam to produce a true spirit of religion, love of Allāh and moral righteousness in an age of crass materialism. The qualities like; the moral and spiritual excellence of the Shaikh (Raḥ.'A), his unflinching devotion to Allāh, the efficacy of his sermons, the inspiring and regenerating influence exercised by him over the people in his own time and the upright character and moral rectitude demonstrated by him, present Jīlānī as one of the most eminent God-fearing persons born in the world of Islam.

His miracle of miracles lay in his inspiring and impressive teachings which made thousands to turn away from the lust of power and wealth and to inculcate the true spirit of faith through introspection and purification of the soul.

Extremely solicitous of eradicating the moral laxity and viciousness produced by ever-increasing opulence, luxury and indolence in the metropolis of Islam, the Shaikh (Raḥ.'A) sometimes came out with the most severe criticism of the then society giving expression to his heartfelt misery over the sinful ways of the people.

The unfailing and penetrating vision of the *Tawḥīd* or Unity of Allāh had conferred upon Jīlānī (Raḥ.'A), the sublime piety which produces an absolute resignation to the will of Allāh. Profound knowledge of the religious lore and meticulous observance of the Traditions of the Prophet (SAW), aided by the grace of Allāh, had unveiled the mysteries of the celestial world to the Shaikh (Raḥ.'A), who had reached the stage where potential of discrimination between *ḥaqq* (truth) and *bāṭil* (untruth), divine intuition and demoniacal imposition is born in man.

We learn from his sermons that social instability and moral deterioration are the result of excessive materialistic outlook in life. He adopts a moderate attitude with regard to the question of free will and holds that one should neither fall a victim to the creed of *Jabriyyah* (determinists) nor to that of *Qadariyya* (indeterminists), instead one should regard that actions belong to Allāh in the point of creation and to man in the point of *kasb* (acquisition). Spiritual peace which is indispensable for a mystic cannot be said to be complete unless he is trained in the school of adversity. Mystic intuition gives the recipient the knowledge of *ḥaqīqat* (reality) that is not possible to gain through reason. *Taṣawwuf,* according to Jīlānī (Raḥ.'A.) is not the result of discussion or talk but that of hunger and privation.

Taqwā, 'adl, moral rectitude, denial of worldliness, self-denial, generosity, *faqr, ṣidq, ikhlāṣ* (sincerity), self-mortification, endurance in affliction, *tarahhum,* identification of saṭānic ways, hypocrites and their fate, harmful effects of vices and the blessings of virtues, *thubāt* (firmness) in the path of Allāh, *tawbah* (repentance for sins), *tashakkur* (gratefulness), *ājizī* (contrition), *tawḥīd* (oneness of Allāh), *shirk* (polytheism) and its various forms and their ill-effects are some of the recurring themes of his sermons.

Jīlānī (Raḥ.'A) emerged as a reformer and reviver of high repute being possessed of sublimated soul. He left deeper imprints on the socio-religious outlook of the people who flocked to him, with great reverence, in thousands at a time when the Islamic world was witnessing the emergence of crusaders, their eastward march, precipitation of rivalry among Saljūq rulers and emergence of *Sabā'īs* under the leadership of Hasan bin Sabā. The number of his audience rose up to seventy thousand (70,000) and as many as four hundred (400) inkpots were counted among his audience who noted down his discourses, sermons, and *naṣā'iah* (advices). Besides this, works of the Shaikh, including *Fatḥ-i Rubbānī, Futūḥ al-Ghaib, al-Ghunyah li-Ṭālibi Ṭariqi'l Ḥaqq, Risāla Maktūbāt, Kibriyat al-Aḥmar* and *Jila'l-i Khaṭīr*, proved a source of inspiration for millions of people all over the world. His teachings were disseminated to different parts of the world even during his lifetime and were transmitted by the subsequent generations even to the remotest corners of the world. With the passage of time certain principles were formulated on the basis of his discourses and *āthār* which gave rise to one of the renowned Ṣūfī *silsilās*, the Qādiriyya *silsilā*, formed after the name of the great Shaikh. The *silsilā* attracted many other people towards its fold and soon a number of offshoots came into being throughout the world in general and the Indian subcontinent in particular.

The influence of the teachings and personality of the Shaikh still continues to be felt in quite a significant section of Muslim society throughout the world.

Appendix A

Chronology of Events as Depicted in *Bahjat al-Asrār*

AH 499, middle of the Sha'bān (p. 53). The Shaikh joins a party who with Hammad al-Dabbas are going across the water of the *masjid* of Rusa-fah for Friday service. Ḥammād pushes the Shaikh into the water. The latter saves his manuscript, but suffers severely from the cold. (*AH 508*) (*p. 115*) birth of his eldest son, Abdul Rahman. *AH 509* (*p. 56*) The Shaikh's first pilgrimage from Baghdad.

At the tower called Umm al-Kurun he meets Adi Ibn Musafir, and they travel together to Makkah, when an Abyssinian joins them. 'Adi Ibn Musafir, who Ibn Khallikān thinks worthy of notice, died AH 557 or 559 at a great age.

AH 521, Tuesday, 16 Shawwal. Jīlānī saw the prophet (SAW) in his dream (p. 25). The prophet (SAW) insisted on the Shaikh's coming forward as preacher. In the form of story told by Dhahabi the ascetic Yūsuf al-Hamadāni also gives Jīlānī this advice. The same year (p. 29) the merchant Abū Muzaffar al-hasan Ibn Najm Ibn Ahmad of Baghdad comes to Ḥammād al-Dabbās, and is warned by him that if he starts his journey he will be killed and his goods robbed. Jīlānī then promises him that he will get safely to Damascus. Ḥammād afterwards meets this merchant in the Suq al-Sultan of Baghdad, and tells him that his success is the result of 17 prayers of Jīlānī.

AH 522, Shaban (p. 114): Birth of Jīlānī's son Abd al Wahhāb.

AH 526: Jīlānī and his pupils take part in building of wall of Baghdad. Jīlānī heads the people of Azaj Gate Quarters.

AH 528, Dhul-Qa'dah (p. 115): Birth of his son Abd al-Razzaq.

AH 529, Dhu'l-Hijjah 27 (p. 53) Wednesday: The Shaikh visited the grave of Hammād al-Dabbās in the Shunizi cemetery, whom he found with royal robes and crown in his grave, but unable to move his right hand, which had given Jīlānī the blow mentioned above, thirty years before. By Abdul Qādir's mediation the hand was restored.

AH 529 (p. 94): The Shaikh's class attended by Abu'l Hasan Sa'd al-Khair Ibn Muhammad Ibn Sahl sa'd al-Ansari al-Andalusi (ob. AH 541).[1] The Shaikh spoke on any subject to which the thoughts of his hearer were directed.

AH 537 (p. 81): The daughter of Abu Sa'd 'Abdullah Ibn Ahmad Ibn Ali Ibn Muhammad al-Baghdadi al-Azaji was snatched away by the *Jinns*. Jīlānī compelled them to restore her.

AH 539 (p. 115) Rabi'al awwal: Birth of his son Mūsā.

AH 543, (p. 58) Friday, 5 Rajab: The Shaikh was visited by Baqa Ibn Battu, a saint scarcely inferior in reputation to Jīlānī.

AH 546 (p. 50): Visit of the same with several other famous saints. A servant who refused to eat at Shaikh's order was struck down dead, and afterwards restored to life at the saints' request.

AH 548 (p. 81): Abū'l Khalil Ahmad Ibn Asad Ibn Wahhab Ibn 'Ali al-Muqri al-Baghdādi heard a sermon, on the office of *qutb*, delivered by the Shaikh.

---

1. Ibn Khallikān, *Wafayāt al-A'yān*, tr. De Slane, vol. I, p. 661.

ah *549 (p. 62)*: The Shaikh, being invited to a meal by Abū Ghalib Fadl-Allah Ibn Ismā'il al Baghdādi, cures a son of his host who was deformed and blind.

AH *550 (p. 49)*: The saint Ali Ibn-Idris al-Ba'qubi was brought to Shaikh and gives him a garment. Birth of Shaikh's son Yaḥya.

AH *552 (p. 72) Saturday night, 9 Rabi Thani*: Vision of a mysterious person flying through the air.

AH *553 (p. 58)*: The Shaikh recites some verses to Abu'l Qasim 'Umar Ibn Mas'ūd al-Bazzar and Abu'l Hasan 'Ali al-Muqri.

(p. 25): The Shaikh recounts the vision of the prophet seen in AH 521 to his sons and al-Bazzar.

AH *555 (p. 67) Sunday, 3 Safar*: The Shaikh by throwing a wooden shoe rescues a caravan from robbers at a distance of 23 days' journey.

AH *556 (p. 76) Friday, 15 Jumada ii*: Al-Bazzar went to the *masjid* with Abdul Qādir.

(p. 49): Al-Bakūbī brought for the second time to Abdul Qādir.

AH *558 (p. 98)*: Jīlānī sent a servant to buy material at a *dīnār* a yard off the draper Abul Fadl Ahmad Ibn al-Qasim Ibn Abdan al-Qurashi.

AH *559 (p. 18)*: Visit of mysterious persons flying through the air at night to see the Shaikh.

(p. 56): Shaikh recounted his pilgrimage to Abu'l-Mafakhir al-Mukhtar al-Husaini.

(p. 63): In the presence of Abu sa'd al-Kailawi Jīlānī healed a crippled and crippled a sound child.

(*p. 73*) *Muharram*: Jīlānī warns his audience in time that the roof is about to fall.

AH *560* (*p. 77*): Abu 'Abd al-Malik Dhayyal desires and sees a miracle in Shaikh's stick.

(*p. 79*): Jīlānī performs a miracle in the presence of Abu'l Hasan Ali Ibn Ahmad Ibn Wahb al-Azaji.

AH *561* (*p. 101, etc.*): Visit to Muwaff aq al-din and Abd al Ghani. They remain with Jīlānī for 50 days till his death in *Rabi'ii.*

Appendix B

(a) Chronology of 'Abbasid Caliphs

Abū 'Abbās as-Saffah	132-136/749-754
al-Manṣūr	136-158/754-775
al-Mahdī	158-169/775-785
al-Hādī	169-170/785-786
Hārūn ar-Rashid	170-193/786-809
al-Amīn	193-198/809-813
al-Māmūn	198-218/813-833
al-Mua'tasim	218-227/833-842
al-Wāthiq	227-232/842-847
al-Mutawakkil	232-247/847-861
al Muntasir	247-248/861-862
al-Musta'īn	248-252/862-866
al-Mu'tazz	252-255/866-869
al-Muhtadi	255-256/869-870
al-Mua'tamid	256-279/870-892
al-Mu'tadīd	279-289/892-902

al-Muktafī	289-295/902-908
al-Muqtadir	295-320/908-932

(b) Buyid Suzerainty 320-447/932-1055

al-Qāhir	320-332/932-934
ar-Raḍi	332-329/934-940
al-Muttaqī	329-333/940-944
al-Mustakfī	333-334/944-946
al-Mutī	334-363/946-974
at-Ta'i	363-381/974-991
al-Qāir	381-422/991-1031
al-Qāi'm	422-476/1031-1075

(c) Saljūq Suzerainty from 447/1055 to 590 /1194

al-Muqtadī	476-487/1075-1094
al-Mustazhir	487-512/1094-1118
al-Mustarshid	512-529/1118-1135
al-Rāshid	529-530/1135-1136
al-Muqtafī	530-555/1136-1160
al-Mustanjid	555-566/1160-1170
al-Mustadī	566-575/1170-1180
al-Nāṣir	575-622/1180-1225
al-Ẓāhir	622-623/1225-1226
al-Mustansir	623-640/1226-1242
al-Musta'ṣīm	640-656/1242-1258

Bibliography

Primary Sources

Abū'l Faraj, Muhammad Fadl al-Din, *Al-Khairāt al-Qādiriyya*, (Awrad Ar), Ms. (ORD Srinagar), no. 1444.

Abū'l Ma'āli, *Tuhfat al-Qādiriyya*, Ms. (O.R.D Srinagar), no. 2239.

'Ali bin Muhammad, *al-Aḥkām al-Sultāniyya*, Ms. (ORD Srinagar), no. 274.

Anon, *Bada'i wa Karāmāt-I Ḥaḍrat Shāh Ni'amatullah Qādiri*, Ms. (ORD Srinagar), no. 2891.

Anon, *Manāqib Shaikh 'Abdu'l Qādir Jīlānī*, Ms. (ORD Srinagar), no. 634.

Anon, *Muntakhab Tafrih al-Khaṭir Fi Manāqib al-Shaikh 'Abdu'l Qādir*, Ms. (ORD Srinagar) no. 2785.

Anon, *Tarjama Khulāṣatu'l Mufākhir*, Ms. (ORD Srinagar), no. 2147.

Attar, Farid-ud-Din, *Tadhkiratu'l-Awliya*, Ms. (ORD Srinagar), no. 223.

Bābā Naṣīb, *Rīshī Nāma*, Ms. (ORD Srinagar).

Baladhūrī, Abu'l Hasan Ahmad bin Yaḥyā (d. 279/892), *Futūh al-Buldān*, Egypt, 1319 (AH).

Chisti, Baba 'Uthmān, *Ishghāl Ṭarīqa Qādiriyya*, Ms. (ORD Srinagar), no. 470.

Dāra Shukoh, Muhammad, *Sirr-i Akbar (Siru'l Asrār)*, Ms. (ORD Srinagar), no. 99.

Darwish, 'Abdul Qādir, *Manāqib-I Ḥaḍrat-i Pir*, Ms. (ORD Srinagar), no. 3189.

Daughlat, Muhammad Haidar, *Tārikh-i Rashīd-ī*, Ms. (ORD Srinagar), no. 573.

Dehlawi, 'Abdu'l Ḥaqq bin Saifu'd-Din, *Akhbār al-Akhyār fi Asrār al-Abrār*, Ms. (ORD Srinagar), no. 538.

Dehlawi, 'Abdu'l Ḥaqq Muhaddith, *Sharh-I Futūḥ al-Ghaib*, Ms. (ORD Srinagar), no. 2639.

———, *Zādu'l Muttaqīn*, Ms. (Rampur).

———, *Akhbāru'l-Akhyār*, Delhi, 1914.

Didah Mari, Khwaja Muhammad A'zam, *Wasilat al-Wasūl Ila Dayār-i al-Rasūl Shaikh 'Abdu'l Qādir Jīlānī*, Ms. (ORD Srinagar), no. 672.

Ghawsu'llah, Abu'l Ma'āli Muhammad, *Tuḥfat al-Qādiriyya*, Ms. (ORD Srinagar), no. 2910.

Ghazzālī, Abū Ḥāmid (d. 1111), *Kimyā'-i Sa'ādat* (3 vols.), Ms. (ORD Srinagar), no. 169-71.

———, *Iḥyā 'Ulūm al-Dīn*, Cairo, 1957.

———, *Kimiyā'-i Sa'ādat*, Lucknow, 1873.

———, *Naṣiḥat al-Mulūk*, Tehran, n.d.

Gibb, H.A.R; *Islāmic Society and the West*, London, 1960.

Gisudaraz, Sayyid Muhammad, *Tarjuma-i 'Awārif al-Ma'ārif*, Ms. (Gulbarga).

———, *Tarjuma-i Risālai Qushairiyya*, Ms. (Salarjang), Hyderabad.

Hujwīrī, Abū'l Hasan Ibn 'Uthmān, *Kashaf al-Maḥjūb*, Ms. (ORD Srinagar), no. 1734.

———, *Kas͟haf al-Maḥjūb*, Lahore, 1923.

Ibn al-Athir, Izzud-din Abū'l Hussain'Ali bin Muhammad (d. AH 630), *Al-Kāmil Fi'l-Tārīk͟h*, (ed.) C.J. Tornbargh, Leiden, 1851-76.

Ibn Kathir, 'Imādud-dīn Abū'l Fida' Isma'il Ibn 'Amar (d. 744/1372), *al-Bidāyah wa An-Nihāya*, Matb'a us-Sa'dah, Egypt (1932), vol. XII, pp. 149, 207, 208, 252.

Jāmī, Abdur Rahman bin Ahmad, *Nafaḥāt al-Uns*, Ms. (ORD Srinagar), nos. 111, 167.

Jawhar, Ghulam Husain Khan, *Tārikh-i Dil-Afrūz*, Ms. (Asfiya).

Jīlānī, Shaikh Sayyid Abdul Qādir, *Chahal Kāf*, Ms. (AMU).

———, *Fatḥ-i Rubbānī*, Ms. (Raza and AMU).

———, *Futūh-al-Ghaib*, Ms. (AMU, Raza, Salar, Phaidi, Asiatic, Asifiyya and ORD Srinagar nos. 2302 and 3042).

———, *Al-G͟hawthiyya* (*al-Mukhatabatu'i G͟hawt͟hiyya*), Ms. Raza).

———, *Al-Ghunyah Li-Ṭālibi Tariqi'l*, Ḥaqq (*Ghunyat al-Ṭālibīn*); Mss. (AMU, Hamdard, Khuda Bakhsh, Asiatic, Raza, Tonk, and Pakistan).

———, *Jila'al-K͟haṭir*, Ms. (Raza, AMU).

———, *Kanz al'-Ibād Fi Sharh al-Awrād,* (Arabic), Ms. (Peshawar).

———, *Al-Kibriyat-al Aḥmar,* Mss. (AMU, Asifiyya, Buhar and Pakistan).

———, *Al-Maktūbāt,* Ms. (AMU, J. Millia, Phulwari, 'Abdu'l Salam and Khuda Bakhsh).

———, *Al-Qaṣīdat al-Ghawthiyya,* Mss. (AMU, Jame' Asifiyya, Abu'l Khair, Phulwari and Khuda Bakhsh).

———, *Risāla al-Bayān al-Asrār,* Ms. (Peshawar).

———, *Risālat al-Ghawthiyya,* Mss. (Raza, Āsifiyya, Khuda Bakhsh, Asiatic, Tonk, Madras, Phulwari, Hamdard, Nadwah and Jami').

———, *Risāla al-Ilhāmiyya,* Ms. (Jami').

———, *Risāla Naw Dah Naw Nām,* Ms. (AMU and Asifiyya).

———, *Risāla-i Ṣamdiyya,* Ms. (Phulwari and Balkhiyya).

———, *Risāla al-Waṣiyah,* Ms. (Khuda Bakhsh).

———, *Risāla Wasl-I Ḥaqq,* Mss. (Pir Wa Madya and State Archives Allahabad).

———, *Tuḥfat al-Qādiriyya,* Ms. (Furqaniyya, Phulwari, Abu'l Khair, Deoband, Khuda Bakhsh and Asifiyya).

———, *Kibriyat-i Aḥmar Wa Kalām-i Miyan Mustafa,* MS. (ORD Srinagar), no. 2261.

———, *Dalā-il-i Khairat,* Ms. (ORD Srinagar), no. 2206.

———, *Kibriyat al-Aḥmar,* Ms. (ORD Srinagar), no. 2206.

———, *Qasidah Ghawthiyya,* Ms. (ORD Srinagar), no. 2206.

———, *Panj Surah wa Kibriyat-i Aḥmar,* Ms. (ORD Srinagar), no. 2258.

———, *Kibriyat al-Aḥmar* (Sharh by Khwaja A'ezam Didahmari), Ms. (ORD Srinagar), no. 29.

———, *al-Karas al-Oula Min al-Mawāhib al-Rahman,* Ms. (ORD Srinagar), no. 2614.

———, *Ghunyat al-Ṭālibin* (Sharh by 'Abdullah alias al-Basib), Ms. (ORD Srinagar), no. 1911.

———, *Dīwān-i 'Abdu'l Qādir* (Pr.), Ms. (ORD Srinagar) no. 674; Also nos. 836, 920.

———, *Miftah al-Asrār* (Pr.), Ms. (ORD Srinagar), no. 734.

———, *Badra Qatu'l Īmān* (Du'a, Adhkar), Ms. (ORD, Srinagar), no. 1328.

———, *Fathu'l Basā'ir,* Ms. (ORD Srinagar), no. 1329.

———, *Ahda Wa Arba 'eyn Isman,* Ms. (ORD Srinagar) no. 1471.

———, *Fath-i Rubbāni* (Urdu tr. under the title *Fayḍ-i Subḥānī),* Kutbkhana Rahimyya, Deoband, n.d. Also, tr. in Urdu by: Merrthi Maulana Āshiq Ilahi, under the title, *Fayūḍi Yazdānī,* Rubbani Book Depot, Delhi, n.d.

———, *Futūḥ ul-Ghayb* (Eng tr. M. Aftab-ud Din Ahmad), Kitab Bhavan, Delhi, 1990.

———, *Futūḥ al-Ghaib* (Persian Commentary by Shaikh 'Abdul' Ḥaqq Muhaddith), Lucknow, 1881.

———, *Ghuniyat ul-Ṭālibin* (Urdu tr. Arman Sarhadi), I'tiqād Publishing House, Delhi, 1987.

———, *Ilhāmāt-i Ghawthiyya* (tr. Urdu, Haji Hafiz Pir Ji Ataullah), Calcutta.

———, *Fuyūdat-i Rubbāniyya,* Delhi, 1329 AH.

Kashmiri, Mahwi, *Madih-i Shāh-i Jilān;* Ms. (ORD Srinagar), no. 572.

Khākī, Bābā Dāwūd, *Dastūru's-Salikīn;* Ms. (ORD Srinagar), no. 741.

———, *Rīshī Nāma,* Ms. (ORD Srinagar).

Mas'udi, Abū'l Hasan Ali bin Husain (d. 345/956), *Murūj udh Dhahab wa M'adin ul-Jawhar,* 1877.

Mattu, Bahau'd-Din, *Ghawthiyaa* (Verse), Ms. (ORD Srinagar), no. 52, 999.

Mattu, Mulla Bahau'd-Din, *Khamsa Bahā'iya* (*Rīshī Nāma, Sultani, Ghawthiyya, Naqashbandiyya, Chistiyya*), Ms. (ORD Srinagar), no. 558.

Mir, Sayyid Muhammad Husain, *Futūḥat-i Qādiriyya* (Pr.); Ms. (ORD Srinagar), no. 30.

Mishkat-I, Bābā Dāwūd, *Asrār al-Abrār,* Ms. (ORD Srinagar), no. 40.

Muhammad Dārā Shukoh, *Majma'ul Bahrain,* Ms. (ORD Srinagar), no. 187.

Multani, Shamsu'd-Din Abū'l Fateh Muhammad, *Makhāzinu'l Qādiriyya* (written in tenth/sixteenth century), Ms. (AMU).

Munshi, Sikandar, *Tārikh-i 'Ālam-i Ārā-i 'Abbāsi* (Parts I, II, III), Ms. (ORD Srinagar), nos. 151, 152, 153.

Nuri, 'Abdu'l Wahhab, *Futūḥat-I Kubrawiyya,* Ms. (ORD Srinagar).

Qādiri, Muhammad Ghawth, *Muqadimāt-i Sulūk,* Ms. (ORD Srinagar), no. 657.

Qādiri, Muluk Shah Siddīqī, *Risāla-Ghawthiyya*, Ms. (ORD Srinagar), no. 2908.

Qushairi, Abū'l Qasim, *Ar-Risālat al-Qushairiyya*, Cairo, 1959.

Rāwandi, Abu Bakr Muhammad bin 'Ali (d. 599/1202) *Rāhat Us-Ṣudūr Wa Āyāt Us-Surūr*, ed. Muhammad Iqbal, London, G.M.S., 1921.

Sadi, Muhammad Sadiq Shihabi, *Manāqib-I Haḍrat Ghawthal-Thaqalayn (Tafrih al-Khatir)*, Ms. (ORD Srinagar), no. 2911.

Sayyid Kashmiri, *Rawḍu'l Akhdar Sharh-i Kibriyat-i Aḥmar*, Ms. (ORD Srinagar), no. 2119.

Shabistari, Muhammad, *Gulshan-i Rāz*, Ms. (ORD Srinagar), no. 656.

Shah, Wali Ibn Malik, *Sharh-i Ghawthiyya*, Ms. (ORD Srinagar), no. 622.

Shaikh, Faridu'd-Din, *Surūr's-Sudūr*, Ms. Maulana Azad Library, A.M.U.

Shaikh 'Abdur Rashid, *Tārikh-i Qādiriyya*, Ms. (Khuda Bakhsh Library, Patna and Riza Library, Rampur) written in 1150/1737.

Shaikh Abu'l-Fayyad Ghulam Rashid, *Ganj-i Arshadi*, Ms. (AMU).

Shaikh, Yasin Muhammad, *Sanad-i Silsila Qādiriyya* (Ar.), Ms. (ORD, Srinagar), no. 2158.

Shamsamud-Dawla, *Baharistān-I Sukhun*, Ms. (Asafiya).

Shattanaufi, Nuru'd-Din 'Ali bin Yusuf, *Bahjat al-Asrār wa Ma'din Al-Anwār*, Cairo, 1301/1384.

Shattanawfi, Shaikh Abu'l Hasan 'Ali bin Yusuf, *Bahjat al-Asrār*, Ms. (ORD, Srinagar), no. 112(A).

Shattari, Muhammad Ghawthi b. Hasan b. Mūsā, *Gulzār-i-Abrār*, Ms. (AMU).

Siddīqī, Malūk Shah, *Sharh-I Risāla-Ghawthiyya*; Ms. (ORD, Srinagar), no. 112(B).

———, *Tuḥfah Qādiri*, Ms. (ORD, Srinagar), no. 1107.

Suhrawardi, Shaikh Shihābu'd Din 'Umar, *'Awārif al-Ma'ārif*, Egypt, 1289/1872-73, tr. H. Wilberforce Clarke, 1891, rpt., New York, 1970.

———, *Awārif al-Ma'ārif*, Ms. (ORD, Srinagar), no. 272.

Tarahbali Ahmad Sa'id, *Risāla Qādiriyya*, Ms. (ORD, Srinagar), no. 1868.

Tusi, Nizam al-Mulk, *Siyāsat Nāma*, Tehran, 1320/1902-3, Eng. tr. H. Darke, *The Book of Government*, London, 1960.

Yafi'I, Afifu'd-Din Abdullah bin Asad (b. in Yemen, settled at Makkah in 718/1318 and d. there in 768/1367), *Khulāṣat al-Mafākir*.

Secondary Sources

'Abdu'l Haiy, *Nuzhat al-Khwāṭīr*, Urdu tr., Lahore, 1965.

'Abu'l Hasan b. Muhammad b. Habibu'llah, *al-Aḥkām al-Sultāniyya*, Beirut, 1978.

Abu'l Khair Muhammad (ed.), *Kalimat-I Ṭayyibah*, Delhi, 1309/1891-92.

Ad-Dinawari, Abu Hanifa Ahmad bin Dawud (d. 288/901), *Akhbār ut-Tiwal*, 1918.

'Afifi Abu'l-'Ala, *The Mystical Philosophy of Muhiy'd Din Ibnu'l 'Arabi*, Cambridge, 1939.

'Ali, Abdullah Yusuf, *The Meaning and Commentary of the Holy Qur'ān*, USA, 1946.

Allami, Shaikh Abu'l Fadl, *Akbar Nāma*, Calcutta, 1873-87, Eng. tr. H. Beveridge, Calcutta, 1897–1921.

———, *Ā'in-i Akbarī*, Lucknow, 1892, Eng. tr. vol. I, by H. Blochmann, 2nd rev. edn. by D.C. Phillot, Calcutta, 1939, vols. II and III, tr. by H.S. Jarrettand revised by J.N. Sarkar, Calcutta, 1948.

Ālūsī, Sayyid N'oman, *Jalaul-'Aynain*, Egypt, AH 1298.

Amir Khwurd, Sayyid Muhammad bin Mubarak, *Siyaru'l-Awliya*, Delhi, 1302/1885.

Anjum, Ghulam Yahya, *Hindustān Mein Silsilā Qādiriyya Kay Bāni*, Abdul Wahhāb Jīlānī, Delhi, 1999.

Ansari, Abu Isma'il 'Abdullah al-Harawi, *Ṭabaqāt al-Sūfiyya*, Kabul, 1962.

Arbali, Shaikh Muhy-ud-Din, *Bastān un-Nazir Tarjama Tafrih al-Khaṭir*, Allahabad, n.d.

Arberry, A.J., *An Introduction to the History of Sūfism*, London, 1942.

———, *Sūfism: An Account of the Mystics of Islam*, London, 1950.

———, *Muslim Saints and Mystics*, London, 1964.

———, *Revelation and Reason in Islam*, London, New York, 1957.

Asqalani, Ibn Hajr (d. AH 582), *Ghibṭaṭ al-Nāzir fi Tarjamat al-Shaikh 'Abdul-Qādir* precisely referred as *Ghibtah* in the text, Eng. tr. E.D. Ros, 1903.

'Attar, Farid ad-Din, *Manṭiqat-Tair*, ed. G. de Tassy, 1864.

———, *Tadhkirat al-Awliya*, ed. R.A. Nicholson, 2 vols., London, 1905-07.

———, Tadhkiratul-Auliya (Part I & II), Eng. tr. Bankey Behāvī, Kitab Bhawan, New Delhi, 1993.

Aziz Ahmad, *Studies in Islamic Culture in the Indian Environment*, Oxford, 1964.

Badāyūnī, 'Abdul Qādir, *Muntakhab al-Tawārīkh*, Calcutta, 1864-69, vol. I, English tr. G.S.A. Ranking, Calcutta, 1895-99, vol. II, W.H. Lowe, Calcutta, 1884-98, vol. III, T.W. Haig, Calcutta, 1899–1925.

Barthold, V.V., *Four Studies on the History of Central Asia*, vol. I, Leiden, 1956.

Barthold, W., *Turkestan Down to the Mongol Invasion*, 2nd edn., London, 1928.

Bilgrami, Ghulam 'Ali Azad, *Rawḍatu'l Awliya*, Aurangabad, 1892-93.

Boyle, J.A. (ed.), *The Cambridge History of Iran*, V. Cambridge, 1968.

Browne, E.G., *A Literary History of Persia*, 4 vols., London and Cambridge, 1902-24, rpt., Cambridge, 1957.

Bundari, (d. 632/1226), *Zubdat un-Nusrā wa Nukhbat ul-'Usrā.*, ed. M.T. Houtsma, Leiden, 1889.

Burckhardt, Titus, *Introduction to Sūfī Doctrines*, Lahore, 1959.

Dārā Shukoh, Sultan Muhammad, *Safinatu'l Awliya*, Kanpur, 1900.

———, *Risāla-I* Ḥaqq *Numā*, Tehran, n.d.

———, *Hasanatu'l-'Ārifīn*, Amritsar, n.d.

———, *Sirri Akbar*, Tehran, n.d.

———, *Majma'u'l-Bahrayn*, Tehran, n.d.

Dehlawi, 'Abdu'l Ḥaqq Muḥaddith, *Madariju'n-Nubūwwa*, Lucknow, 1867.

Dehlawi, Amir Khusrau, *The Nūh Sipihr: A Historical Mathnawi on the Reign of Mubārak Shah*, ed. Muhammad Wahid Mirza, Calcutta, 1949.

Dehlawi, Hamid B. Fadlu'llah, *Siyaru'l-'Ārifin*, Delhi, 1311/1893.

Dehlawi, Shah Wali Allah, *Al-Qawl al-Jamīl fi-Sawa us-Sabīl*, Delhi, n.d.

———, *Hujjatullah al-Bāligha, Karachi*, n.d.

Dhahabi, Shams ud-Din (d. 748/1348), Tadhkiratu'l Ḥuffāẓ, *Dai'ratu'l Ma'arif*, Hyderabad, AH 1355.

Didamari, Muhammad A'zam, *Waqi'āt-i Kashmir*, Lahore, 1303/1885-86.

Drewes, G.W.J., *De mirakelen Van Abdoel Kadir Djaelani*, G.W.J. Drewes, and Poetabatjaraka, Bandoeng, 1938, a Summary of contents in places amounting to almost a complete translation of the Javanese

Version of *Hika'yat 'Abdul Qādir Jīlānī*, which is based on al-Yafe's Arabic *Khulasat al-Mafakir*.

Dughlat, Mirza Haidar, *Tārikh-i Rashīdī*, Eng. tr. E. Denison Ross, London, 1898.

Ghulam Murtada, *Basātinu'l Salātin*, Hyderabad–Deccan, 1310/1892-93.

Ghulam Sarwar, *Khazīnatu'l Āṣifiya*, Lucknow, 1873.

Gisūdarāz, Sayyid Muhammad, *Khatima*, Ethe, 1856.

———, *Wujūdu'l 'Āshiqin*, Ethe, 1859.

———, *Asmāru'l Asrār*, Ethe, 1861.

Hallaj, Abu Mansūr, *Kitab al-Tawāsin*, ed. L. Massignon, Paris, 1913.

Harawi, Nimatallah b. Habibullah, *Tārikh-i Jahāni Wa Makh Zan-i Afghāni*, Dacca, 1960.

Hasan Shah, *Tārikh-i Hasan*, vol. III, pp. 61-62.

Hasani, 'Abdul Haiy, *Nuzhat al-Khawāṭīr*, Hyderabad–Deccan, 1955.

Hasrat, B.J., *Dārā Shukoh: Life and Works*, rpt., New Delhi, 1980.

Hodgson, Marshall G.S., *The Order of Assassins: The Struggle of the Early Nizari Isma'ilis against the Islāmic World*, The Hague, 1955.

Ibn al 'Arabi, Shaikh Muhy-ud-Din, *al-Futūḥāt al-Makkiyya*, 4 vols., Bulaq, 1293/1876-77.

———, *Fuṣūṣ al-Ḥikam*, ed. Abul 'Ala, Afifs, Cairo, 1365/1946.

———, *Muhāzarat al-Abrār*, 2 vols. Cairo, 1305/1888.

———, *Risālat Rūh al-Quds*, Quds, Cairo, 1281/1866.

———, *Tarjumān al-Ashwāq*, ed. and tr. R.A. Nicholson, London, 1911.

———, *Al-Asfār 'an Risālat al-Anwār*, with commentary by 'Abd al-Karim al-Jili, Damascus, 1348/1929.

Ibn al-'Imād, *Shazarāt al-Dhahab*, Cairo, 1351/1932.

Ibn al-Jawzi, *Talbīs Iblīs*, Cairo, 1340/1922. tr. D.S. Margoliouth, "The Devils Delusion", *Islamic Culture*, 12, 1938.

Ibn al-Jawzi, *al-Muntaẓam fi't Tārikh al–Mulūk wal Uman*, 7 vols., Hyderabad, 1357-59/1938-41.

Ibn Baṭṭūṭa, *Riḥla*, Cairo edn., al-Matba 'at al-Aẓhariyya, 1346/1928.

Ibn Baṭṭūṭa, *Riḥla*, tr. H.A.R. Gibb, Hakluyt Society (i) 1956 (ii) 1962.

Ibn Khaldun, *The Muqaddimah*, tr. F. Rosenthal, 3 vols., New York, 1958.

Ibn Khallikān, Ahmad, *Wafayāt al-A'yān wa Anba' az-Zamān* ("Obituaries of the famous," a biographical dictionary), Cairo, AH 1275, 1299, tr. Baron MacGuckin de Slane, 4 vols., Paris, 1842-71, rpt. 1961.

Ibn Khurdadbeh, *al-Masālik wa'l-Mamālik*, ed. de Geoje, *Bibl. Geogr. Arab.* IV, Leiden, 1889.

Ibn an-Nadim, M.B. Ishaq, *Fihrist (Index)*, ed. G. Flugel, Leipzig, 1871-72.

Ibn Taymiyya, *Minhāj as-Sunna Un-Nabawiyya fi Naqd-i Kalām a'sh-Shi'a wa'l Qādiriyya*, 4 vols., Bulaq, 1321-22/1903-04.

Ikram, Shaikh Muhammad, *Āb-i Kawthar*, Lahore, 1975.

———, *Rūd-i Kawthar*, Lahore, 1975.

———, *Mawj-i Kawthar*, Lahore, 1975.

Isfahānī, Abū Nu'aīm (d. 1038), *Hilyat al-Awliya wa Ṭabaqāt al-Āṣfiya*, 10 vols., Cairo, 1351/1932–1357/1938.

Jahangir, the Emperor, *Tuzuk-i Jahāngiri*, Ghazipur and Aligarh, 1863-64, Eng. tr. A. Rogers, ed. H. Beveridge, London, 1909-14, reprinted, New Delhi, 1978.

Jamī, Maulana 'Abdu'r Rahman, *Nafaḥāt al-Uns*, Tehran, 1336/1947.

Jawhar, Ghulam Husain Khan, *Gulzār-I Āṣfiya*, Bombay, 1308/1891.

Kalabādhī, Abū Bakr, *Kitāb at Ta'ārruf Li Madhhab at Taṣawwuf*, Cairo, 1934, ed. and tr. A.J. Arberry, Cambridge, 1935.

Karkhi, Gul Muhammad Ma'ruf, *Dhikr al-Āṣfiya fi Takmilat Siyaru'l-Awliya' Dar Manqabāt-I Shams al-Hudā*, Delhi, 1312/1894.

Khafi Khan, Muhammad Hashim, *Muntakhab al-Lubāb*, Calcutta, 1850-74.

Khaja Khan, *Studies in Taṣawwuf*, Chennai, 1923.

Khaki, Bābā Dāwūd, *Wirdu'l Murīdīn*, Lahore, 1894

Khan, Muhammad 'Abdullah bin Haji Roushan, *Maqāmāt-i Dastagīrī*, Kanpur, AH 1286.

Khatib, *Tārikh-i Baghdad*, Cairo, 1931.

Kirmani, Shaikh Abu'l Ma'ali Qādiri, *Tuḥfatu'l Qādiriyya*, Sialkote, 1317/1899.

Kissling, H.J., *The Role of Dervish Orders in Ottoman Empire, Studies in Islamic Cultural History*, ed. G.E. Von Grunebarum, Chicago, 1954, pp. 23-35.

Macdonald, D.B., The *Religious Attitude and Life in Islam*, Chicago, 2nd edn. 1912.

———, *Development of Muslim Theology, Jurisprudence and Constitutional Theory*, New York, 1903.

Makki, Abū Ṭālib (d. CE 998), *Quwat al-Qulūb*, 2 vols., Cairo, 1306/1888-89.

Molvi, Ghulam Ahmad, *At-Taḥqīq al-Jalay an-Nasbi-i as-Sayyid al-Jilay*, Hyderabad, n.d.

Mufti, Mawlana Azizu'r Rahman, *Tadhkira-i Mashā'ikh-i Deoband*, Bijnor, 1950.

Mufti, Mohmmad Ghulam Sarwar, *Khazīnatu'l-Āsfiya*, Kanpur, 1894.

Muhammad 'Awfi (13th century), *Lubāb ul-Albāb*.

Muhmmad Latif, *Awliya-i Lahore*, Lahore, 1962.

Muhammad Miyan, *'Ulamā-i Hind kā Shāndār Māḍī*, 4 vols., Delhi, 1957-60.

Muhammad Tayyjib, *Dāru'l 'Ulūm Deoband*, Karachi, 1972.

Mujeeb, M., *The Indian Muslims*, London, 1967.

Munir, E.J. Simore and Aini, Mehmmed 'Ali, *Abd-al-Ḳādir Gilānī*, Paris, 1967.

Mustawfi, Hamdu'llah, *Tārikh-I Guzīda*, ed. E.G. Browne, Leiden, London, 1910.

Nadvi, Abu'l Hasan 'Ali, *Saviours of Islāmic Spirit*, vol. I, Eng. tr. Mohiu'ddin Ahmad, Academy of Islamic Research and Publications, 1986.

Nanawtawi, Muhammad Qasim, *Qibla-Numā*, Deoband, 1969.

Nasr, Sayyid Husain, *Ideas and Realities of Islam*, London, 1966.

———, *Sūfī Essays*, London, 1972.

——— (ed.), *Isma'ili Contributions to Islāmic Culture*, Tehran, 1977.

Nicholson, R.A., *The Mystics of Islam*, London, 1914.

———, *The Idea of Personality in Sūfism*, Cambridge, 1923.

———, *Studies in Islāmic Mysticism*, Cambridge, 1921.

Nizami, K.A., *Some Aspects of Religion and Politics in Medieval India during the Thirteenth Century*, 2nd edn., Delhi, 1974.

Nizami, Khaliq Ahmad, *Ḥayat-i Shaikh 'Abdu'l Ḥaqq Muhaddith Dihlawi*, Delhi, 1953.

Nizami, Khwaja Hasan, *Muḥfil Nāma Giyārhawin Sharīf*, Delhi, 1336/1918.

Palmer, E.H., *Oriental Mysticism: A Treatise on the Sūfistic and Unitarian Theosophy of the Persians*, 1867, rpt., 1960.

Qādiri, 'Abdu'l Qādir, *Tafrij al-Khaṭir fi Manāqib Sayyid 'Abdul Qādir al-Jilāni*, Cairo, AH 1300.

Qādiri, Sayyid Ahmad Arūj, *Shaikh 'Abdul Qādir Jīlānī ki Zindagī kā Aṣlī Kārnāma*, Markazi Maktaba Islāmi, Delhi, 1988.

Qādiri, Shah Ni'amatullah Wali, *Rasā'il-I Ni'amatullah Walī*, Ivanow, 1239-40, Tehran, 1937.

Qanungo, K.R., *Dārā Shukoh*, Calcutta, 1935.

Qudusī, I'jazu'l-Ḥaqq, *Tadhkira-i Sūfiyā-i Sindh*, Karachi, 1959.

———, *Tadhkira-i Sūfiyā-i Punjab*, Karachi, 1962.

———, *Tadhkira-i Sūfiyā-i Bengal*, Lahore, 1965.

———, *Tadhkira-i Sūfiyā-i Sarhad*, Lahore, 1966.

Quraishi, Abdur Razzaq, *Mirza Mazhar Jāni Janān aur unkā Kalām*, Bombay, 1966.

Rafiqi, A.Q., *Sūfism in Kashmir*, Delhi, 1977.

Rahman Ali, *Tadhkira-i 'Ulamā'-i Hind*, Lucknow, 1914.

Razi, Amin Ahmad, *Haft Iqlīm*, Tehran, n.d.

Rinn, L., *Marabouts et Khouan*, Algiers, 1884.

Rizvi, S.A.A, *Muslim Revivalist Movements in Northern India in the Sixteenth and Seventeenth Centuries*, Agra, 1965.

———, *A History of Sūfism in India*, vol. I, Delhi, 1978, vol. II, Delhi, 1983, rpt., 1992.

———, *Religious and Intellectual History of the Muslims in Akbar's Reign*, Delhi, 1975.

Sanauallah M.F., *The Decline of the Saljūqid Empire*, Calcutta, 1938.

Saunders, J.J., *The History of Medieval Islam*, London, 1965.

Schimmel, A., *Mystical Dimensions of Islam*, Chapel Hill, 1975.

Shabistari Saadud-Din Mahmūd, *Gulshan-i Rāz*, ed. and tr. E.H. Whinfield, London, 1880.

Shah, Iqbal Ali, *Islamic Sufism*, London, 1933.

Shamsamud-Dawla, Shahnawas Khan Mir Abdur' Razzaq, Nawab, *Ma'asir u'l-Umarā*, Calcutta, 1888-91.

Sharif, M.M. (ed.), *A History of Muslim Philosophy*, 2 vols., Wiesbaden, 1963.

Sh'ara'ni, 'Abdul Wahhāb, *al-Ṭabaqāt al-Kubrā*, Egypt, AH 1305.

Shustari, Qādi Sayyid Nuru'llah, *Majālisu'l-Mu'minīn*, Tehran, 1299/1881-82.

Sihalawi, Mulla Nizamud-Din, *Manāqib-i Razzāqiyya*, Lucknow, 1899.

Sindhi, M. 'Ubaydu'llah, *Taṣawwuf kay Ādab wa Ashghāl*, Lahore, 1946.

Siraj, Shaikh Abū Nasr, *Kitābū'l Luma'e Fi at-Taṣawwuf* (Urdu tr. Sayyid Asrar Bukhari), I'tiqad Publishing House, Delhi, 1991, Eng. tr. and ed. R.A. Nicholson, Leiden, London, 1914.

Sirhindi, Shaikh Ahmad, *Maktūbāt-i Imām-i Rubbānī*, Karachi, 1392/1972.

Sirhindi, Shaikh Badru'd-Din, *Ḥaḍaratu'l-Quds*, Lahore, 1971.

Sirhindi, Shaikh Muhamad 'Ubaidu'llah, *Khazīnatu'l Ma'ārif*, Karachi, 1973.

Smith, M., *Studies in Early Mysticism in the Near and the Middle East*, London 1931.

———, *The Sūfī Path of Love*, London 1954.

———, *Readings from the Mystics of Islam*, London 1950.

———, *An Early Mystic of Baghdad*, Cambridge, 1920.

Smith, W. Cantwell, *Islam in Modern History*, Princeton, 1957.

Subhan, J.A., *Sūfism: Its Saints and Shrines*, rev. edn., Lucknow, 1960.

Subki, Taju'd-Din, *Al-Ṭabaqātu sh-Shāfi'yya al-Kubrā*, 6 vols., Cairo, 1324/1900.

Sufi, G.M.D., *Kash'īr* (2 vols.), Lahore, 1940-49.

———, *Islamic Culture in Kashmir*, Delhi, 1979.

Sulami, Abu 'Abdur Rahman, *Kitāb Ādāb as-Ṣuḥba*, ed. M.J. Kister, Jerusalem, 1954.

———, *Ṭabaqāt as-Sūfiyya*, Cairo, 1372/1953, Eng. tr. and ed. J. Pedersen, Leiden, 1960.

Tabataba'i, Ghulam Husain Khan, *Siyar al-Muta'akhirīn*, Lucknow, 1282-83/1866.

Tadifi, Muhammad Ibn Yahyā, *Qalā'id al-Jawāhir* (Composed about AH 980), Cairo, AH 1303.

Tarachand, *Influence of Islam on Indian Culture*, 2nd edn., Allahabad, 1963.

Trimingham, J.S., *The Sūfī Orders in Islam*, London, Oxford, New York, 1971.

Underhill, E., *Mysticism: A Study in the Nature and Development of Man's Spiritual Consciousness*, New York, Paperback, 1956.

W. Braune, *Die Futūh al Ghaib des 'Abd. Al-Qādir*, Berlin, 1933.

Yafi'I, 'Abdullah b. Asad, *Mirat al-janan*, 4 vols., Hyderabad, AH 1337-39.

Ya'qubi, Ahmad bin Abi Yaqub (d. 284/897), *Tarikh*, 1833.

Zaehner, R.C., *Hindū and Muslim Mysticism*, London, 1960.

Research Articles in Reputed Journals

Ahmad Aziz, "Religious and Political Ideas of Shaikh Ahmad Sirhindi", *R.S.O.* XXXVI (1961), pp. 257-70.

Amedroz, H.F., "Note on Some Sufi Lives", *JRAS* (1912), pp. 551-86.

Anderson, S., "Dervish Orders of Constantinople", *M.W.*, XII (1922), pp. 53-61.

Andrews, G.F., "Islam and the Confraternities in French North Africa", *Geog. Journ.*, XLVII (1916).

Anjum, Ghulam Yaḥya, "Bari Saghīr mein Silsila Qādiriyya, Tarvij wa Ishā'at", *Fikr-o-Nazar*, Islamabad, vol. XXXIII, no. 2, Oct.-Dec., 1995.

———, "Silsila Qādiriyya Qor Iskay Bānī Par Taṣānīf Kā Ijmāl-I Jā'izah", *Fikr-o-Naẓar*, Islamabad, vol. XXXVI, no. 1, July-Sep., 1998.

Ansari, Muhammed, "The Doctrine of Divine Command: A study in the Development of Ghazali's view of Reality", *Islāmic Studies*, Islāmabad, vol. XXI, no. 3, 1982.

'Arnakis, G.G., "Futuwwā Traditions in the Ottoman Empire; Akhis, Bektashis Dervishes and Craftsmen", *Journal of Near Eastern Studies*, XII, no. 4 (October 1953).

Bhatnagar, Ishwar Chandra, "Mystic Monasticism During the Mughal Period", *Islamic Culture*, XV (1941), pp. 76-90.

Browne, E.G., "Notes on the Literature of the Hurufis and their connection with the Bektashi Dervishes", *JRAS*, 1907, pp. 533-81.

Hekmat, A.A., "Les Voyages d'un Mystique Persian au Kashmir", *J.Asiat.*, CCXI (1952), pp. 53-66.

Ivanow, W., "The Sources of the Nafaḥāt", *JRAS*, 1922, pp. 385-91.

Kissling, H.J., "The Sociological and Educational Role of the Dervish Orders in the Ottoman Empire", *Memoris of the American Anthropological Assn.*, no. 76 (1954), pp. 23–35.

Khan, Majid. A., "Taṣawwuf Kee Haqīqāt", *Al-Furqān*, Lucknow, April 1978.

Lewis, I.M., "Sufism in Somaliland", *BSOAS* XVII (1955), 581–602, XVIII (1956), pp. 146-60.

Macdonald, B.D., "Emotional Religion in Islam as Affected by Music and Singing", *JRAS* 1901, pp. 195–252, 705-48; 1902, pp. 1-28.

———, "The Life of al-Ghazzāli", *J. Amer. Or. Soc.*, XX (1899), pp. 71–132.

Margoliouth, D.S., *The Devil's Delusion*, Eng. Tr. of Ibn al-Jawzi's, "Naqd al-'Ilm wa'l 'Ulamā aw Talbis Iblīs" in *Islāmic Culture*, Hyderabad, IX (1935) – XXII (1948).

———, "Contributions to the Biography of 'Abdul-Qādir of Jilān", *JRAS*, 1907, pp. 267–310.

Miller, McE. W., "Shi'ah Mysticism: The Sūfis of Gunabad", *M.W.*, XIII (1923), pp. 343-63.

Nicholson, R.A., "A Historical Inquiry Concerning the Origin and Development of Sūfism", *JRAS*, 1906, pp. 303-48.

———, "The Goal of Mohammadan Mysticism", *JRAS*, 1913, pp. 55-68.

———, "The Lives of 'Umar Ibnu'l-Farid and Ibnu'l 'Arabi", *JRAS*, 1906, pp. 797–824 (as given in Ibn al-'Imad's *Shadharāt*).

Nizami, K.A., "Some Aspects of Khānqāh Life in Medieval India", *Studia Islāmica*, VIII (1957), pp. 51-69.

———, "Naqashbandi Influence on Mughal Rulers and Poltitics", *Islamic Culture*, XXXIX (1965), pp. 41-52.

Riazu'l Islam, "A Survey in Outline of the Sultanate Period", *J. Pakistan Hist. Soc.*, III (1955), pp. 201-08.

Sadler, A.W., "Visit to a Chishti Qawwali", *M.W.*, III (1963), pp. 287-92.

Siddīqī, M.Y. Mazhar, "The Role of 'Ulamā' in the Spread of Islam in the Indo-Pak Subcontinent — A Critical Appraisal", *Journal of Objective Studies*, vol. 3, no. 1, 1991.

Takle, J., "The Approach to Muslim Mysticism", *M.W.*, VIII (1918), pp. 249-58.

Weir, T.H., Eng. tr. of 1st Part of "Natījatu'l Taḥqīq" by Abū 'Abdullah Muhammad al-Dilā'I (d. 1089), *JRAS of Great Britian and Ireland*, 1903, pp. 155-66.

Zhukovsky, V.A., "Persian Sufism", *BSOAS* (1928-30), pp. 475-88.

Index